THE EX-BOYFRIEND YARD SALE

Finding the formula for the cost of love

Haley McGee

CORONET

First published in Great Britain in 2021 by Coronet
An Imprint of Hodder & Stoughton
An Hachette UK company

1

A CIP catalogue record for this title is available from the British Library

Hardback ISBN 9781529391497
eBook ISBN 9781529391503

Typeset in New Aster by Hewer Text UK Ltd, Edinburgh
Printed and bound in Great Britain by Clays Ltd, Elcograf S.p.A.

Hodder & Stoughton policy is to use papers that are natural, renewable
and recyclable products and made from wood grown in sustainable
forests. The logging and manufacturing processes are expected to
conform to the environmental regulations of the country of origin.

Hodder & Stoughton Ltd
Carmelite House
50 Victoria Embankment
London EC4Y 0DZ

www.hodder.co.uk

This book is dedicated to anyone who has ever wondered if the cost of love is worth it.

A word to the reader: all names and identifying characteristics have been changed. Certain events have been reordered, others have been reimagined to protect the privacy of others. Some characters, objects and scenes are composites and some other elements are fictional.

PART ONE

TAKING STOCK

1. THE DEPTH OF MY DEBT

*"What can be added to the happiness of a man who is
in health, out of debt, and has a clear conscience?"*
Adam Smith

Waiting at the red light, it hits me. Maybe I could get five
hundred pounds to have sex with someone?

It comes as a calm thought. A moment of suspension amidst
a flurry of anxiety as I rush along the high street in my new
neighbourhood in London.

I don't like this route, but I have to traverse the city on the
diagonal to save time.

I'm late and I've been working up a sweat, worrying. About
money.

I glance at my reflection in a shop window.

I think I could probably get five hundred pounds to have sex
with someone.

I'm in pretty good shape.

I've never given birth.

I've had sex with fewer than twenty-five — definitely fewer
than thirty — people, ever. That's got to be worth something.

The light is taking ages to change while traffic is stopped
in all directions around me. I've been in the UK for a year
and a half and I still don't understand how the crosswalks
work. Just as I place a foot off the curb, a horn blasts and a
man in a red car whips past, calling me an idiot. I step back
and wait.

3

Although at five hundred pounds a pop, I'd have to do it twenty times.

I imagine cold fingers peeling off my underwear. Then promptly shake it from my brain.

I can't I can't I can't I can't I can't.

I pass the supermarket.

A homeless guy asks me if I can spare a pound.

Without pausing, I toss him a, "Sorry, man."

"You can't spare one pound?"

Over my shoulder I confirm, "No. I can't spare one pound."

I turn back in time to dodge dog shit smeared across the pavement.

I can see the bank now. And it hits me.

Maybe I could get a thousand pounds to have sex with someone?

I think I could probably get a thousand pounds to have sex with someone.

I check the time on my phone and pick up the pace, ducking around a trio of mothers strolling with their broods.

Although for a grand I'd probably have to spend the night.

And I'd still have to do it ten times.

That's ten evenings.

Ten evenings is essentially two entire working weeks of my life.

Plus, my boobs are small. My labia's messy. I don't understand the politics of pubic hair. I'm not confident enough in my sexual prowess to charge that high a price. And what would I wear? Where would I advertise?

The Internet. The Internet; you advertise these things on the Internet.

I catch my reflection in the side-view mirror of a grocery delivery truck.

Oh god — would I have to post my picture?

Shuddering, I expel the thought.

I can't I can't I can't I can't I can't

I arrive at the bank and it hits me.

Although, if I'm one rich person's exact type, maybe could I get ten grand for one night.

Ten grand would change my life.

The door is heavy. I knock myself off balance prying it open. Then reprimand myself, I must not be a squishy-armed woman. I must be strong enough to open doors.

I enter the bank.

I'm directed up the stairs to a little room where I sit in a green upholstered chair and I ask for a line of credit.

Casilda, my financial adviser — or rather, the employee who happened to be free when I arrived — is pregnant.

She asks to see my UK tax returns. Careful not to aggravate the temperamental zipper on my backpack, I pull out a file folder and pass her the pages, explaining that I only have one set of taxes because I moved to the UK a year and a half ago.

She taps the pages on the desk, getting the corners straight before laying them down in front of her.

She narrows her eyes. "And why do you want a line of credit?"

"Well, I'm . . ." My heart is knocked sideways in my ribcage. Tears brew in my cheekbones. But I laugh. "Uh, I'm in debt and I . . ." Searching for the words that will stop me from crying, my eyes drift to the window. Not a blue scrap or sunbeam in the July sky, just endless diffused off-white.

She's flipping through my documents, scrutinising them. Already this is not going how I'd planned it. How did I plan it? I didn't plan it. That's the problem. I assumed everything would just work out. I didn't take any of the right steps; that's why I'm here.

I take a sharp breath in through my nostrils and sit up straight. "I moved here from Toronto and it's been a more expensive transition than I expected."

Casilda nods. "So easy to underestimate costs. Especially with the exchange rate."

I tell her I arrived in London with savings, but I've managed to burn through them.

She smiles sympathetically.

"And now," I shake my head and roll my eyes, "I'm racking up debt on my Canadian credit card. And I . . ." My word supply dries up. Everything important has dried up — cash flow, work prospects and romance. The ledger of my life is a big fat zero.

Casilda asks how much debt is on the credit card.

I buy some time by pretending I need to check the statement. "About ten thousand pounds' worth," I whisper, referring to the top corner of my most recent bill. "And my interest rate is 19.25 per cent, so I thought . . ." Trying to get something right, this time I make sure my bills are neatly aligned before handing them over.

She takes them from me and swivels in her chair to face her computer screen. "It's a bit tricky because you don't have much banking history here."

My poise pours out from some undetectable, unstoppable leak in my body. "I actually had good credit before the move. I have those statements too." I begin searching for my flush bank statements from several years ago.

Casilda halts me and explains that because this is a UK bank, they're only concerned with my banking history in the UK.

No sooner can I utter a protest, she has a new window open on her computer and another question for me. "What do you do for a living?"

"I'm self-employed."

"Oh, that's nice."

"Sometimes." I yank my mouth into a wide self-deprecating mail-slot smile.

She regards me expectantly, her fingers suspended above the keyboard.

"I'm an actor and a writer and I make solo shows — one-woman shows — and I take them on tour. And I also do a lot of voiceovers. Actually, that's been my bread and butter."

"Voiceovers?"

I tilt my head and turn it on, "Tune in Friday at eight on ITV-Be."

She laughs and asks where else she may have heard my voice.

"I did a dog food advert a while ago and lots of stuff for a cable channel in South Africa."

"Amazing," Casilda says as she types.

"That's why I'm here actually. Sorry, I meant to say. I did a voiceover job that was supposed to pay thirteen thousand pounds. It would have cleared my debt and given me a buffer." The instant I catch Casilda's eye, I impel myself to smile. She rubs her belly absent mindedly. "I just moved from a house where I was lodging with a couple in their seventies into a new flat because I thought I had that money coming in. I'd signed the buyout contract and everything, but right before the ad was meant to air, the client changed their mind."

Casilda winces as I say this. I'm not sure if it's me or if her baby's just kicked. "The arts are so volatile," she offers. She tells me her father was a musician in Poland and that watching him struggle after they moved to the UK was what convinced her to get a steady job.

I tell her the worst part is that my thirteen-thousand-pound advert was for a gambling company. "Serves me right for thinking I could luck out of having to work hard to pay off my debt."

"I imagine you work very hard."

"Sometimes." I don't tell her I was standing in a sopping wet bikini on the bank of the Hampstead Heath Ladies' Pond on a Tuesday afternoon when my agent called to inform me that the advert had been pulled. I just say, "I made the mistake of resting on my laurels." More like blithely lallygagging around as a bon vivant, thinking you'd been the winner of a windfall. "My grandma always told me not to count my chickens before they hatch."

Casilda defends me, saying, "Yes, but it's understandable." She clicks on a few dropdown menus while studying my tax return. She wants to know if she's seen me on TV.

I explain that I was working almost exclusively in the theatre before I moved. I want to brag about how busy and in-demand an actor I was in Canada, that I walked away from a year's worth of work to relocate to London, but I've learned that my résumé is meaningless on this side of the pond. Instead I tell her that I'm doing a lot of improvised comedy at the moment and offer her free tickets to my show on Thursday.

She doesn't respond to this but asks if I moved to the UK with a partner.

"No." I press my tongue against the back of my teeth. "No, I moved here alone."

"That's brave."

"I don't know if it was 'brave'. I moved here shortly after a break-up." I moved here after one of many break-ups, with the same person, but I don't say that.

She says she's sorry.

"Oh, it's okay. He had to go. It was—" I make a gentle farting noise and give the thumbs down.

Casilda looks bemused by this. "So it's not as though you are someone's dependent?"

"No." I feel myself slipping into a memory trance, about to relive my most recent goodbye with my ex, T; the way he smoothed my halo of frizz outside the airport.

Casilda cuts my reverie short. "You're not married or common law, now?"

"No. I'm alone."

She asks which UK visa I'm on and I tell her I've just switched over from a Tier 5 Youth Mobility visa to a Tier 1 Exceptional Talent visa. She adjusts her wedding ring and turns to face me. She wants to know if my parents own property in the UK — if they have any banking history here. They don't.

"Right. And are they — your parents — are they financially solvent?"

"I don't know how much savings they have. But, my dad's a retired professor, so — it's not corporate money or medical money but it's — yeah, they're middle class. They're not struggling."

She pushes herself back from her desk, sliding my documents to one side. "Could they lend you some money?"

I shake my head.

She raises her eyebrows.

"No." The harshness of my tone surprises me.

"Alright." She pats her stomach as if to say *quit it* to the baby and swivels away from me again.

Her fingers tap at her keyboard. I pick at the cuffs of my fraying jean jacket. Out of the window I watch as a tiny patch of blue sky is swallowed up by a mass of grey clouds.

When she's done crunching my numbers, Casilda turns back towards me. "Unfortunately you don't meet the criteria for a line of credit."

I cry. When she passes me a tissue, I reassure her. "It's okay. I actually really like my life." This is a lie, but I've got to have something. I lie and cry easily. I'm an actor. I'm thirty-one. I wipe the tears from the edges of my eyes, sniff snot back into my nose.

"Honestly Haley, I'm not supposed to say this, but, ask your parents to lend you some money."

I shake my head again. "They'll tell me to come home."

"But if it's only a buffer you need to get through a tricky time—"

"I can't," is all I manage to get out before honking my nose.

She commiserates, telling me London's a stupidly expensive city, and returns my useless documents.

Hurrying to close my backpack and get out of there, I snag the zipper. Casilda stands with her hand held out to me. I take it in mine and shake it.

She encourages me to come back in six months' time and try again. She'll be on maternity leave but one of her colleagues will be able to help me. She wishes me good luck. I leave the bank with my bag open.

THE LEDGER

Love	Not over my ex, T
Money	– £10,284.71 in debt
	£1,238.73 in bank
Career	No jobs lined up, no prospects & no auditions

Total	0

2. ASSESSING MY ASSETS

Asset, noun
1. a useful or valuable thing or person.
2. an item of property owned by a person or company, regarded as having value and available to meet debts, commitments, or legacies.

Dignity, Haley.

My mother's voice rings in my head as I lean against the bank's thick walls, fiddling with the zipper on my bag. Dignity. Don't be a crying woman on the high street.

I roll my shoulders back and start to walk.

When I was sixteen, my high school boyfriend weaselled out of our relationship to date someone new and even though I was aware of this betrayal, months later I wanted him back. "Dignity, Haley," my mum recommended from across the kitchen table. "Go where you're wanted." Which I understood to mean, only go after boys who like you.

I've always loved words. Perhaps because a sure-fire way to grab my English-professor father's attention was a request to look one up in his multi-volume *Oxford English Dictionary*. In any case, I've long been in the habit.

Dignity is defined as:

1. the state of being worthy of respect.
2. a calm or serious manner.
3. a sense of pride in oneself, self-respect.

It seemed like a good thing to aspire to, and so with a thick black marker I wrote the word "Dignity" on a piece of cardboard, surrounded it with stickers and stuck it on my bedroom wall among my many collages. It was the first thing I saw upon waking and the last thing I saw before nodding off to sleep.

The concept has clung to me through the intervening years. I thought of dignity again as I wheeled my suitcase through Heathrow's arrivals a few weeks ago. I was returning from a couple months in Canada, where I'd been touring one of my solo shows and trying again with my on-again off-again non-boyfriend boyfriend, T. We'd given it another go at his request. He believed he was capable of change and thought us both being in Canada could be a good way to start again. He wanted to try to commit — to forge an unconventional relationship with me. He'd convinced himself of this theory while in my absence, but in practice, he reverted to his old refrain. And so, after two meagre months on again and two sessions with a couples' therapist, T and I returned to our original roles: me wanting more and him wanting less.

The night before I flew back to the UK, he told me he had changed his mind; he couldn't commit after all. He still needed more time in the same city but didn't know where he wanted to live. He said, long-distance relationships are imaginary — they're not real. He lives in four cities. London isn't one of them.

Maybe I should have called it quits right then, but I refused to reveal my devastation and held out hope he'd at least cop to loving me before I got on the plane. Besides, he wasn't cruel about it; he was in knots. He didn't want what we had to end, he just couldn't see a way to commit further.

In the morning he doubled me on his bike all the way to the airport in Vancouver. I wore his T-shirt. He wore my backpack on his front and I balanced on the rat trap, holding his stomach with one hand and clutching the seat post with the other. Midway through the ride, we got smoothies at an outdoor market before having sex in a bathroom on the bike trail. By the time I was back on the rat trap, I had acid reflux from the apple in my smoothie and spent the remainder of the ride dry heaving and burping.

When we got to the airport, he smoothed my halo of frizzy hair and said, "You sweet thing."

After almost three years of long-distance on-again off-again, he still hadn't told me he loved me, and he wouldn't agree to the label of boyfriend.

And so, dignity. When I got back to the UK, I ended it.

That's what I'm thinking about as I take the long way home. Trying to retrace my steps to understand where I made the first wrong turn, how I could have prevented having so little to show for myself.

On Dickenson Road I pass a couple encircled by grocery bags, kissing at the front door of what I presume to be their home. A hydrangea the colour of watermelon in full bloom augments the scene. They're both wearing leather sandals.

I push down the torrent of I have nothing I have nothing I have nothing. I itch to get drunk, but I don't want to spend the money. I text my friend Milo, *Drinks tonight? I'm dancing with the demons. Wheee! x*

Home. Langdon Park Road. Navid's compact flat is carpeted and clean. He's owned it for several years and I'm his most recent tenant. Of the four flats in our building, I'm the only inhabitant who works from home. Situated on a residential street in the north end of the city, its large west-facing windows make this flat a tiny oasis of tranquillity and warmth.

In London, the possibility of living alone isn't available to me. Especially since the gods have taken a vacuum to my work life and I now face an empty calendar. But I like this carpeted cocoon I've wound up in.

Navid's dishes are piled high in the sink. Pina the cleaner is coming tomorrow. Even so, I methodically place the plates and cutlery in the dishwasher, put a pellet in and listen to it hum.

If Navid was my boyfriend I'd be infuriated by his wilful inability to put his dishes in the dishwasher, but as his flatmate, I've chosen to not be annoyed by it, as it's his only irritating quality.

"Now, Visa," I say out loud.

Milo texts back, *Oh dude. Bad time at bank? Drinks sure. 8pm? Or Franco Manca? My treat. I can come to you. x*

I reply, *Yes pizza. I'll meet you there then! x*

Being a good friend is Milo's modus operandi. Not just to me, to everyone he knows. I met him at the Edinburgh Festival Fringe about a year ago, in the queue for a bao truck. He hates being alone, which means he's always down for meals and taking in artsy stuff.

In the bathroom I squeeze the blackheads on my nose for all they're worth, collecting the pus on a square of toilet paper, watching my collection grow. I have to pee so badly my teeth tingle. Sometimes I hold my pee in just to savour the power and relief of releasing it with force.

As I wash my hands, I stare at my face in the mirror, fixing my closed-lip smile so I can bear to see what's looking back. You can do this. You have to do something to right this ship-wreck. You can't not do anything.

I call Visa. Sitting at my tiny desk with my recent bills in front of me and my phone on speaker, I enter my security infor-mation and wait until a real person arrives on the line.

In my friendliest, shit-together voice I ask if they can decrease my interest rate from 19.25 per cent to "something like eleven? I think I have a friend who has it for eleven."

The agent goes quiet as he examines my file. I listen to the rumble of other voices in the background, imagining a vast room lit by fluorescent lights, rows of people sitting at desks speaking into headsets, consoling customers about their lost and stolen credit cards. The agent says since I'm maxed out, they can't decrease my interest rate until I can prove I'm able to pay off my bill.

"But I'm paying four thousand dollars a year in interest on this balance."

"Unfortunately that's how interest works."

My armpits get moist and my tone sharpens. "I understand how interest works, but it seems to me that 19.25 per cent is highway robbery, especially since I have been a loyal customer, with good credit. Until recently."

"Yes, I can see that; however—"

I cut the agent off to explain that it's the move, the exchange rate, that I've had a job fall through, that I'm not in a civil partnership, I can't ask my parents and work is slow. "And now, my credit card is maxed out. My chequing account will be in overdraft. I don't have a savings account. And my rent is due."

The agent says he appreciates where I'm coming from and he's sorry to hear I've fallen on hard times.

"It's not 'hard times', it's just . . ." I gaze out the window into the flat across the road. "What do you suggest I do?"

"I put my card in the freezer. I know that sounds stupid, but I do."

I laugh. "Too late."

"Guess so."

I seize the opening and begin to bargain. "Could you not charge me interest this month? Could I have a grace period, so I can get ahead of this?"

He says he'll have to check with his manager, but he believes if I can demonstrate that I'm actively taking steps to pay down the bill then they may be able to waive my interest fees for a month.

Without thinking, I exclaim, "I'm going to sell some things! I'm going to have a yard sale."

As I say this, I look around my room and realise the only things I could sell, the only things I own that are worth anything, monetarily, have all been given to me by my different ex-boyfriends.

While the Visa agent goes to check with his boss, I take stock. I've got a ukulele and a bike and a sapphire necklace. I've also got a vintage typewriter and a handmade porcelain and mango wood jewellery box.

"So, Haley, I've spoken with my manager." I sense a smile in his voice.

"Yes?"

"And as a one-time exception and a gesture of goodwill, we will waive this month's interest charge."

"Oh, thank you so much," I say talking over him. My shoulders drop and I place both my palms on my heart.

"You don't have to pay this month's minimum payment. But next month, you need to pay the cumulative minimum, and we'll start charging you interest again."

"THANK YOU." I say it in all caps. I say it as if I've got both hands on the agent's shoulders and I'm forcing him to make eye contact with me. I want this to land. I am grateful.

I hang up the phone. Get up, walk into the living room, throw a few punches into an imaginary punching bag, do some fancy footwork, raise my hands to the ceiling and say, "Thank you." I'm not religious but in my less cynical moments I subscribe to the notion that gratitude begets good things, even if those things are just good feelings. Then I lie down on the cream carpet in a patch of afternoon sunlight.

I'm having a yard sale. "The Ex-Boyfriend Yard Sale" springs into my mind. I chuckle out loud, then roll over, rock up, and begin gathering my goods for sale, laying them out on the sofa.

I have a vintage Olympia Splendid 66 portable, manual typewriter, housed in its original leather case, with the instruction booklet and cleaning brushes. Never been used by me.

There's the Hora ukulele, made in Romania, which is sadly missing a string.

Probably the most expensive object is the white gold, sapphire and diamond necklace, strung on a white gold chain. Only worn twice. Good as new.

The porcelain and mango wood jewellery box was crafted by a semi-famous ceramist in Finland.

And then of course my bicycle. A 10 speed ladies' bike, the

letters on its low crossbeam read "Free Spirit" — a Sears Canada model, which, as I discovered when taking it for a major tune-up, has its own slightly different sizing for each of its parts, making them very difficult to replace.

I wonder if I can sell my "well-loved" denim Herschel backpack. It was made in the era before the company went mainstream. I figure that integrity might matter to someone, so I add it to my line up.

Stepping back, I behold my bounty, these talismans of invested time and emotion that ultimately did not pay off.

Not wanting to let my fickle assets out of my sight, I sit on the floor, leaning against the TV stand, my laptop cooking my thighs. I've gone to Google to investigate the going rates for similar objects online.

I'm a third generation yard sale aficionado. I've been visiting them and hosting them my entire life. My maternal grandfather had a basement filled with treasures and bric-a-brac and my aunt Harlow took up the torch with unbridled fervour. Harlow collects almost everything (coins, soapstone carvings, pottery, Royal Family memorabilia, 1950s kitchen appliances, bone china, period costumes, cameras, sheet music for organs, craft supplies, stickers, nutcrackers and vintage swimwear to name a few). Together they indoctrinated me. Many Saturdays of my childhood were spent cruising for signs pointing to yard sales, hunting down treasures in the rubble.

As an adult, when I asked Harlow why yard sales, she said it was because no matter how little money you have, they make you feel rich. While I love this feeling as a buyer, it occurs to me that the traditional front lawn yard sale will not deliver me the best bang for my buck. Or best buck for my bang.

The notion of my neighbours standing on my stoop, haggling over my vintage typewriter, gives me the heebie-jeebies. I don't want them diminishing the value of my precious objects — how could they ever truly appreciate their worth when they don't know the stories attached to them? Plus, yard sales aren't really a thing in the UK — they have "car boot sales" and I don't have a car. Nor do I have a yard. The front "garden" is a tiled area sunken below street level that belongs to the people who own the garden flat. No, the objects will have to go online, where hobbyists and connoisseurs will comprehend them and fork out dough for their cachet. I suffer a modicum of ancestral guilt at this decision but needs must.

My phone rings. It's Ollie, my childhood best friend. I've known him since we were seven. We walked home from school together, feeding our mutual affinity for cross-country running, embroidery-floss bracelets and reading books with female protagonists. Since then we've seen each other through umpteen phases of disparate popularity and opposing interests and now our relationship is familial, we're bound by our shared history.

"Ollieeee!" I say, drawing out the "e" part of his name as I always do.

And he responds in kind, matching my intonation and holding on to the "ley" part of Haley.

Ollie's been calling more than usual since he arrived in Ghent for a research project. Ironically, he followed *my* mother's footsteps into a career in molecular biology. I fill him in on what I'm up to, running him through the objects for sale. He wants to know why there is nothing in the collection from my high school boyfriend, who Ollie got to know quite well. Exasperated, I remind him that the most expensive thing that ex got me was a ticket to see Matthew Good Band, and since we were broken up by the time the concert rolled around, I didn't go.

"Oh yeah," he says, and then we both go quiet.

Ollie was a first-hand witness to the cataclysmic nature of my first heartbreak. Even now, he holds a certain reverence for it. Also, Ollie's going through a divorce.

"He did make me a mix tape."

"That's good."

"No one is going to want to buy a mix tape from 2002,

featuring the music of Phish, Counting Crows and Blink 182."

Ollie rattles off lyrics about a movie sneak preview, and we laugh. And then he probes, "What about T? What did he give you?"

"He only paid for flights. Oh, and I have his T-shirt. It's a second-hand Royal Canadian Navy T-shirt."

Ollie says, "You should see if you could sell those things too."

We talk about it and decide I should write descriptive Gumtree posts for each of the items — posts that include a little too much emotional information — to see if I can convince someone out there my stuff is worth more than it would be on my front lawn.

"And how about I title each post 'The Ex-Boyfriend Yard Sale'?"

"That's *great*." Ollie is sparing with his praise and even more sparing with his artistic green lights. "Also, it's the Internet — there is a buyer for everything." One of Ollie's exes did a brief stint as an editor in the online porn industry, so he knows. "If the price isn't right, you don't have to sell, but you might be surprised by what people are willing to pay for stuff they want."

I tell him, "I did see a similar typewriter on Etsy for four hundred and forty dollars. Plus shipping."

"Exactly."

When we hang up, I close my laptop and open my notebook. In block letters with pen I write:

INVENTORY FOR THE EX-BOYFRIEND YARD SALE
Mix Tape
Necklace
Ukulele
Bicycle
Typewriter
Backpack
Jewellery Box
T-shirt

I've got eight items from eight different ex-boyfriends to price, post and sell to the highest bidders.

3. SYSTEMS MANAGEMENT

"... the systems approach to management, is based on the idea that 'everything is interrelated and interdependent'."
Smriti Chand

I meet Milo at Franco Manca's in Kentish Town. As he places his phone, wallet and multi-tool on the glass tabletop, I press my back into the exposed brick wall. Milo is a golden retriever of a man right down to his big, soft paws — positive, dependable, chummy with everyone. Occasionally, I wonder what it would be like to sleep with him, but it's more a scientific query rather than a buried desire. I knocked the question mark out of our orbit by enlisting Milo's insight into my various dilemmas with T, and Milo is in a five-year relationship. Any romantic tension has been successfully relegated to the friend zone.

Milo eats posh pizza whenever possible but otherwise maintains being a foodie is the laziest of hobbies. We often meet at Franco Manca's.

Inhaling my droopy crust margherita, I wallow about the bank and my credit card debt.

"Ah dude," he says, "I can help you."

"Milo. I don't want your money," I say hurriedly, waving my hands.

He assures me he'd never offer it. "Never lend to friends. No—" he turns his phone to me, displaying a colour-coded spreadsheet — "I have a system."

"Tell. Me. Everything." I top us up from our carafe of house wine.

"Okay," he says, leaning back and closing his app, "so, I was terrible with money. Like terrible, terrible, till I was in my mid-thirties—"

"Aren't you like thirty-seven?"

"I'm thirty-nine, McGee, but yeah, till about two years ago I was shite."

"But haven't you been living in Julie's flat for years?"

I've only met Milo's girlfriend Julie once. She's a copywriter and he's a freelance lighting designer for bands and corporate trade shows. They live in one of the six flats her family owns in east London. I'm finding it difficult to take his financial advice terribly seriously and say so.

Milo's Scottish accent amplifies. "McGee, I have never accepted a *penny* of her parents' money. I was raised to pay my own way. When you accept favours there are always strings attached." He insists that without fail he's deposited his share of the flat's market value into Julie's parents' account every month.

"Okay, okay. Very admirable."

"Fuck off," he laughs. "But I was still shit with money. Like literally bricking it sometimes when the first of the month would roll around. Because I was secretly in debt on my credit card. It was bad."

"Oh my god, it's the worst."

"The worst. Felt like absolute shite. And I actually went — wait for it." He slurps up the better part of a slice and chomps it like a camel.

"I'm waiting."

He exaggerates his chewing, swallows and pronounces, "To Debtors Anonymous."

"What, like AA?"

"Yeah, but for people in debt."

"Did you have a gambling problem?"

"No. Some people there did, but no. It was great. And they got me doing this thing that has literally saved me." He leans forward. I'm on bated breath. "Every morning, when I get up and have my coffee, I write down everything I spent the day before into a notebook. And then on Saturdays, I enter all of that spending into the spreadsheet I showed you. And then at the end of the month, I look at where my money is going and where I can save."

I nod slowly. I love this system. (Ollie says I'm obsessed with systems management.) I'm also bracing myself for what this system will uncover. "It's going to be all coffees and eating out isn't it?"

"Well, you'll see. It's super interesting. And it really gives you a picture of how much you need to earn to afford your life."

I dot chili oil onto my plate and twizzle my crust through it. "I'm going to have to get a Joe-job," I grumble.

"A what?"

"A temp job, a pin job, a shitty job that you do to earn cash, that is flexible and easy and that you can drop in a heartbeat when something better comes along. A Joe-job. A job for an average Joe."

A real boasting point for me is that I have earned my living entirely as an artist since I was twenty-five. I've never been rich, but I was living off my art and those optics dazzled me. It often meant rocking up to new acting gigs deep in the red and using the first few pay cheques to get back in the black. It was "fiscally irresponsible", but the money always came, and I owned all my time.

I talk a bit about my plan to sell my items. Milo says it's a good start, but my focus should not be a Band-Aid solution. My aim should be to remedy my relationship with money once and for all.

He pays for the meal. The night has turned soggy but neither of us wants to call it, so we meander down to Camden and along the canal.

Milo describes the categories he sorts his expenses into and explains that he tracks his income on an adjoining spreadsheet. He waxes on about the importance of building up a capital base and the eventual necessity of diversifying my portfolio. Milo doesn't ask a lot of questions, but he does drive me home. When I get out, I thank him.

He says, "Thank DA," and hollers that tracking spending is the reason he was able to afford his car.

I begin tracking the next morning.

4. THE PRICING PREDICAMENT

*"The moment you make a mistake in pricing, you're
eating into your reputation or your profits."*
Katharine Paine

"What if I told you I suffered a flesh wound for the necklace?"

"Did you?"

"Well, sort of."

I'm strolling around Hampstead Heath with Fi, my best friend in London. She, like Navid, works from home on Wednesdays, and so sometimes I meet with her to escape the noise of the TV which Navid keeps on a low rumble all day, while simultaneously watching YouTube videos on photo editing.

"John Lewis — no." Fi pulls her dog away from a splattered ice cream cone on the pathway. John Lewis is a rescue. His previous owners named him after the department store. Fi and her husband Ru tried to change his name — John Legend, John Junior, Don Luis, Brutus, Ron Vesuvius, Johan, Amazing Khan — but John Lewis is the only thing the dog responds to.

"Okay, well get this," I say. "When I went to visit the guy who gave me the necklace, I took a bus. I was at acting school in Toronto and he was at police college in a city 120 miles away. On the bus, someone had wedged a box cutter — a scalpel — between the seats. But I didn't notice the blade till I moved to get comfortable, and the knife sliced through my new jeans—"

Fi sucks air through gritted teeth.

"—through the flesh of my bum, drawing blood."

"Love! That's awful."

We head into a wooded portion of the Heath where tall ivy-licked trees shade us from the midday sun.

"I know. So, do you think that flesh wound increases or decreases the value of the necklace he gave me for my nineteenth birthday?"

She pauses to let John Lewis sniff the myriad of dog markings surrounding us. "How big is the diamond?"

"Tiny. It's mostly sapphire."

"Do you reckon it was ethically sourced?"

"I highly doubt it. I also believe it was paid for with money he made selling marijuana."

She releases John Lewis from his lead and laughs. "Increase, I guess, because you suffered pain and had to, what, get stitches?"

"I had to mend my jeans."

Fi's a pragmatic person. I suspect she said increase because she wants to make me feel good. I take it. And carry on.

"Now what if I told you that the guy who gave me the necklace is the person I 'gave' my virginity to — increase/decrease?"

"Increase. John Lewis — NO." She trots towards John Lewis, who's entangled in a shrub. I follow hot on her heels. This is what I've been grappling with as I attempt to post the objects online, and I need an external perspective.

"Okay, and what about the fact that the demand for sapphires has gone up by two thousand per cent since Kate Middleton started wearing a sapphire ring?"

"Increase, definitely. Hold this." She passes me her coffee cup and gets down on the ground. The smell of barista-made latte floods me with jealousy. I'm down to the sludge of my homemade brew in one of Navid's reusable mugs. After one week of money tracking, my outgoings on booze, dining out and coffees from cafés surpassed my rent. Navid's cafetière is now in daily use, as I've cut coffee culture from my life. £2.40 per day x 365 = £876, versus a bag of coffee from Sainsbury's at £4 lasting two weeks. 26 weeks x £4 = £104, which is a saving of £772.

Fi yanks John Lewis away from the garbage he was mowing down on, attaches the lead to his collar and scolds him for being a scrounger. "Sorry. I swear he's going through a rebellious phase."

"One last question, then I'm done."

She gestures for me to go on.

"What if I told you that my first thought when I opened the necklace was, 'Now I can never break up with him'?"

Fi stops in her tracks and looks at me.

"Increase/decrease?"

"Did you really think that?"

"Yes. I then proceeded to do thirteen shots in an hour. My knees started giving out on the dance floor. I was kicked out of a nightclub before midnight. And I threw up in the cab on the way back to his dorm."

"A rager."

I tell her how good natured he was about it all. How he stayed up all night, sitting on the edge of the bathtub while I cleaved to the toilet, cajoling me to drink water between bouts of vomiting, and how the next day he kept saying, "Babe, you had a classic nineteenth birthday."

"Nineteen was the drinking age?"

"Yeah."

She tilts her head up, squinting into the sun, and considers. "Decrease? Although I guess it's terrible to feel trapped. Does a bad feeling make it decrease or increase?"

"I don't know."

Fi polishes off her coffee and lobs the cup into a bin on our path.

Here I'm hit with a genuine predicament. Does a miserable time mean front lawn, barter me down, hell I'll give it away for free, it's worthless junk? Or should I be compensated for my suffering? Should I be seeking financial retribution? And if that's the case does that mean that the objects that have positive associations should be given away for free? Or are they the most precious? Should they be kept under glass — preserved as priceless relics of unspeakable bliss?

"I don't know how to price any of my things given all the factors in play."

She lets John Lewis off his leash again. He bounds towards a group of dogs tussling. "Yeah, it's a conundrum."

"I mean, there's got be some formula or equation or algorithm out there, somewhere, that could take into account all the ways we invest in our romantic relationships and spit out a price for the material things we're left with when a romance dies — a formula for the cost of love."

Fi points at me. "Now *that's* something people would pay for."

"Oh my god. Can you imagine?"

John Lewis is trying to hump a dog that isn't interested, and we go running to intervene, both of us shouting, "John Lewis — NO!"

Having schooled him on the necessity of consent, we walk up to the lookout.

"This is what scares me about motherhood," Fi says. "How do you raise a decent bloke?"

"Wait — are you pregnant?"

Fi goes quiet. Then says, "I don't think so but, uh, it's going to happen." She reveals that after almost twenty years, she's gone off the contraceptive pill. She's been with her husband for a decade. It's time.

I admire Fi. Her job as a television producer isn't her passion, but she works her ass off and then savours her weekends popping off to Europe, hosting political supper clubs, baking elaborate confections and seeing every important film. Our friendship works because we openly acknowledge that we don't want the other's life.

We look down at the rooftops of central London. Although she's ambivalent about the baby, the sex she and Ru are having while trying to make a baby is the hottest sex they've ever had.

"It's like, sex 2.0. It's like ... like teenager gropey but with this kind of deep, soul-touching element." She shrieks as she wraps up her description.

I widen my eyes, clasp her arm and avow, "It sounds terrific."

Even after all this time, Fi's still really attracted to her husband. She asks about my foray into the dating apps.

I cover my face with my hands and make squirming noises. "I deleted the apps!" I uncover my eyes sheepishly but keep my hands over my mouth. "People wrote to me, but I never wrote back."

"Love ..." Fi admonishes me playfully.

"I'm not ready! I'm just not."

She asks me if I miss T. We haven't spoken about him since I told her it was over.

"I wasn't getting what I wanted. He had to go. And I'm so tired of being sad about him, I feel kind of impervious to it now."

"Yeah, but do you miss him?"

I pull lip balm out of my purse and rub it over my lips.

"It's okay if you do."

Wiping the edges of my mouth, I nod. "I miss him as a presence in my life, as a person I talked to — as a person who knows me. And I have this low-grade fear that it's T or no one."

Fi tells me that's nuts.

I tell her that during my first break-up with T, my mum and I saw *Crazy for You*, the Gershwin musical revue. One of the lead characters isn't having any luck in love and so, dismayed, she belts out her disappointment, singing, "They're writing songs of love but not for me."

"Of course, it's a musical, so in the end she lands a devoted man."

"Naturally," laughs Fi.

"Anyway, after the show, I sobbed on a bench outside the theatre, asking my mum what if there really were no songs of love for me?"

"Oh no!"

"That's basically how I feel after every break-up now."

"What did your mum do?"

"She hugged me and promised she would love me."

"So sweet."

"I know."

"But it's not the same!"

"I know. Then I got mad at her for trying to give me advice when she's only ever been single for a couple of months in her entire adult life. How could she know what it's like to worry that you're somehow deficient or that love doesn't exist for you — that you're some kind of love idiot who lacks the capacity for it?"

"Fuck, being a parent is thankless." Fi turns the conversation back to T and nudges, "So, do you miss *him*? Or just having someone? The hope that you weren't going to be alone forever?"

I consider this. "I miss the potential future I could have had with him. And I miss being adored by someone — as rickety and haphazard as his adoration was. And I miss being a person who has a person. And I like T. He's . . . an exceptional human."

"But you were unhappy a lot of the time."

"Because he wouldn't commit. But what's the alternative? I'm just supposed to find a ho-hum dum-di-dum guy who is reliable, but who I can't stand talking to? And settle because something is better than nothing?"

"Right. But he's an Eeyore and you love to laugh."

"Who doesn't love to laugh?"

"You laugh a lot. You laugh a lot when you talk with people Haley, but when you talk about T you moan and groan and pull the flesh on your face."

Fi has an annoying, uncanny way of exposing my cracks. It bothers me that I don't give it back hard enough.

"Anyway." I change the subject. "What if I made a piece of digital art with the stuff from my exes?" I say. "Like a website, with research about the objects themselves and the personal story behind each one. People could make bids, like at an auction, and then I'll sell them."

She inhales, energised. "You should ask your ex what he paid for the necklace. You should ask all of them, actually."

"Oh god."

She revs up. "It's such a good idea. I mean, are you on good terms with your exes?"

Though Fi feels like an old friend, I've only known her for the last year. These gaps of knowledge shock me when we stumble upon them. I tell her I'm not on bad terms with most of them, but none of them are actively in my life as friends.

"See if they'll talk to you. And record your interviews."

"And then put them on the website?"

Fi scrunches her face and makes a humming noise. "What if you made it into a show?" Her eyes widen. "Haley. This is your next show." She tells me to make art that capitalises on my talent. "That's what will sell your objects."

"Oh! Like a live auction? I can sell tickets to the auction where I'll tell the stories about the different objects and then sell them off one by one."

Fi closes her eyes. "The problem with that is then you can only do it once. What if you never sell them? What if you make it a show that you can perform a lot?"

"And it's all about the objects and a formula for the cost of love?"

She nods. "Yes."

John Lewis wants to be picked up, disgruntled at being left out of the conversation for so long. We make our way towards the tennis courts.

Sitting on the grass, watching athletes chase balls, I can't stop thinking about the show.

"It's not too salacious talking about my exes?"

"Anonymise everything," Fi says definitively. "Change details, names, conflate people — swap out the real objects for imaginary ones. I mean, that sounds like something I'd pay to see."

"I need a math whiz to work with me."

"Lemon squeezy."

"*The Ex-Boyfriend Yard Sale*. That's the title." I hold my breath for her approval.

"It's fucking golden."

5. CAN I GET A MATH WHIZ?

"Mathematicians aren't satisfied because they
know there are no solutions up to four million
or four billion, they really want to know that
there are no solutions up to infinity."
Andrew Wiles

Navid paces in the living room. Arsenal is playing and he's on edge.

Navid works in finance and has a passion for architectural photography. We'd never be friends if we weren't flatmates because we run in such different circles, but I like him. He's a generous conversationalist and loves to joke around. Plus he's an excellent cook. He's in a long-distance relationship and describes the eighty-inch TV in the living room as his sanctuary.

"Do you have money on this?" I ask, poking my head in the doorway.

"Get in!" He shouts at his sanctuary and then turns to me. "It's not the money. It's the pride."

I scurry past the TV and settle on the floor with my laptop.

I type "how to make a formula" into Google. Nothing definitive rises to the top of the search. It's all threads and message boards and geek sites. The first link I open begins with a long post from 2013 by someone with the username ScarsRememberBrandy who writes:

It's difficult to know how deep or complete an answer to give, because this is a very open-ended question. It's also a question more about science than mathematics.

What follows is a stream of words and phrases, entirely indecipherable to me. My eyes bounce over the passage, a stone skipping on water until it inevitably runs out of force and sinks.

model originates with first principles . . . structure of the phenomenon . . . natural periodicity . . . data you collect . . . in the case of 2b the growth is linear . . . definistic models . . . Fourier analysis . . . polynomial fitting . . . regression analysis . . . stochastic phenomenon . . . Box–Jenkins method . . . heuristic measure . . . Akaike Information Criterion (AIC) . . . don't 'overdetermine' the system.

By the time the commercial break rolls around, I'm dumbstruck by both the jargon and swagger of ScarsRememberBrandy. I turn to Navid, who is now seated on the sofa, sipping a Trappist beer in an ornate bottle.

"Navid," I venture, "do you know how to create a mathematical formula?"

He lowers the volume. "Depends. What for?"

I tell him I'm trying to price some stuff from my exes to sell, but I want to do a bit of a cheeky thing and factor in the time and emotional costs of the relationship, as well as the monetary value.

Ever jovial, he teases me. "Haley? That's crazy. Why you gotta do that?"

"It's — it's for a show I'm making, about love and money."

"Different life!" he exclaims. "Alright, first make a list of all the things that affect the price — those are your variables."

I begin typing.

- *How long the relationship lasted*
- *Who broke up with who*
- *Who paid for more things during the relationship*
- *How good the sex was*
- *How hard he made me laugh*
- *Ratio of fun to misery*
- *How long it took to get over the relationship*
- *How much he paid for the object in question*
- *Is there appreciation or depreciation on the object, if it's an antique/vintage*
- *How much I cried during the relationship*

At the next commercial, I report to Navid that I've got ten variables.

"Now assign each of them a value from one to ten, and then take an average," he instructs.

But this doesn't satisfy me. "I want something nuanced," I say. "Some factors are more important than others."

"Well then," he parries, "you need to create a ranking system, so that the most important thing is — how many variables do you have?"

"Ten," I remind him.

"So the most important one could be multiplied by ten, or point one. That will weight some more strongly than the others."

"But it's more complicated," I insist. "Like romantic gestures are only valuable if before and after them the person was reliable." As I say this, I add those two variables to my list. "Otherwise, a romantic gesture is a selfish act, a performance, and should have negative worth."

"Define romantic gesture."

"Like in *The Notebook* when Ryan Gosling hangs off the Ferris wheel threatening to kill himself, or the guy with the cue cards in *Love Actually*."

"Cloe loves those movies."

34

Cloe is Navid's girlfriend. They've been together for about six months, after meeting at a mutual friend's wedding. She lives in Greece. Navid is hoping he can convince her to move to London; he can't move because the money he earns here is so much better than what he'd earn there. Though I disagree with his logic, it's another thing I keep zipped up about, because if he moves, I'd probably have to move out too, and I really don't want that.

"So although those romantic gestures are juicy, it's the day-to-day stuff that gives a relationship meaning."

"You women. Oh my days," he shakes his head jokingly. Another arena of Navid-behaviour I would not tolerate from a boyfriend but do from my landlord/flatmate. I worry this makes me a bad feminist.

I give Navid an example from my life. "So, shortly after I met one of my exes, he surprised me on my lunch break at rehearsal with an expensive porchetta sandwich. The sandwich was not to my taste, but I was charmed by the gesture. However, in the months afterwards, he stopped calling when he said he would, showed up late, flaked on our plans, often forgot his wallet when we went to dinner — basically, I couldn't rely on him."

"Why buy the cow when you can get the milk for free?" chants Navid.

I roll my eyes.

"Just saying." Navid wiggles his fingers as if sprinkling fairy dust. "Give him some demerit points for letting you down."

"But, see, that's arbitrary."

"But it's for a show, right? It doesn't have to be real mathematics."

I smooth the carpet with my hand and let out a sigh.

"Keep it simple," he concludes.

I don't want simple. I want beautiful math. Navid takes a call from a friend in his fantasy football pool and shit-talks on speakerphone while gesticulating wildly. I think, what about factoring in how useful the object has been and whether or not I'm still friends with my ex? I make a few more notes in my Word doc.

I decide to kill two birds with one stone and reinstall the dating app on my phone, changing my bio to read: *I'm particularly interested in meeting someone who works with numbers — math, finance, economics, stats, etc.*

Through squinted eyes, holding the phone at a distance, I write opening lines to my matches as fast as I can:

Nice hat

ENFJ

Turkey?

You Canadian too?

Is this at the Boogaloo?

Are you really a math teacher?

My mouth fills with a tacky taste knowing that my qualities are about to be enumerated. I fret about how I'm representing myself in my digital shop window. With most of the people I've loved, if I only saw the pictures they'd likely post on a dating app without my knowing anything about them, I'd probably swipe no. And so, to negate this possibility, I dole out my yeses liberally. I close the app.

Nearing the end of the second half, the other team scores, tying the game. Navid's swearing and praying under his breath, standing stone still, hands on his knees, willing Arsenal into victory. His relationship with the sport suddenly strikes me as private.

I scoot behind him and head to the bathroom. I'm a night shower person. I can't sleep without one to punctuate my day, wiping my slate clean. A physical and symbolic cleansing. I like them hot. So hot that no one I've showered with has been able to stand the heat.

T has a walk-in shower in one of the apartments he stays in. When we showered there together the temperature was too high for him, the sex was too dry for both of us and the nozzle was too small to share. One of us was always left outside the stream, rubbing our triceps.

I don't want to think about T. I want to think about my new show. With my finger I write numbers in the condensation on the shower door as I conjure up my to-do list:

1. *Contact theatres about helping me develop the show*
2. *Reach out to all math-minded people I know*
3. *Research Joe-jobs — put feelers out — ask friends*

But my mind keeps drifting back to sex with T. I get out of the shower, steaming, and vaguely turned on.

The sofa in the lounge and my bed share a wall, so I lie on my nun cell's minuscule patch of floorspace to masturbate. Probably overkill, but I want to mitigate any possibility of the wall quaking, jiggling or getting a knock. After my requisite three orgasms, I get up, dry myself off and admire my flushed cheeks in the mirror. Then I fling on some pajamas, wrap my housecoat tight and join Navid on the sofa.

Navid is now watching a propulsive reality TV show in which exceptionally beautiful twenty-year-olds must be coupled up or risk being kicked off an island. To my shame, I find the show compelling, and not just ironically or as a sociological document. But as with all reality TV, you can't give it your full attention. I check my replies.

The math teacher wrote back. *Ha. Yes I am. 6th form. What do you do?*

Hot potato! I reply as quickly as I can. *I'm an actor.*

Have I seen you in anything?

Probably not, I just moved here from Canada.

Impatient with this chit chat, I type, *What are you doing this Friday?* I'm supposed to get some money for a voiceover I did months ago on Friday. And I want to get this formula sorted. In three strokes the math teacher and I have arranged a date.

He writes, *I'll pick you up at 6:30. Good?*

I'm about to reply with a thumbs-up emoji, but then decide to change it out for a *yes* before settling on a simple *Sounds good!* I'm toying with deleting the exclamation point when the Skype app begins to ring on my phone. "Oh fuck, fuck," I say, scrambling to get up.

"What?" asks Navid.

"I have a meeting — a call — with someone in Toronto." I never tell Navid I'm doing therapy on the other side of the thin drywall. Add it to the list of things I withhold from him. I bolt into my room, closing the door with a thud.

"Hi — sorry," I whisper furtively, "I lost track of time."

"That's alright Haley. Do you need a couple minutes?"

"No. No. I'm fine," I reassure Thea, sliding into my desk and putting my earphones in.

Thea has been my therapist since I was twenty-five. She lives in Toronto, but I like her too much to end it, so we do long-distance therapy. She's no bullshit and deeply empathic — not that she's ever hugged me, but she's the kind of person who'd hold you tight while you sobbed onto her chest till you felt better, then tell you that you're trapped in a prison of your own making, and give you the tools to deconstruct it. She was a professional jazz singer before becoming a therapist and the most intuitive person I've ever met. From the get-go I felt at home with her.

As I settle behind my desk, I come out with it. "I think I have to stop our sessions for a while." I bite the skin on the pad of my thumb.

"Oh — okay." She pauses. "I'm not trying to convince you otherwise, but tell me more?"

"I didn't get the line of credit and I've got to get back to the bare essentials. Not that this isn't essential, but it's not food and board . . . and I just really fucked up with my lavish . . . well not lavish . . . but living like a person who earns more than I do and stupidly expecting that it would be okay."

"I don't think you were stupid Haley. You thought you had some money coming from a voice job, no?"

"Yeah, but it's not like I worked for that money. That money was a fluke — a get-out-of-jail-free card."

We circle this for a while until she asks, "Do you *want* to stop therapy?"

My whisper strains in the back of my throat, "No. But it's not feasible."

Thea offers to carry on with me for as long as I need, deferring payment till I'm more financially stable.

I'm working hard to muzzle my sobs so Navid doesn't hear. "Really?" I choke.

"I'll keep track, and when you've got your money under control, we'll work out a plan for you repay me."

I eke out another, "Really?"

"I know you're good for it." The certainty with which she says this winds me.

I do my best to say thank you without sobbing again. When I catch my breath, I tell her that I have to swallow my pride, roll up my sleeves and get a Joe-job. "I have to go back to being a pleb."

She reminds me that any Joe-job will be temporary. "And," she assures me, "we're going to work on your relationship with money."

In bed that night, as always, I spoon my pillow and reflexively imagine it's T. Which is annoying. Just as I'm slipping off, I'm jolted awake. My date! *Sorry,* I write him. *I forgot I had a call at 10pm. (Canada). Yes 6:30 is good. See you then.*

6. THE WASTE

"Humanity is the rich effluvium, it is the waste and the manure and the soil, and from it grows the tree of the arts."
Ezra Pound

The faint smell of burning hair is a familiar accompaniment to this primping ritual. I'm twirling my locks around a ceramic curling iron when the math teacher's text arrives.

I'm so sorry to do this but I'm running late, can we meet at the club? I'll buy you an Uber?

I release my hair cautiously, careful not to scald my neck. *All good. I'll take the Tube*, I write, adding a smiley face.

The math teacher proposed the plan for our evening so quickly, I'm certain it was cut and pasted from his notes.

We're meeting at his club in Covent Garden for "cocktails and crudités" and then going to see an improvised show in the West End. When he suggested it, I didn't tell him I perform improv myself.

I spend way too long putting myself together. My hair alone takes an hour. I dab my T-zone with foundation. I do my face like one of my many former flatmates — a retired model turned furniture restorer — trained me to do. White eyeshadow brushed up to my eyebrows, pink on the lids and charcoal with a small, firm brush along the line of my lashes. Blush on my cheekbones and a tiny bit in the centre of my chin. I'm going for effortlessly captivating and carefree.

When I go to the bathroom to check myself in the flat's only full-length mirror, I gargle a splash of Navid's mouthwash. The look I've pulled together is like my cooking: good, considering it's been concocted by me. I don't pluck my nipples or alter my pubic hair. I need obstacles in place to ensure I don't sleep with him. Though I'm not thrilled with my internalised patriarchy, today I'm using it to my advantage.

I had several years of dilly-dallying with strangers, trysts and flings and one-night stands while touring, and though I'm glad to have given my eighty-year-old self something to look back on and delight in, I'm done with it. I've had my fill from the all-you-can-eat buffet and now I want an à la carte meal that satiates my finicky palate.

I pack my notebook, a couple of pens, my lipstick and portable phone charger into my purse. At the Sainsbury's Local on Archway Road — the only grocery store within a ten-minute walk of Navid's flat — I stop to buy mints and get some cash out. This sixty pounds takes me into overdraft. My heart clenches. I'll be fined but I want to be prepared and self-sufficient.

The math teacher is waiting in the foyer when I arrive. A flat cap frames his grinning face. Inviting and non-threatening. A beta male.

His club's bar appears opulent, though it's hard to distinguish if the furnishings are actually expensive, because it's so dimly lit. We sink into a velvet sofa beneath a chandelier. I wriggle out of my jean jacket. He leaves his cap on and passes me a cocktail menu.

We squint at the menus for a moment before he asks, "Would you have a martini?"

"I'd have a dry gin martini with a twist of lemon."

"That's very specific."

I shrug. "I've had too many things go awry with olives in this country."

He laughs and heads to the bar, returning moments later followed by a server in crisp black trousers and shirt — an outfit

I'll soon be sporting if my catering contact pulls through. I've got an interview on Skype tomorrow afternoon. We order our drinks.

"And some crisps and guacamole!" squawks my date.

I rearrange the throw pillows pushing me to the edge of the sofa and get down to business. "How did you come to be a math teacher?"

"Maths."

"Pardon?"

"It's maths," he explains, "with an 's'."

"What? No, it's not."

"In America you say math—"

I cut him off, "I'm not American."

"Canadian, American, same thing," he says with a toss of his hand.

"No, it's not." My brow's furrowed and my back's up.

The martinis arrive. He raises his to me. "Cheers."

"Cheers." My smile is laboured.

We sip carefully. "Sorry if I offended you."

"It's—" I search for a way to correct him that won't tank the evening. With my best, laid-back, west coast vibes, I speak for my nation. "You just can't say that to a Canadian. You can't tell us that our country is the same as another one, especially not the US. It's really . . ."

"Imperialist?" he offers.

"Yes."

"Sorry for that. I was only . . ." He bats his hand in front of his face as if swatting away a fly. "I'm sorry."

In a good-natured tone I rattle off that we also have universal health care, really good public education and strict gun laws.

He says, "I only meant to say that, in Britain, the short form for mathematics is maths not math. Maths with an 's'," he clarifies. "The plural. I wasn't trying to mansplain your nation to you."

"I see. I see. Got it."

I take the tiniest sip, rationing my martini. I'm not a good drinker. I like drinking. I like the way everything softens and becomes funnier after one glass of wine, but I'm a cheap drunk.

Must keep the filter on tonight. Must not talk about T, heartbreak, money, debt, work disappointments or loneliness.

"So how have you found the move here?"

"Lonely — wait, no. Tell me about being a *maths* teacher first." I add the "s" to make peace.

"Right. So, after I graduated from Cambridge—"

"Excuse me," I channel the voice of a middle-aged woman and pretend to look at him over a pair of glasses.

He laughs uncomfortably. "A lot of people in my family went there, so . . ."

I blurt out, "My dad was the first person in his family to go to university." Which is true, but my parents are academics. Why am I flexing some kind of proletariat muscle, some false blue-collar pride, when I grew up in the middle class?

"Right." He tells me that after graduating with a maths degree he followed his girlfriend at the time — (already talking about exes. Noted.) — to South Korea, to teach English. She had massive student debt and wanted to pay it off quickly. And he'd never been to that part of the world, so they went there for a year. "She ended up falling in love with one of the other teachers at our school — a lifer — and she still lives there. They have two kids now." Greedily scooping guacamole, he shovels tortilla chips into his face. Still crunching, he tells me that he actually really liked teaching, so when he came back to the UK, he got a Master's in education before doing his teacher training. "Slightly overqualified. Bit difficult with my family as they really wanted me to work for our company. But I'm the bleeding-heart liberal maths teacher, not a manager of corporate construction projects." He washes down his snack with a gulp and sets his empty glass down on the table. Period. "And that's me."

His mouth is the opposite to T's. Where T's lips are thin and his teeth are movie-star straight, the math teacher has full lips and gappy teeth.

"Another round?"

"I'm okay for now." My glass is 85 per cent full.

"Do you mind if I—?" he asks, already waving down our server.

Into his third martini, I broach the topic. "Do you know how to create a mathematical equation?"

He wipes his pillowy lower lip with the back of his index finger. "No, no. My turn to ask you a question. How are you still single?"

"Uh. I . . . Really?"

"Yeah."

"I'm not sure. Probably chose badly?" Of course, I have other answers in my arsenal, like, my work has been my priority, my parents' relationship freaked me out about being in relationships, and with most people I feel I can only bring a percentage of myself to the table, but I eschew the truths for self-effacing vagueness.

An alarm beeps on his watch. "Bottoms up."

I'm relieved when he insists on paying the bill, which he does by making a gesture to the server, who bows. Apparently that's all it takes to charge it to his account. As he holds my jean jacket for me, I thank him and make it clear that I'll get the next drinks.

My date deftly manoeuvres us through the tiny, cramped theatre lobby to a less busy concession stand below. When he asks me what I want to drink, his breath is hot on my cheek and he touches the small of my back.

I tilt my spine to create a gap. "I'm getting these. What do you want?"

"G&T."

We sidle up to the bar together. I pay with cash and pass him his drink, noting that his cap is still on. The paradox of his self-assuredness with the evening's schedule in conjunction with his evident discomfort about balding fascinates me. In this moment, I decide, henceforth, that men who can grapple with their hair loss and own it will be at the top of my list of potential mates.

During the show he keeps his hat on and his hands to himself. At the interval he asks if I want another drink.

"No, but let me get you one."

"No, no. You got the last one."

"In that case," I tell him, "I'm going to go to the washroom."

He holds me close to him with his hand on my back. "What's that?"

"Toilet," I over-enunciate.

"Ah." He dismisses me, not wanting to think about me and the toilet.

T was a poo prude too.

The line snakes through the bar in the basement. I'm glad for the long wait. I check my bank statement on my phone. Hallelujah, the money for the voice job I did several months ago has arrived. I've got wiggle room.

When I get back upstairs, the math teacher is swilling the final dregs of one of the three gin and tonics balanced in his hands. "Here," he says, taking his puckered lips off a straw. "For you."

"Oh — no, I don't—"

"Go on."

"I'm not a very good drinker."

"At least hold it so I can put this down."

I take the plastic tumbler from him. He deposits his empty cup on top of a trash bin, spins around and clinks my glass. "Cheers."

I smile. It was a good pirouette. "You a dancer?"

He sways into me, his wet lips brush my ear, but he doesn't whisper. "You'll see."

The bell dings and we take our seats again. He laughs bois-terously throughout the second half and his arm slithers to the back of my chair. I spend the remainder of the show weighing whether it's worth giving it another hour, for a last-ditch effort to grill him about how one creates an algorithm. The injection of cash in my account makes it easy to agree when he recommends that we return to his club for a nightcap.

The bloodshot London Eye leers at us from across the Thames as the math teacher orders himself a whiskey and a beer. I order another G&T and slap my card down. "On me. On me, on me. Please."

"Alright. Got myself a sugar mama." He winks at the nonplussed bartender, who ignores his quip. I hear myself give him a pity chuckle.

We're thrust into each other's personal space thanks to the dinner-plate sized cabaret tables. Our knees keep knocking. A woman in a black dress sways on stage, a mic in hand, mostly singing to the band behind her. None of the people sitting on the rooftop are really here for the jazz.

After his toast "to possibility" and the clinking of glasses, I fight the booze haze setting in and say, "I really want to talk about math."

"You mean maths." He points a finger gun at me and sloppily pulls the trigger.

"Sure. Maths."

He leans in. "What do you want to talk about?"

I lean back. "I want to know how you create a formula."

"Like you plus me?"

"No, like a real mathematical formula. I'm curious."

"I'm curious about me and you." He's got one hand on the back of my stool and the other on the table in front of me.

"Well, we'll see." It comes out more seductively than I intended. I'm suddenly aware that my bladder is going to burst. "Toilet."

When I come out of the bathroom he's there.

"Wasn't sure if I was supposed to follow you." He snatches my waist and draws me in. Kisses my mouth. His lips are soft, but he kisses hard.

The coat-check attendant is in my eyeline. I don't resist his kiss, but I don't get into it either, although unfortunately, I'm an inadvertent tongue slipper.

He tugs me close to him and bends me back, licking the underside of my tongue.

Out of habit I press up onto my tiptoes, even though with this fellow I don't need to. I entertain this outpouring of passion until I hear him say, "Come home with me."

"No."

"Come on."

I rest my forearms on his shoulders. "No." I smile.

"Why not?"

I step back, so my hands hold him at a distance. "Because I don't know you."

"Seriously?"

"Yes."

He closes the gap, kissing me again.

A group of women on a hen-do file past us into the loos. Their presence snaps me to attention. I retrieve my phone from my purse. "I'm going to get an Uber."

"I'll get it."

I glide to the elevator and push the button. Inside he nuzzles into my face and paws at my midriff. Under the awning, the app is slow to load. It's raining and the prices are surging. He boasts about his love-making lexicon. I hail a black cab.

"Don't leave me here."

"I can drop you off at home."

He climbs in behind me.

I tell the driver I'm going to Langdon Park Road in Highgate. "N6."

"No," my date interjects, "we're going to Primrose Hill."

"We're making two stops."

The math teacher kisses my neck and my cheek, pleading with me to go home with him.

The cabbie looks in the mirror, making eye contact with me. "Look mate, she's not going home with you, so we're going to drop you off first."

The math teacher slurs his address and the driver floors it. My body brushes against his with every turn and he holds my thigh with his hands. I oscillate between kissing him back and squirming away from him.

When we get to his flat, the cabbie barks, "This is you, mate."

"Come in with me," he simpers.

"No."

"Mate. She's not getting out of the car."

The math teacher misjudges the distance to the curb. Recovering, he hovers with a Shakespearean knee inside the cab and sways in the door. "Well this has been . . . a waste of . . ." He doesn't finish the sentence. Just slams the door and the driver takes off. Of what? I wonder. Money? Time? Maybe effort? All of the above?

"He's a prick, love."

"Awful," I agree and let my body slump.

"What you doing out with a bloke like that?"

"To be honest? I thought he could help me with a math formula I want to make. He's a teacher."

"Fuck's sake, wouldn't want him near my girls."

"Me neither."

The cabbie mumbles a retching noise and zooms me home without the GPS. I pay for the cab ride with what's left of my cash.

The flat is dark when I get in. Navid must be asleep. I strip naked in the bathroom and turn the shower on. As the water heats up, I inspect my naked profile in the full-length mirror. I completely failed my artistic and mathematical mission. But I did well in that I didn't succumb to his desire — I didn't go along to get along. I hug my naked self and whisper, "Thank you thank you thank you. You did good babe. You did real good."

7. RETURN ON INVESTMENT

Return on investment is a ratio between the net profit
and the original capital cost of an investment. The
higher the ratio, the more bang for your buck.

I race along the aspirational side streets of Highbury. The leaves are changing and I've just turned thirty-two. The voice work only comes when it comes and it's still not coming that often. But I'm working. I've been Joe-jobbing for a couple months. I carry a small spiralbound notebook in my purse where I diligently record my daily spending, entering the figures into a spreadsheet on Saturday mornings. I think about *The Ex-Boyfriend Yard Sale* constantly, but the project's been dormant since my hapless date with Mr. Maths. And tonight, I have an improv comedy show. It begins in twenty-six minutes.

I bound up the pub's rickety stairs two at a time. Breathless, I swing open the door to the green room, a small chaotic space littered with empty pint glasses, backpacks and denim jackets and a carpet that's never been hoovered. My team warms up by playing games called Zip Zap Zop, Bunny-Bunny and Follow the Follower. I'm keen to be silly after a day of being repeatedly told I had cervical cancer.

I don't. One of my Joe-jobs is medical role play for physicians training in obstetrics and gynaecology. Today they were being tested on breaking bad news. Four doctors per hour, for six hours — twenty-four times I was told I had cervical cancer. Then I had to cry so the examiner could assess their bedside manner. My face is puffy and there's now a pain in my right ovary. The other Joe-job I landed is at the catering company — they service small gallery openings, which I find more degrading but less psychologically disruptive.

Top Forty tunes blare through the speakers. A bell is rung and an Irish accent bellows, "The house is now open!"

I do a style of improvisation called the Harold. I don't get paid to do these shows, but I auditioned to be part of this team. We're called Inappropriately Attired. I get nervous for performances and take them seriously. A Harold lasts between twenty-three to thirty minutes and begins with three improvised monologues, inspired by a random word suggested by an audience member. Carrot and banana are surprisingly common suggestions. The aim is to take the word and free associate until you hit on something you have some strong opinion on or an interesting anecdote about.

For example, if the word was banana, I might step forward and say, "Banana makes me think of condoms, which makes me think of sex. The last time I had sex was with my ex, T, while he was doubling me on his bike to the airport. Well — not on the bike — but we stopped and did it in a public washroom."

I'd riff on this for about a minute. Then there would be two more monologues, performed by different members of the team, followed by three two-person scenes inspired by the monologues, a silly game, then three more scenes and another silly game and finally a scene where we tie up all the threads.

From the wings, I listen to the host riling up the audience. When he announces us, we jog onto the small stage and assume our spots on the backline, where the members of the team stand throughout the show when they're not in a scene. It's a full and raucous crowd, a combination of fellow improvisers, pals of performers on the bill tonight and punters from the pub below.

I stand on the backline, listening intently. Our designated player says, "All we need to get started is a word."

"TINDER!" caws a husky voiced woman, lifting a pint glass.

I push past the teammate who always steps forward to monologue regardless of the word. I've got this one. I regale the audience with a two-minute rendition of my date with the math — sorry, "maths" — teacher, ending with, "So if anyone knows an honourable maths whiz who would be willing to help me out, let me know after the show." There's laughter and hoots and applause.

The show speeds by. My teammates take the piss out of my newfound favour for openly balding men and my misuse of a dating app for a research project. Seeing my foibles reflected through this comedic prism makes me weep with laughter from the backline. They genuinely make light of it all, and this lifts my spirits tremendously.

Queuing at the bar afterwards, I'm tapped on the shoulder. An amiable guy shouts over the noise, "I have a mathematician for you."

Just then the bartender prompts me with a surly, "Yes?"

I order a half-pint of cider, which is the cheapest booze available here, and turn to my new companion. "And for you?"

The buoyant youngster asks for a pint and offers me cash.

"No. No. You got the math whiz. I got the drinks."

We sit at the corner of a large wooden table surrounded by animated improvisers one-upping each other and jesting. The math whiz is this guy's girlfriend, Gemma. She has an honours degree in Math and Philosophy, she grew up doing amateur dramatics with her family and is up for zany projects. He sends the email introducing us halfway through his pint.

I lift my feet off the floor and pedal a small imaginary bicycle in celebration. "Thank you so much. This is amazing."

I head home when I polish off my cider, rather than get another. My good mood seems fragile and I want to preserve it. I save £1.50 and take the fifty-five-minute walk in the balmy September air.

8. SECURITY DEPOSIT

Think of your security deposit as a personality fee
and then do whatever you want to your home.
Amy Sedaris

Gemma and I meet at a café in Aldgate several weeks later. When I arrive, she's already sitting at the table in the window. In front of her, a flat white, a notebook and a graphing calculator are laid out in neat lines.

Nerves surge in my gut as I approach her. Since arranging this date, I've plunged back into the project with a kind of born-again ardour. I wave. She tosses her long ponytail over her shoulder and pushes back her chair to rise and greet me.

"Thank you so much for meeting with me."

"Pleasure." Her hand is warm and her Geordie accent is soft.

We get right to it. The first thing she tells me is that, contrary to my assumptions, formulas, equations and algorithms are not interchangeable terms. This is in response to the email I'd sent her, where I'd said I was looking for "help creating an equation/algorithm/formula".

Out of her backpack she produces a metal case, from which she removes an expensive-looking pencil. Clicking the top of it with her thumb, she begins to write in her notebook. "An equation is something that you're trying to balance on either side."

"$y = mx + b$?" I ask.

"Well, that's tricky. Depending on how you engage, it's both a formula and an equation."

I remember $y = mx + b$ vividly because it's linked to sex. For a brief period in grade nine we had a student teacher named Mr. Colleth, a riveting combination of nerdy made attractive by simply being slightly older and marginally taller than the boys in our class. His speech was peppered with the phrase, "Uh okay so", and his teaching style included incorporating our ideas more than was helpful. He'd been put in charge of teaching us Slope, also known as $y = mx + b$.

Sometime during his practicum with our class, a group of us fourteen-year-old girls found ourselves at a sleepover and talk turned to Mr. Colleth, primarily what it would be like to have sex with him. "Uh okay so I'll just, lift this and — you tell me what — or, sure, I have a thought, uh okay so, I want your ideas here, if it's alright with you, uh okay so . . ."

This collective role-playing quickly escalated to one of us cawing out, "Mr. Colleth! Mr. Colleth! Show me the slope of your penis!"

As if by groupthink, we all joined in, a chorus of virgins executing our best approximations of orgasmic tones, chanting "why equals em ex plus bee!" until the mother of our host came down to the basement to tell us to be quiet.

I don't tell Gemma any of this. I watch her draw on the graph-paper pages of her notebook, until it clicks for me.

"Oh, like positive five on one side of the equals sign becomes negative five on the other side."

"Exactly." She shows me her notebook where she's written:

$$2x + 3 = 0$$
$$2x = -3$$
$$x = -3 \div 2$$

"An equation says two things are equal. This equals that. What is on the left of the equation is equal to what is on the right. And it's like a scale that you always want to keep balanced. So, if you subtract three away from one side, you have to subtract three away from the opposite side." She explains that solving an equation, which contains variables, or unknowns such as "x", is a process of figuring out which numeric values for the unknowns make the equality true.

Checking to make sure I've understood, I point to her book. "So, solving the equation here is about figuring out what number the x equals?"

"That's right. Now, an algorithm is a broader term and is essentially a set of instructions, like a recipe. Whereas a formula calculates something for a specific purpose and gives you an answer. Formulas are always true, no matter what values are entered. And for me—" she takes a sip of her coffee "— a formula is a representation of a relationship."

My heart swells. "That's what I want." I swig my now-cool peppermint tea. The beautiful math I long for is on the horizon. I give Gemma the rundown on my pricing predicament, explaining that I've been doing research on my various objects from my exes, and now need to enlist the expertise of a math whiz to help me create a *formula*.

Smiling, she interrupts. "Sorry, can you remind me what the formula is *for* exactly?"

"To price the objects from my exes."

"Right, but why?" She cocks her head to the side, her mouth frozen in a perplexed grin.

"The formula is actually for a new show I'm writing, about love and money. It's called *The Ex-Boyfriend Yard Sale*."

She chuckles, picks up her pencil again and clicks the top with her thumb. I take this as a signal to carry on.

"I've been wondering if and/or how we can ever turn sentimental value into cash — if we can ever convince another person to value our sentimental objects as much as we do? I've also been thinking about how the context of where we place objects, like in a yard sale or an art gallery, can radically change their worth. And, well, basically, I'm interested in *how* we quantify love — if there's some mathematical way to know if the cost of love is worth it."

She's been nodding along, taking notes. "Cool. And where will you present the show?"

Tap-dancing, I say, "I'm not sure yet, exactly, but I'm in talks with a few theatres. And I'm in the process of securing funding for the project."

"That's brilliant."

"Yes." I fold my hands in my lap and bow my head. I mean, I could theoretically be doing all those things. It isn't a gigantic fabrication. I don't want to enter into my work with Gemma under false pretenses. But she's excitedly scribbling notes on graph paper. I can't spoil this. I clear my throat and look up. "Yes, I think it has the potential to be a really fun and interesting project."

"And, what's your timeline?"

Nonchalantly I say, "It's looking like it'll be on stage within the next year."

Gemma orders another coffee. When she returns, she hasn't sat down before she asks if I have a sense of which variables I'd like to include in the formula.

For this I am prepared. Whipping out my laptop, I lean over the table and read a list considerably longer than the one I'd shared with Navid:

- *How much the ex paid for the object in question*
- *The appreciation or depreciation of the object in question as determined by an appraiser and market research via posting the objects on Gumtree*
- *How much thought he put into the gift — if it was a gift*
- *The value of the big life lessons the relationship taught me*
- *How much baggage I left the relationship with*
- *Practical skills imparted from the ex (i.e. how to make pancakes without a recipe)*
- *Useful cultural knowledge acquired from the ex (i.e. Jane Campion's oeuvre)*
- *Rites of passage in the relationship*

- *How many good stories they contributed to my life story*
- *Am I friends with them now?*
- *Biggest romantic gesture*
- *Reliability*
- *Key highs versus key lows*
- *How long the relationship lasted*
- *Who broke up with who*
- *The ratio of fun to misery during the relationship*
- *The time spent pining before we got together*
- *How long it took to get over the relationship*
- *Percent of the relationship that was long distance*
- *How good the sex was*
- *The calibre of the "poetry"/romance*
- *How hard he made me laugh*
- *How often and badly we fought*
- *Who paid for more things during the relationship*
- *Was there ever unspeakable bliss?*
- *Was I in love?*
- *What was the intensity of the love?*
- *How much I cried during the relationship*

When I look up from the list Gemma's staring into the middle distance, her eyelids fluttering. Not sure what to do, I keep talking.

"For 'how much I cried', I was wondering if some kind of crying tax should be applied or deducted, to account for my exes' suffering, on any objects given to me before 2012, which was when I began psychotherapy."

Gemma drums her fingers for a moment, before cracking a smile. "Sure," she says, "we can do something like that."

"Great. And then for stuff that isn't always present, but when it is, it really colours how you view a relationship, like being cheated on or cheating on someone, I was wondering if there was a way to include these kind of wild cards?"

"Absolutely." Gemma says we'll use all my variables, also known as data points, figure out how to weigh them and how they relate to each other, to create a formula that will determine a genuine price for each of my objects.

"Gemma," I say. "This is a great plan."

"How many objects do you have?" she asks.

"Eight. Seven. Eight? I — my most recent ex was never technically my boyfriend, so I'm not sure." I zing through the fundamental details of my saga with T. Wrapping up with, "But even though it lasted three years, because the majority of the relationship was long distance, he felt that it was actually kind of imaginary, or not real."

She withdraws the pencil from her ponytail and scribbles in her notebook again. "This is considered to be one of the most beautiful pieces of maths. It's called Euler's Identity." She pronounces Euler as "oilers", like the Edmonton Oilers. After a pause, she pins me with her eyes. "Do you know about imaginary numbers?"

"I vaguely remember the little 'i' from grade-eleven math, but I don't know what it does."

"So, Euler's Identity brings together seemingly disparate strands of mathematics in a distilled way. It looks like this." She slides her notebook to me:

$$e^{i\pi} + 1 = 0$$

"Euler was asking, 'what happens to a positive number when we raise it to an imaginary power?'"

Gemma speaks quickly. "So, i represents the square root of negative one. It stands in for something that doesn't compute. Meaning, if you try to enter the square root of negative one on a calculator, you'll get an error message." She demonstrates this using her calculator. "Using an i allows us to open up a whole other realm of working with numbers, but these numbers are imaginary."

Her words wash over me. I make listening noises but I'm not entirely comprehending. I'm snagged on *e*.

"*e* is the base of natural logarithms, which are used a lot in calculus," she explains. "It was discovered by a friend of Euler, a guy called Jacob Bernoulli, who was working on the principles of compound interest. *e* is 2.7 something something something — lots of decimal points." Her painted fingernails play a scale on an imaginary piano.

I read Euler's Identity out loud: "*e* to the power of *i* times pi plus one equals zero." My eyes move from the *i* to the zero and back again. "So, something can come to equal nothing, if even just part of that something is imaginary?" I put my elbow on the table and drop my head into my hand. Don't cry.

"I was only saying, there are imaginary numbers that could be useful if we're trying to express imaginary components." Placing her empty cup in the saucer she says, "Euler's is the pop ballad of math — cliché but undeniably, well, beautiful."

I close my laptop and we talk next steps. I'll conduct some market research, collect the data for my data points and enter it all into a spreadsheet. She'll look into some "mathematical models that may be of use" and we'll reconvene in a couple weeks.

As she closes her pencil case, I make myself say, "So, in terms of paying you, keep track of your time and when the funding comes through, I will—"

She cuts me off, assuring me that's just fine. She's keen to do something "arty".

So it's agreed. Gemma is going to help me to create a mathematical formula that spits out an accurate value for the material things we're left with when a relationship ends. A formula that turns sentimental value into cold hard cash. A formula for the cost of love. So we can all know if it was worth it.

PART TWO

PRICING

9. THE SPREADSHEET

*"Spreadsheets are corporate poetry; when
constructed elegantly enough, they can be used
to communicate sophisticated ideas to audiences
who wouldn't otherwise be receptive to details."*
Eric Seufert

"Can you help me make a spreadsheet?"

It's Sunday morning. Navid is watching a nature documentary about the ocean, and sorting receipts.

"Put the eight objects across the top and the variables down the side. And use Excel."

My task now, having defined all the variables relevant to the cost of love, is to enter all the data for each of my objects into a spreadsheet. The spreadsheet is the middle ground where I drop off my emotions and experiences and Gemma picks them up and transforms them into numbers, and eventually, a cash price.

There's a lot to do to get the project up and running. The great news is that I've got Camden People's Theatre on board. Their artistic director, Sam, is the only London-based artistic director who has demonstrated a remote interest in my solo shows. The day after meeting Gemma, I wrote to him about *The Ex-Boyfriend Yard Sale*. He was really excited by the idea and particularly keen that I interview all of my exes, so "contact exes" is on my to-do list. I also have to write a grant application. For that, first I have to rustle up support from a few other theatre companies, in order to then request funds from the Arts Council to support the development of the show, which includes paying collaborators — who I have yet to find — renting rehearsal space, covering design costs, marketing, Gemma's fee, supplies, and buying some time away from my Joe-jobs.

I also need to fill in the spreadsheet. There are the simple numerics: how old I was during the relationship, how long the relationship lasted, how much each ex paid for the object in question. Then there are variables that can only be answered in words, like the most significant rite of passage I experienced in the relationship or the big life lesson I gained from my time with an ex, while other data points require me to think back (how good the sex was, for instance). And for those that are impossible to recall, I'm delving into my personal archives, combing through old diaries, emails, social media messages and bank statements, collecting hard evidence of how I paid for these relationships in money, time and emotion.

And then there are straight-up unknowns connected to the market value of each item, that require sniffing around online for comparable items or testing what kind of offers my items get in the online marketplace. I am flummoxed by the market research component. It should be simple — post my items online and track the offers that roll in — but the more I consider it, the more hiccups I encounter. My brother has been working as a market research analyst for the better part of his twenties, and so we're meeting on Skype later to talk about setting up a proper market research study.

In the meantime, I plod on with my data entry, sitting on the living room floor.

As I input my data, the spreadsheet stretches into a dissatis-fying shape. My sentences rather than neat numerics, and my inability to be succinct, mutate it into a lopsided, janky mess. But this is my data for now and so I leave it.

Object	Age	Who broke up with who	Rite of passage	LDR %	Length of rel.	Cost of phone bills	How good sex was	Biggest romantic gesture	Price of Object @ time of purchase	Current market value — waiting for offers on Gumtree	Biggest life lesson I learned
Mix Tape	16–17	Him	First love	2%	10 mos.	0	n/a	Made me a mix tape	£0.25		Love is conditional
Necklace	17–19	Me	Losing virginity	85%	1 yr. + 8 mos.	$1,697	8	"I Love You" Post-its all over dorm room	£150		If you want out, don't stick around waiting for things to revert
Ukulele	20	Me	First time taking morning-after pill	0%	4 mos.	$0	7	Wrote me a song	£55		You need to know people before you dive in
Bicycle	21–24	Me (on his behalf)	First time breaking up with someone on their behalf	26%	2.5 yrs.	$658	5	Wooden sculpture in dressing room	£173		A relationship is a third entity
Typewriter	25–26	Him	Getting played	43%	6 mos. spread over 12 mos.	$327	6	Porchetta sandwich	£62		If everyone warns you about someone, listen
Backpack	26–27	Me	Living with a partner	64%	1 yr.	$424	8	LD starter pack	£43		Just because you professed love early on, doesn't mean you have to stay
Jewellery Box	28	Me	Physically afraid of partner	89%	8 mos.	$196	6	Valentines abroad	£31		I don't want a teacher, I want a partner
T-shirt	29–32	(On/off) Him, Me, Him, Me	Driven crazy by unexplored potential with someone I love	76%	3.5 yrs. with 6 mos. silence	$217	9	Flew me to NYC	£1		Just because you love someone, doesn't mean you should be in a relationship with them (?)

63

Tracking my daily spending for the last four months has made me acutely aware of how much of my earnings I thoughtlessly pissed away in restaurants and coffee shops. Now, entering the astronomical sums I spent on phone bills talking with my exes before the ubiquity of Skype and WhatsApp, I groan.

Navid asks what's up.

I relay the embarrassing figures.

"Nah," he says. "You gotta enjoy your life."

I sigh. "I enjoyed too much without earning it."

He waves off my self-reproach. "It's all about balance."

I suspect my austerity measures may be getting to him. I'm home far more frequently whipping things up in the kitchen, which is normally his domain.

I reach a saturation point with my amorphous spreadsheet, despairing that everything takes eight times longer than I allot for it.

Navid advises me to get out of the house.

On the Parkland Walk, a tree-canopied, long-abandoned rail path stretching from Finsbury Park up to Alexandra Palace, I swing my arms and formulate the stock letter to my exes. Navid's flat is two minutes from an entry point to this once dangerous and seedy place, now a haven filled with dog walkers, cyclists and joggers. By the time I reach Ally Pally, I'm ready to fire away. Beginning at the beginning, from a bench, looking down on the city, my fingers tremor and my pulse quickens as I draft and send the following:

Dear Mix Tape,

Hi! I hope you're well.

I've been thinking about you recently. I'm making a new solo show called The Ex-Boyfriend Yard Sale. It's an experimental piece in which I try to figure out the value of various objects based on the stories and feelings associated with them. How their value increases or decreases based on all the ways I invested (time, emotion, money), or didn't, in the romantic relationships they came from.

In the show I want to talk about the mix tape you gave me and my experiences with you. Of course, I will change your name and any identifying details.

I was wondering if you might be willing to have a short Skype call (I've moved to the UK!) with me to talk about the tape?

I understand this might be really weird, and if you're not into it, I completely get it.

Sending you my best,

Haley xo

I don't have an email address for Mix Tape, so he receives the above through an Instagram direct message.

Even though I walk briskly through dusk, I get cold.

£ + ♥

"So my plan is to post my objects on Gumtree, eking out little bits of emotional context, and see what kind of offers I get."

When I told my brother Kian I was making a new show and requested that he help me with market research, his initial response was, "God, I'm glad you're finally gonna make sure the show will sell before you write it." After I explained that wasn't quite what I meant, he reminded me, "Art is a business, Hales."

Kian's feedback to my first solo show was, "Honestly Haley, I could appreciate the art of it but it's the weirdest fucking thing I've ever seen." When I was on tour with that edgy, subversive show in rural Canada, playing to a confounded, white-haired crowd, my brother snapped me out of my shame spiral with, "So the seventy-plus crowd isn't your demographic. Is that really something to be upset about?"

My brother and I share a sense of humour. Our value systems and life paths differ but what makes us laugh is the same. If he wasn't my brother, I'd want to be friends with him, even if I'm not sure he'd want to be friends with me. He lives in Vancouver now, working a corporate job where he specialises in analysing data from focus groups to help corporations maximise their profits. When I asked him if he loved his ex-girlfriend, he said he thought so, but also reminded me that romantic love, as we understand it today, is an idea largely developed in the eighteenth century, and may just be a kind of religion we've all bought into.

When you keep that in mind, what is love?

It's midnight here and 4 p.m. in his time zone. He cracks his neck and begins.

"So what you want to do, is make sure you include the same kinds of details for each object. Its age, one to three USPs—" Seeing my blank expression, he specifies, "Unique Selling Points. One hundred per cent organic materials, one of a kind, handmade, water resistant — something that makes it special and worth paying for."

"What's my USP?" I ask.

"Honestly, that's what I thought this call was going to be about, and I think that's a more worthwhile pursuit, Hales. Approaching your art stuff with an idea of: who is this for, and why do they want it?"

Referring to my notes, I ask, "What other variables should my posts always hit on?"

He says it doesn't really matter as long as I'm consistent. "And be *brief*. No one wants a novella. Two hundred words — max."

I write that down and circle it. "Then I take an average of the offers and put it in the spreadsheet?"

"It's better to take the median. Don't take the mean." He explains that the trouble with means, or averages, is that they can be skewered by outliers. "A median is going to be a cleaner read."

Later I'll learn that an outlier is a piece of data that is very different from all the others in a set, that doesn't fit the same pattern. If you include them in the average, they can miscon-strue your data, leading to misguided decisions. I'll wonder if I'm an outlier; thirty-two, single, in a rented room, sleeping in a single bed, never having lived with a partner for any signifi-cant period of time.

Getting my head around it, I say, "So if I get nine responses to an ad on Gumtree, the four lowest are on one side, the four highest are on the other side, and the number that is smack in the middle is the median."

For the most unbiased response in my study, he recommends that I refrain from including an asking price because by includ-ing one, my emotional info is afforded less influence. "That being said, anyone who is looking for a shovel, for example, is going to have the prices of other shovels in their head when they look at your shovel. So what you're trying to answer with this data is, 'Do people give any fucks about my love?'"

"Or my pain," I say. "But the big question is, can I convince another person to pay for my sentimental value?"

He lays out the best practices for my market research study. "Post each object you have on Gumtree. You have to be sneaky about it. Post one item. Leave it up for a week or two, take it down, post another — maybe even from a different account each time. See what the offers are."

We talk about other things for a while.

He tells me he's got a Tinder date lined up this week. I've hit pause on online dating since the math teacher. I'm concentrat-ing entirely on earning money, paying down debt and getting *The Ex-Boyfriend Yard Sale* off the ground. I tell him I won't be home for Christmas this year. I blame it on the money, but the real reason is that it's too depressing.

I've been trying to break the pattern for years. I love Christmas baking and the mulled wine and decorating the tree and the wintery activities and the rum cakes and the carols, but Christmas Day itself has become a stale re-enactment year after year. I long for my own Christmas with my own family, even if my own family is just me and my partner, instead of returning to the strained conversations and feigned excitement at receiving oven mitts for the sixth year running and the looming sense that we're all sat in the same configuration and the only thing that's changed is the elasticity of our skin.

Kian asks why I'm not using the dating apps but doesn't buy any of my reasons for avoiding them. "Hales. What are you so scared of?"

Anything to escape my current dating life as a topic. I ask why a market research approach to my general work is wise.

"You're a person who looks at things emotionally," he tells me. "Your work as an artist, your solo shows — the ones I've seen — seemed to be about an emotional exchange. Driven by, 'does someone like me' — the audience, that director, a critic?

"Everything is judged from that lens and from the emotional exchange between your work, you and another person. That's one way to look at life: Does someone like me? Another way to look at life is: Do I *need* this person to like me? Are they giving me money? Are they really the right customer? That's the business lens of what you're doing."

He says he thinks there's an aversion to looking at art in that way; it seems impure or unartistic. "But in a weird way, I think it can make you feel better about what you're doing. Because you're kind of missing the point if you're getting your sense of being loved from your working life. Your work —" he pauses — "should support you financially. Yeah, you can get people to like you, but if they're not paying you for what you're doing, you're not really advancing your goals or making this a career."

We talk about my target demographic. When I ask if he thinks this might be a commercially viable show, my brother flicks his fingers through his hair before looking down the barrel of his laptop camera. "I don't know. Break-ups and money are topics most people can relate to, so that's good. Just talk normal. And invest in strong marketing."

"Kian. Message received." And it is. I am ready to earn. I am ready to create something that people will pay for. I want to make something popular and economically successful.

Over the next few days, I pen my posts:

Personalised Mix Tape from my high school sweetheart. Circa 2002 for nostalgia fiends!
This lovingly made mix tape was a gift from my high school boyfriend and includes his original "liner notes" and album art, as well as some commentary between tracks.

This is a perfect oddity for someone who loves buying old postcards at flea markets, tripping upon grocery lists or old diaries, collecting found treasures by the side of the road — or audiophiles who feel nostalgic for the lost era of the original mix tape.

The cassette features tunes by Phish, Counting Crows and Blink 182, as well as lesser known bands such as Tabitha's Secret. In good working condition.

A fun novelty for you from my own romantic vaults. Could this relic of teenage love be a valuable addition to your collection? Is this historical specimen worth anything to you?

Lovely and delicate, 10K White Gold Sapphire & Diamond Necklace — perfect for September babies.
This necklace is a sapphire and diamond, set in white gold and strung on a white gold chain.

Specs are: 10K white gold, round diamond, sapphire.

It was given to me as a nineteenth birthday gift in 2003, from my boyfriend at the time. I have only worn the necklace once. At the time he gave it to me, I was terrified of losing it, knowing it must have been very expensive for him. (He was nineteen, in school and working two part-time jobs (and probably selling marijuana!?)).

If I'm being totally honest, the necklace was never really my style, though it is my birthstone.

We broke up in 2004, but I felt guilty about getting rid of the necklace because it was such a generous gift and I hurt the guy who gave it to me. I have moved with it eight times! Including across an ocean.

If you have any September babies in your life who might like this classy piece, write me a note. It's a lovely necklace and now only has good vibes associated with it. Original box included.

Pick up in north London or we can discuss courier.

Hora Soprano Ukulele, made of walnut, with case — beginner's classic uke!

Made in Romania, this soprano ukulele measures in at 21 inches (53 cm) and features a solid wood spruce face, a walnut plywood back and eclipse, and a maple neck. Delicious.

It was a gift from a guy I dated briefly in university. He'd learned on it, before buying himself a better quality ukulele. I never learned to play — I gave up after "Somewhere Over the Rainbow".

I don't know that it's a particularly "good" instrument. It's missing a string and needs to be tuned.

No bad energy. The relationship didn't last long. It's been played periodically over the years by friends, but mostly unused.

It's a great beginner's uke and I'd love for someone who'll actually play it and enjoy it to have it. I have the case for it and I'll chuck in a "learn to play the ukulele" book that I have along with some picks.

When we broke up I gave him £57 for it. But make me an offer.

Pick up in Highgate/Archway area.

Most charming Free Spirit Bicycle — made in Canada
This Free Spirit, 10 speed bicycle was a birthday gift from a boyfriend at the time.

It's a Sears Canada model.

Over the last ten years I've paid to replace the seat, the tires, the innertubes, the entire back wheel, the brake pads, the handle-bar grips. And I've added a bell, a basket, a rat trap and a milk crate and a fender.

This overhaul was sadly a result of abandoning the bike in a snowbank the winter I found out my ex was dating a friend of mine.

Haven't ridden it in a couple years. Needs a tune up.

1960s Vintage Typewriter — Olympia ultra-portable — works perfectly/never been used (by me)
This is a stunning German-made Olympia Splendid 66 portable manual typewriter in perfect condition. It comes with its original case and accessories (manual, cleaning brushes, etc.) and even the ribbon remains in good condition. Start writing today!

I have never used it. It was a Christmas gift from an ex who broke up with me shortly after, and who I later discovered was cheating on me.

Because I'd wanted this typewriter for such a long time I held onto it, but the humiliation of the experience kept me from using it . . . so it's just been sitting there.

Anyway, it's been years and we've made our peace, we're almost friends. Now I'm ready to let the typewriter go.

Do you want this charming machine? It needs a good story. And it makes a satisfying clicking sound.

He told me he paid £100 for it at an antique shop. This model goes for upwards of £250 on Etsy. Make me an offer.

Original Denim Hershel Backpack — well loved

The OG. This is a piece from before the brand went mainstream and started mass producing their bags with shittier materials.

My ex-bf was hurting for cash when he got me this backpack for Christmas, but he knew I needed a new one (the one I was using had a rip in the bottom) and that I would have never spent money on getting something this nice for myself at that time.

I travelled the world with this backpack — Mongolia, Kosovo, Finland, to name a few! It's a well-loved bag. Now the zipper is broken, and the seams are torn, the colour's faded and the fabric's worn.

With some love it'll be back in working order. A modern classic. A recent vintage. Great for collectors and lovers of denim.

Gorgeous and functional Handmade Porcelain & Mango Wood Jewellery Box

Handmade by my ex, a Scandinavian ceramicist. He left this three-tiered, intricate and beautiful box at my apartment as a place to house his weed when he came to visit me. But you could use it for jewellery or spices or trinkets.

The split with the ceramicist was not good — we haven't spoken since and I feel weird about keeping his box around.

It's a truly gorgeous and well-made piece. The tiny drawers each have a delicately carved porcelain tile on the front and pull out easily, and the lid opens with a vintage brass hinge. It seems a shame to have such a lovely thing collecting dust at mine, or to end up in a dumpster . . . I need it outta my flat!

If you're not superstitious, and you love ceramics, this is for you.

Vintage Royal Canadian Navy T-shirt, circa 1970

A vintage RCN T-shirt purchased circa 2002 at a Value Village by my ex, who wore it for years before giving it to me in 2016 as a nightshirt.

Authentic vintage item. Threadbare and pily but no rips or holes.

I can't sleep in it anymore but don't want it to go to a landfill.

£ + ♥

A couple days later, I'm in the basement of the Radisson Hotel just south of Warren Street Station, in a maid's costume. I'm performing in a murder-mystery dinner theatre-show, thrusting a bawdy adaptation of a Sherlock Holmes tale onto a group of unsuspecting colleagues who were expecting a civilised dinner on their company's dime.

I glug cheap white wine in the "dressing room" to prepare for the scene that falls between their main course and dessert, in which I jerk off a feather duster. It pays one hundred and fifty pounds a night, so.

As I tighten my frilly apron, I check my phone. Luis Bay, a physicist I'm acquainted with, has emailed me back about *The Ex-Boyfriend Yard Sale*.

He's only available to speak right before the voice job I have on Thursday, so I agree to Skype with him then.

A few days later, I video call him from a bench in Soho's Golden Square, surrounded by pigeons. Luis holds a PhD in physics from Harvard, he was a visiting scholar at Oxford and he's written several books, one of which was referred to heavily in a play about physics I did in Toronto.

First of all, Luis tells me that, essentially, what I am dealing with here is economics, not physics. "But," he says, "I'll help you however I can."

He tells me there are two kinds of economics, classical and neoclassical. Classical economics argue that everything has a price, even if it's never been bought or sold, whereas neoclassical economics operates under the principle that sometimes, some things don't have a value. He says that, "Money is truly symbolic and abstract, except for when we, people, agree to give it a value. What makes money perfect is that it doesn't have a history; we don't know where it's been, and that's what makes the system work. Money," he concludes, "has no memory."

"Yeah," I say, shivering in the late November air, "money's cold."

He wonders aloud whether I could include some non-monetary payment in my final price. This is counter to the exercise, but I allow it because he's got the PhD.

When I hang up the phone, another email has arrived. *(No Subject.)* From T. I have to be in a recording booth in twelve minutes, talking about pantyhose. My rabbit heart racing, I open the email and manoeuvre through Soho as I read.

Hello Haley,

I'm writing to you from Sault Ste. Marie, where I've spent the last few months as my brother's health declines. He's on his way out of the world. I know you think there's something more, but I still think dead/over, and that is both a comfort and a horror. My little brother, gone. In truth, I'm just plain sad. Angry too. But really sad.

I've been going to a meditation centre at 5 a.m. every day. And something is shifting.

You've been on my mind. A lot. I'm writing to see if you would be open to a conversation? If not, I'm sorry to intrude.

You've been quiet on social media — I know it's a deceptive gauge for how a person is doing, but with nothing to decipher . . . anyway, I hope everything is going well for you these days.

I miss your voice, in all forms of the meaning.

If I've overstepped, I'm very sorry. If you're willing to speak with me, I'd love that.

Xo T

As I read advertising copy about control tops and reinforced toes with a bright smile, with sassy confidence, with a subtly conspiratorial tone — whatever the client wants — my mind swirls. I oscillate between hoping T wants to get back together, and agitation that he only wants me around when he's down. The client is happy, and the sound engineer will Frankenstein my two best takes together. They shake my hand and I stumble up the carpeted stairs. From the bathroom stall of the studio, I peck a curt reply to T with my thumbs but decide to hold off on sending it till after therapy this evening.

Later that night, I doodle hearts and pound signs on a Post-it note beside my laptop while Thea asks, "What do *you* think T wants?"

"To get back together, but I'm also scared he just wants me to hold his hand through his grief and that I'm being presumptuous." I tell her that I want to talk to him, but I know doing it would be opening Pandora's box. "If I talk to him, I'm entangled and if I'm entangled, I'm fucked."

She reminds me the clearest indicator of someone's future behaviour is their past behaviour. "But," she adds, "there is something to be said for how a big life event, such as the death of a sibling, can shift perspectives and precipitate change." And she believes that people are capable of change.

Midway through the session she's got me compiling a list of my conditions for getting back together, so I'm prepared should T propose it. My terms take up several Post-it notes.

I want to keep the good stuff — the sexual connection, the endlessly rousing conversation — and I want to change everything else. Measures must be put in place to ensure the relationship doesn't zap all my energy. My concern is that it'll distract and detract from the verve I could be pouring into my work, which will then suffer and never pay off, and even with that sacrifice our relationship won't be healthy enough for T and me to have a baby and I'll end up in my fifties with a shitty relationship, no child and a lacklustre career.

As we wind down, Thea says, "Hold your ground. If he can't meet these demands, then you walk."

"Yeah. It's only worth it if it can be on my terms." I sigh. "I feel like an asshole, saying I can either be the lover that he's trying to win back, or his friend. But I can't truly be there for him about his brother, if he wants to win me back."

Armed with my list of conditions, along with the giddy nerves that accompany gambling with the heart, the sense that this exchange could alter the course of my life and a dose of indignation, I write T a brief email that says I'm very sorry to hear about his brother and I'm free at 6 p.m. tomorrow to speak on the phone.

£ + ♥

The call comes at 6 p.m. on the dot. It's been five months since the last time we spoke. I'm in the nun's cell, at my desk, my notes and a freshly brewed ginger tea in front of me. I hear T straining to control his breathing.

"Hi."

I smile at the familiar abruptness of his speech. "How are you doing?" I coax.

"I'm . . . you know. Nervous."

"I'm so sorry about your brother."

"Yeah. It's not a surprise but it's . . . fucking awful." He exhales. "It's so good to hear your voice."

I lie down on my tiny bed for a moment.

He wants to know about me. I'm embarrassed, but I admit to him that the voice job for the gambling company didn't come through and I'm doing penance, paying off my debt by working Joe-jobs. What I don't admit is that the Joe-jobs are actually just covering my day-to-day living expenses. I only make dents in my debt when voiceover money arrives, usually two hundred and five pounds per job.

"Tell me about you," I say.

But he wants me to keep talking, so I describe *The Ex-Boyfriend Yard Sale*. When he asks if he's featured, I say, "It's hard to know if I should include you because you were never technically my boyfriend."

"But I was," he protests, "whether we had the label or not. I was a fucking idiot, Haley. I was scared. I was . . ." His voice trails off.

My guts twist like a wet towel being wrung out. I pull my knees into my chest to still my innards and offer, "If I was going to include you, I would sell the T-shirt you gave me — the one I wore on the way to the airport."

"Huh," he says, and then he talks about his brother, holding his brother while he cries, petrified of not getting to be alive, crying because he doesn't have the energy to rage. His brother has been on a very strict diet for the last year, but now that the cancer is in his liver and it's just a matter of time, he wants to eat things that give him pleasure. T fed him a chocolate-glazed doughnut yesterday. T says the other big thing about being back home after so much time away is witnessing his parents' relationship and the life they built together — "this simple, domestic, wholesome life in tandem" — up close. This is the longest amount of time he's spent in his hometown since he left as a teenager. He's been on the road as long as he could do anything about it — sailing, teaching white-water rafting, working as a French translator, painting murals, before becoming a journalist and now, here he is, espousing the value of settling in one place. "And the only person I want to do it with is you."

I hold my breath.

"I love you, Haley."

I'm silent for a while. He listens. And then I smile and say, "Okay." I've been waiting years to hear this and now that I have, I'm not sure how to say it back. He doesn't push me.

He has a proposition. "What if I come to London for a month. I'll get my own place and we can start again, with a bit more breath."

I realise this is serious business. I snap up and sit at my desk, focusing my eyes on my conditions. "The thing is T, I love you too, but I don't trust you."

"What would it take?" he asks. "Can I go on probation?"

"I'm concerned," I say carefully, "that you're lonely and sad, and that those things are clouding your vision."

"I know. I know it might seem that way but it's really not."

"But I'd understand if you wanted me around as a supportive pal during this really brutal time."

He asserts, "Haley. That's not what I want."

I fumble my way through explaining that I can either be the lover he's trying to woo back or a sympathetic ear — not both.

"I want partner — lover," T corrects himself hastily.

"Think about it."

"I don't need to."

I'm jittery and I want to pace but I stay seated, my feet on the ground. "I am willing to entertain the possibility of getting back together, but, *but* —" I interrupt his expressions of excitement — "you have to hear me out."

"Yes. Of course. Anything."

"I don't want to faff around. I want something serious. I'm thirty-two. I want to have a baby."

"I want that too."

"Then here's what it will take," I say, keeping my finger on the top item on my list. "First of all, I want to be with someone who likes himself."

He weeps at this, misinterpreting my self-interest as generosity for his wellbeing.

"I want you to be in regular ongoing therapy."

"I agree. I agree." His tone is ebullient at the fact that I haven't outright refused him.

"Once a week, not for a year, for a long time. And you have to stick with it, consistently."

"I know, you're right. Yes. I will do that."

"I want to be in contact with you every day. I want to Skype regularly, at least once a week — I want this to be planned and not slotted in around other stuff. I want you to tell me that you love me."

"I do love you."

Vindicated, righteous and marshmallow-kneed, I tell him, "I want you to say it, a lot. I need to hear it—"

"I'm so sorry I didn't say it before. I'm so sorry, Haley."

"I can't have fear and neurosis running this relationship. You need to get a grip. No more telling me 'it should be light'. You need to take responsibility for the fear and anxiety you bring to the table."

"I agree."

"I need you to be firm and solid, no more retractions. No more ground shifting. No more saying one thing one day and changing your mind the next. I need a man of his word. If you're in, you're in."

"I'm in."

"I need you to acknowledge that I live in the UK. I'm not going to change my mind and I don't want you forgetting that and asking me if I want to live in Canada in a hypothetical future." I tell him I'm up for an unconventional relationship but if he doesn't want to do long distance he needs to provide solutions.

He says he's planning on getting his British passport — his dad was born in Somerset.

This thrills me, but I retain an officious tone and move on to my next item. "I don't want to repeat the pattern where, when I soften towards you, you withdraw. I want you to let us be close and soft together."

"I *want* to be close to you Haley. I will go on Facebook and change my relationship status today — whatever you need."

"I don't need that, but I need you to be my boyfriend. I need the label to be established between us."

"I'm yours. You want that, I'm in. One hundred per cent. I want it too."

It's hard not to get high off his brazen laying of himself at my feet. Is there anything more tantalising than a grovelling lover? "Well, let's see. Those are my conditions. If you want to be my boyfriend then you need to meet them. And follow through. This all has to be proven over time."

"How can I prove it to you?"

"Being consistent with all this stuff, *over time*. Follow through."

"Right." A beat. "I love you, Haley."

"I love you too." I stick my fingers down the collar of my shirt. My armpits are slick. We plan to Skype in three days.

I hang up, bust open the door to my cell and waltz into the living room, beneficent. "It's back on, Navid. He's coming here for a month and he's getting his citizenship."

Navid maintains his stance that when something ends, it's over, and stretches his arms into a big "Y".

£ + ♥

The following day, on the Tube ride to meet Gemma in Bethnal Green, I read and re-read T's follow-up email:

I can't tell you how good it was to talk with you. I slept better last night than I have in ages. You're good to me and for me. I'm so grateful that you were willing to speak with me.

80

If there's anything from our call that you want to rehash or discuss, just say the word. Regardless of whether or not you decide to give me another chance, I'm going to get back into therapy straight away. You were right about that and so much more. I'm sorry I let my fear stop me from taking the leap. And I regret how heavy that made things between us. I want all the changes you want.

As for "being a guy who likes himself", loving myself feels far off, but accepting myself is a place I can aim for.

I hope you don't mind, I told my brother about our call and I showed him your picture. He's heard a lot about you already but mostly how I've been an idiot. He high-fived me — weakly but still — and told me not to fuck it up.

Things will be different now, Haley. The version of me that saw the world in black and white — long distance isn't real, for example — is dying as my brother does. A sick silver lining. I see now how nuanced life is, all the gradations I missed earlier. I'm ready to create a life for us that is wholly ours and my proposal to come and spend significant time with you in the UK is a start.

You're right, the timing isn't great, but this experience has changed me and I hope you'll allow me the chance to prove it to you. I'm happy to give you as much time as you need to make a decision about me. I'm not going anywhere.

Please forgive me for the grave tone of this letter. But the prospect of winning you back into my life is too important for me to be glib about.

I love you,

T

ps. I bought the T-shirt while on a trip out west at a thrift shop on Salt Spring Island. I believe you wore it as a nightshirt and it seemed right that you should keep it after that. Happy to answer questions about it.

It's dark outside when I step off the bus. Gemma and I find a swish and cosy restaurant on Roman Road. In the soft lighting we pile our wool sweaters and backpacks on the bar stools to either side of us and order nuts and red wine.

I reveal my rat's nest of a spreadsheet. "I'm still waiting on some of the market research and I haven't got through *all* of the data entry yet."

"Do you mind if I . . .?" She slides my laptop across the marble countertop, careful to keep her wine glass a few inches from my keyboard, and makes some cosmetic changes.

I sit tall on my bar stool, bubbling with the prospective T 5.0 love affair, still high off his adulation and prostration.

She says our first task is to now determine how to turn all my qualitative data (words, stories, feelings) into quantitative data (numbers), which can then be pumped through the formula, which will spit out a price. "We need to think about systems of measurement."

"So like – scale of one to ten?" I ask.

"Yes. And should we look at ten as positive and one as negative? Or vice versa?"

I share my joy-verses-suffering quandary with her. Does suffering increase or decrease the value of an item? "I can see in some cases wanting to be compensated for a miserable time, and in other cases, wanting a fantastic time to increase the value of the item because parting with it would be more painful because of its positive associations."

Without missing a beat she says, "Not a problem. We'll make calls, case by case." Gemma scribbles in her notebook. "We need to think about pricing in accordance with your earnings, scaled to your relationship with money."

We decide I should figure out my average hourly income during each relationship, in order to measure how much my time was literally worth at those various points in my life, converted into British pounds, with the correct exchange rate for the given years. We discuss whether or not to take inflation into account.

Gemma says, "It'll be a little more annoying, but it will give us a fairer, less subjective result. And we only have to worry about it for cash amounts connected to a specific time."

Professionalism rounded down by the wine, conversation drifts to our personal lives. I pry into Gemma's dating history.

Before her current partner, she never really liked any of her boyfriends. "I had a scary amount of power in those relationships. I was only in them because the boys expressed interest, and I thought, why not?" She admits that she's never been broken up with.

I tell her I'm very jealous.

She says those relationships don't really count because they all happened before she was twenty.

My laptop's now closed and I've taken out my notebook. We order another glass and I coil my hair up into a concentration bun. While we devour crusty bread, I gnaw on this idea of who broke up with who. "It's better to be the one who ends it instead of the one who gets dumped. Any day. Except, except —" I slather soft butter onto a fluffy sourdough slice — "when you break up with someone *on their behalf*. Like with the guy who gave me the bike; he just got colder and more distant and then I realised he was waiting for me to end it with him. So that needs to be in the formula."

Gemma assures me we'll factor that in but recommends taking a step back before we get granular. "We need a system," she stresses. "I want to work methodically."

We crack on fuelled by booze and the good mood induced by a new collaboration. We start grouping together the various data points. Swiftly we determine that anything to do with the object itself should be in one category, which we name Market Value (MV), and anything to do with time should be in another category, which we call Time Invested (t). For now, we agree to keep the Wild Cards (WC) under one category, and figure them out once we know more.

For details about the quality of a particular relationship we invent a category called the Relationship Index (RI). The RI encapsulates the nitty gritty that can be assessed for just about every relationship, like who broke up with who and the quality of sex.

"So, we have Market Value, Time Invested and the Relationship Index, plus any applicable Wild Cards." We admire our cleanly sorted categories.

Market Value (MV)	Time Invested (t)	Relationship Index (RI)	Wild Cards (WC)
• How much the ex paid for the object in question • The appreciation or depreciation of the object in question as determined by an appraiser, and market research via posting the objects on Gumtree • Who paid for more things during the relationship • How much thought he put into the gift — if it was a gift?	• How long the relationship lasted • The ratio of fun to misery during the relationship • The time spent pining before we got together • How long it took to get over the relationship • Percent of the relationship that was long distance	• The value of big life lessons the relationship taught me • How much baggage I left the relationship with • Practical skills • Rites of passage in the relationship • Good stories contributed to life story • Friends with them now? • Biggest romantic gesture • Reliability • Key highs versus key lows • Who broke up with who • How good the sex was • The calibre of "poetry"/ romance • How hard he made me laugh • How often and badly we fought • Was there ever unspeakable bliss? • Was I in love? & what was the intensity of the love?	• How much I cried during the relationship • Getting played • Damage to my property • Still feel guilty

Putting her pens back in their case, Gemma says, "It's difficult to keep all the ex-boyfriends straight, so let's work chronologically."

I agree. "To simplify," I say, "I won't call them by their names, but instead I'll refer to them by the objects they gave me, Mix Tape, Necklace, T-shirt — although . . ." I press my warm fingertips into breadcrumbs scattered on the bar, collecting them in my palm.

"What?" Gemma searches for my eyes.

"Nothing." I lie. "I forgot what I was going to say." There's no point telling her about T yet. I don't know if he's an ex or a current.

We split the bill and bundle up. All my favourite adults wear backpacks and Gemma is no different. Swerving into each other, laughing, drunk, we make our way to the Tube.

THE LEDGER

Love	T loves me. He's always loved me. I wasn't deluded
Money	Covering my living expenses w/ Joe-jobs, tracking
	– £9,669.32 in debt
	£507.86 in bank
	Thea is allowing me to do therapy on credit. I owe
	her £825.40 ($65 per session x 22 sessions)
	I will save £600 by not going home for Christmas
Career	*The Ex-Boyfriend Yard Sale* is underway:
	– Market research has begun
	– The formula is going to work
	Voiceovers averaging about 3 per month
	Joe-jobs = medical role play & catering
Total	*?? Coming up from zero.*

10. MARKET VALUE

Market value is the price an asset would fetch in the
marketplace, or the price at which something can be
sold, at a particular time in a particular place.

"Delay no more," I say aloud to myself just before tripping on
Navid's new snorkel gear. My coffee sloshes onto the beige
carpet and I spend the next twelve minutes dabbing it with fizzy
water and scrubbing it with baking soda until the stain fades.
Navid's out getting his weekly haircut and I've already completed
my personal weekly budget tracking my expenses. I forked out
some dough to send Christmas cards to everyone who's
employed me or helped me out in my professional life over the
past year, an unforeseen expenditure I hope pays off.

I received a fascinating email from a Master's student at
Goldsmiths University in response to one of my Gumtree posts.
She's writing her dissertation on "cultural hybridity, standard-
isation and the mix-tape culture of the early noughties". She
wanted to know if I had any other mix tapes like the one from
my high school boyfriend. Regardless, her offer was two pounds
for the tape including postage.

After a week of medical role-playing, embodying a Jehovah's
Witness who will only accept a specific type of blood transfu-
sion, I'm hunkering down with *The Ex-Boyfriend Yard Sale* on
my day off. My plan was to crank out my Arts Council England
grant application. I've now got three theatre companies each
willing to give me free space to work on the piece for a week.

These research and development (R&D) weeks will happen over several months beginning in the new year, and the first two will culminate in work-in-progress performances. With the theatres' support and a share of the box office earnings for the second performance lined up, I'm eligible for grant money to develop the show, and given that I need to pay Gemma, it's imperative that I apply. But the deadline is approaching fast, and the one hour a day I've dedicated to writing the application is proving to be insufficient. I have to blitz it.

But I can't today, because today is the only day Mix Tape is available to chat with me. He replied to my Instagram message saying that the project sounded like a "cool idea" but the time difference between London and Bogota, where he now lives, made scheduling tricky.

I pull Navid's ancient boom box off the bottom bookshelf, plug it in and listen to the mix tape from my first love for the first time since I was seventeen. The first song is an echoey live recording of "Loss, Strain and Butterflies" by Tabitha's Secret. When I hear the lyric, "I'm looking for a soul to cling to/Girl what you think about that", I immediately recall my elation of hearing it the first time and the supreme, unabashed purity with which I loved Mix Tape. The concept of being someone's girl, belonging to someone, now chafes against my feminism and need for autonomy, but at that time, it swarmed my guts with pleasure.

I dated Mix Tape for just under a year when I was sixteen. That summer, a small group of us tore around my hometown — Kitchener-Waterloo, a mid-sized university city about ninety minutes west of Toronto — by foot and on the local buses, none of us working or driving yet. When we met, Mix Tape had braces, and paired Hawaiian shirts with basketball shorts. He was more attractive than his slouched posture let on, not yet sure how to occupy his new height or the sudden breadth of his shoulders. I was smitten. All I wanted was to be close to his toneless but slender body, to be entangled in his hairless arms and legs.

My crush on him grew out of our aimless days and enthralling evenings getting drunk and becoming friends. In August we took the bus to the Canadian National Exhibition in Toronto — a gigantic fair with an air show, amusement-park rides and corporate trade convention. His leg brushed mine as we were getting into a hot, metal, bullet-like compartment on a whirl-di-whirl ride. A bolt of energy zinged through me. And though I screamed throughout the ride, it was the thrill of the spark I was responding to.

On the bus home that evening we poked at revealing our feelings for each other.

"I hate it when I end up in the friend zone," he said.

"Me too," I agreed. And without explicitly saying it, when we stepped off the Greyhound at the Kitchener bus terminal, we both knew.

Our first kiss took place in his parents' basement, lying on the tattered, brown sofa, sock feet intertwined, "watching a movie". Sure, some of our peers were having sex, and we'd both kissed people before. We'd both had various three-week, maybe even three-month relationships already, but this seemed different. Kissing symbolised crossing a threshold from the platonic to the romantic *and* into the relationship we'd be in until we died. We were scared. He shifted himself on top of me, and our nervous lips met. It wasn't long before his tongue was jabbing into my mouth, stiff and stirring. His arms shook holding his own weight and I could smell his medicated acne concealer.

It was clumsy and effortful making-out. One thought ran through my mind on a loop the whole time: I can't kiss like this for the rest of my life. Either he has to get better or I have to find someone else.

But I didn't want anyone else. I attempted to demonstrate how I wanted to be kissed with my kissing. What resulted was chapped faces and both of us gasping for air. Yet we persisted.

It was autumn when we first kissed and spring the first time that he touched my vagina. We were co-pilots on a journey to lose our innocence. I was mildly dismayed to be dealt such a boring love story. I'd expected to have a few more boyfriends in my twenties, but missing out on a variety of lovers seemed like a small price to pay for the gigantic windfall of having found the one so early on. As we covered more physical terrain, I wanted more love and devotion from him. Whereas he, I think, wanted more experiences with more partners.

Four tracks in, "Brian Wilson" by the Barenaked Ladies is playing, and it's time for the call. I've slapped on my make-up and I've got the cassette case and my list of questions beside my laptop.

Mix Tape Skypes with me from his living room while his wife makes a lasagne from scratch in the kitchen. They have an open-concept home.

In fifteen minutes, we catch each other up on the last sixteen years. He reminds me that the tape was a gift, but given without occasion, just because. A lot of thought was given to what song flowed into the next, and how the relationship between the various pieces of music conveyed a greater meaning. He'd been obsessed with the film *High Fidelity* and believed a mix was a meaningful gesture.

At the mention of the film, I recall the John Cusack character's monologue about the symbolic nature of his girlfriend's French-cut undies, which had prompted me to buy my own pair of white cotton underpants at a department store. This was an effort to prove to Mix Tape that I liked the things he liked; that we still had things in common when we were obviously growing apart. Is there anything more disheartening than showing off new underwear to a partner with waning sexual interest in you? I write *white underpants* in my notebook and wrench my attention back to what he's saying.

Though the physical cassette itself was stolen from his parents' collection and taped over a recording of an audio drama, he stresses that it took hours to create a mix tape at that point in history. Downloading each song, illegally, and then burning them onto a CD was a temperamental process because the computer so often crashed midway through. And then he had to use one of those CD-cassette boom boxes to transfer the music onto tape, pausing to record his audio commentary in between. I jot down *potentially risking jail-time*, as it was the era of the Napster crackdown. Behind him, his wife lays fresh sheets of pasta on a wooden drying rack.

I read the song list to him. He'd forgotten it and his liner notes entirely. His breathy laugh catches in his throat. It comes out sharp on the word "Yeah" followed by "Oh god". When his iPad runs out of battery, he heads upstairs to retrieve the power cord. On the way to his office he whispers and flips the camera around to show me his sleeping twins in their crib. He plugs in his iPad and stays in his office.

Moving out of the concrete realm of the mix tape itself, I keep my questions connected to the premise of the project. "What were the big gains and losses from our relationship for you?"

He begins with gains, citing "so many firsts". I had decided I didn't want to lose my virginity till I turned seventeen. He never pressured me about it. We don't talk about the fact that we never had penetrative sex but it's on my mind that that was one of the firsts we didn't forge together.

"And for loss," he says, "I guess, a loss of a sense of innocence."

I concur.

"Uh, yeah but for me, more . . . uh." His voice rising, he looks over his shoulder. "When we got together, I thought of myself as a pretty stand-up guy, and then the way, I, uh . . ." He scratches his thumbnail over something that looks like spit-up on his sweater as he continues. "The way I handled our break-up, I learned I was just a piece-of-shit dude, like everybody else."

"But didn't you just like somebody else?"

He sighs.

"You were done!" I cry, almost joyfully.

"Yeah, I was done, but I said I wasn't and—" he looks over his shoulder again — "that break-up was one of the shittiest things I've ever done as a person, and I've always felt really bad about it."

"Oh, you're absolved," I say a bit too loudly, a bit too much of an actress's voice.

"No no, that's not—". He shakes his head.

I notice just how far Mix Tape's hairline has receded, and the depth of the lines etched in his forehead. He looks tired; his shoulders have slid away from his ears over the last sixteen years; he looks like his father.

Mix Tape asks when he can see the show and I half-lie that Canadian dates are TBC. I've written to several theatres in Toronto, but nothing is confirmed yet. And nothing for South America.

I say, "Enjoy your lasagne and your babies."

He laughs, sharp and throaty, and salutes me.

I hang up and shut my computer. The hum of the TV on the other side of the wall lulls me and I sit very still. Stunned. My face is flushed. I yearn to be outside. I should be studiously making notes and entering the data into the spreadsheet, but instead I rifle through my brimming wardrobe, looking for the teenage journals I brought over from Canada.

Triumphant, I open a chunky notebook covered with magazine cut-outs and read:

Mix Tape has another girlfriend. There have been enough clues/hints. I know he does. I don't feel there's any point lying to myself about the matter, clearly, whatever we had was NOT love. It's the stage you (as a teenager) buy into as being love; however, it isn't.

I wish he cared about me the same way I did about him.

I hate that I'm still hating him!

Anyway, there have been perks:

I'm not on the phone with him WASTING my TIME.

He's not around to make me feel badly, guilty or tell me I'm such a jealous person, when clearly I KNEW intuitively exactly what was going on. It really pisses me off that he tried to convince me I was just jealous and paranoid.

He's failing school and he's drinking A LOT. I hope he chokes on his vomit and dies. No, I don't want him to die. That's a horrid thing to say. I just hope he gets caught by the police! And is charged a severe fine! And that his parents get SO MAD at him. I hope he goes NOWHERE! I hate him for hurting me.

I'm not a bad person. I'm not a bad person.

I'm sad.

Oh dear. Enough paper wasted on the dick! I'm sure I'm learning something I'll realise some time from now.

Love, Haley

I had blocked out that, on the night we broke up, I collapsed outside my parents' bedroom sobbing. My mum got out of bed, got down on the floor and rocked me. She said, "If I could take your pain I would." I had forgotten all of it. But he hadn't. And he owned up to it sixteen years later. I had not anticipated this outcome.

Milo calls. When I tell him I can't go to a comedy show because I'm working on my grant application, he persuades me by promising to edit my budget and agreeing to go see the show I want to, an improvised Christmas cabaret that my coach is performing in.

While I wait for Milo to pick me up, I forward the email from the pop music academic to my brother, asking if he'd recommend me seeing if she's willing to barter.

£ + ♥

At the pub before heading up to the theatre, I scarf a quarter chicken roast and tell Milo about Mix Tape's apology and my erasure of the events that are graphically recounted in my teenage journal.

Milo begs to read my diary.

"NEVER!" I pass Milo my laptop so he can look at the budget. It occurs to me that even though the break-up with Mix Tape was more devastating for me at the time, it's more vivid for him now. I say to Milo, "The conversation with Mix Tape made me realise something about break-ups I didn't want to."

"Oh yeah?"

"Dilution does something."

Milo jostles a piece of broccoli into his mouth and raises his eyebrows.

"Because I've had eight break-ups versus his three, my experience with him is watered down."

Milo says he wouldn't know, being a serial monogamist who's dovetailed each of his long-term relationships. "Since I was eighteen, I've had a seven-year relationship, then straight into a three-year relationship, then a six-year relationship that I ended when I met Julie and we're five years in." He's never had to withstand the pain of being single after a break-up.

When he goes to buy another round, I send Gemma a voice note updating her on the call with Mix Tape, and declaring that we need to include this dilution effect in the formula.

Milo returns, drinks in hand, clarifying that he's a burn-it-all-to-the-ground kind of person after a break-up. He can't understand how I'm able to keep all this stuff, let alone converse with my exes.

I tell him I got rid of most of my stuff when I left Toronto. Laid it out on my front lawn and gave most of it away. My parents had downsized and refused to store anything, so my precious items, mostly my childhood journals, went into a storage locker in their town and stayed there for a year until I brought the journals to London.

"$56.89 CAD per month."

Milo does that math on his phone. "You spent $682.68 to preserve your writing."

"I guess we better get that in the formula."

"This is why tracking your expenses is crucial."

I pull out my phone to text Gemma again and see a message from T: *Just saying. I really wish we could have some pancakes right now.*

Milo asks me why I'm blushing.

"T. Being so — hold on, I've gotta respond." I type: *You're on probation. Come here. I love you.*

His response fills my screen with *yayayyayayayayayyayayayay yaayyayayyaya. YAYAYAYYYAYAYAYAYAYAYAYAYYAYAYAYAYAYAYAYY AYAYAYAYAYAYAYAYYYAYAYAYAYAYAYAYAYAYAYAYAYAYAYAA YAYYAYAYAYAYAYAYAYAYAYAYAYYAYAYAYAYAYAYAYYAYAYAYAY AYAYAYAYAYAAY.*

I beam and put away my phone.

Milo says, "Mate, you two are honeymooning hard."

"Maybe we can have dinner with you and Julie? I just told him to book the ticket to come see me." Milo's never met T but I hope he will on this visit.

"Well . . . we'll see. Julie and I are having a bit of a shit time." He says he feels more like her brother than her lover these days. "Too much using the toilet with the door open."

I nod and try to remain focused on him. The new lease T's promises have given our relationship makes me smug, as does the fact that our unconventional relationship will avoid these common pitfalls.

Then I hear him say, "But the big problem is she doesn't talk to me about why she's blue. I don't know what's going on. She's just so quiet. It's like living with a ghost." When I ask if she's depressed, Milo evades the topic entirely. "Right McGee, let's fix this budget then." He adds several lines. "National Insurance, pension contributions, public liability insurance, plus an artist's fee for you. Don't waive that!"

We talk about the timeline for the show and how I want to structure my R&D weeks.

Milo says, "I don't want to sound like an injured ego, but why haven't you asked me to do your lighting design?"

"I didn't think I could afford you!"

He turns the spreadsheet to face me, pointing out the fee included for lighting. "Nice work if you can get it."

"Do you like working with friends?"

"I only want to work with friends."

"I don't know," I say. "I worry it might get contentious." I try to explain that because I struggle to argue with friends, even in a professional setting, I often acquiesce to avoid conflict and then come to not only resent them, but uninvest in the project as a way to cope with not having defended my ideas.

"Well don't do that with me," he says. "Besides, I'll give you a mate's rate."

"Sold."

Milo readjusts his fee in the spreadsheet.

The bell is rung, and we head up to the pub's theatre. My coach kicks off the show by asking who likes eggnog. We whoop and glasses are passed to us. It's an hour of silliness involving elves, capitalism, and family politics. I laugh generously, high on T's imminent visit. Milo laughs incessantly, I presume to escape the gloom of the situation with Julie he's driving back to.

£ + ♥

My conversations with T intensify over the Christmas period. I indulge in the comfort of our familiarity. There's something soothing about spending hours on the phone with a person

96

who shares my accent while I'm far from home. The dinner Fi hosts on New Year's Eve for six couples and myself leaves me feeling like a total outlier; I escape before midnight and ring in the new year via video chat with T from inside a bus shelter. By midnight in T's time zone, his brother has died.

Two weeks later and his romance has dialled down. I've been paralysed by my desires to both tend to his grief and resist falling into the relationship zone with him before he's met all of my conditions. But he's arriving in London this afternoon.

When I open the door, T smiles, a rare sight. He lumbers up the steps, gripping the straps of his bags. I hop in the door frame, trying to keep my sock feet from freezing. He hugs me lightly.

"Come in. Come up," I say.

He manoeuvres his duffle bag as he follows me up the narrow staircase to the second floor. Inside Navid's flat, I sit on the sofa and he eases himself into the armchair.

"Do you want a tea or a coffee or some water? Or I have muesli. Oh, and I bought you a grapefruit!" I leap up to fetch it from the kitchen. Somehow, the grapefruit cottage cheese diet is lodged in T's brain as acceptable breakfast food, though he never eats cottage cheese. "And I also got you a croissant," I call from the kitchen. Ollie says part of being my friend is putting up with my aggressive hosting. I squat to check my reflection in the microwave. "Do you want jam?" I holler.

He's in the doorway.

I lower my voice. "Do you want jam?"

"No. No. That's perfect."

"I got you a grapefruit," I repeat, holding it out to him.

"I'll have it later."

He has his hands around my waist now. I touch his face. He leans down and kisses me. His lips are still cool from his walk from the station.

"You're a little ripe," I whisper.

He backs away, covering his mouth with one hand and holding his upper arm with the other, horrified. Clamping down on wherever the offensive smell might be coming from.

I reassure him I don't mind, trying to close the gap between us, but he holds me at arm's length.

"I'll take a shower."

"Take it after you eat."

"I don't need to eat."

I put his croissant back in the bag. I take a bite of mine but I'm too nervous to eat.

After his shower, he sits beside me on the sofa. I put my arms around him, and we kiss till I'm on my back and he's got his hands on the button of my jeans.

"I'm not there yet," I say as gently as possible.

He retreats, hands in the air.

"Sorry. I have to — you gotta earn that."

"Right. Of course. I'm sorry, I didn't know."

"It's okay."

We sit up, him on one end of the sofa, me on the other. I sip my coffee and push my feet into his thigh. He holds my big toe with his thumb.

"I'm fucked up, Haley. I know I'm not supposed to talk about my brother but . . ."

He tilts his head back to prevent tears from falling.

I crawl to him. He sobs and I rub his back.

"Take how quickly I've come to you after my brother died as a symbol of how much I want this to work with you."

We stay on the sofa like this till the afternoon sun has moved out of the room and we're immobile in the grey of the early evening. I have to pee badly, but I don't want to leave him.

"Do you want to get some pub food in Crouch End? We could go to a movie?"

"I'm so sorry I'm such a fucking mess, Haley." He starts to weep again.

"It's okay." Gesturing towards the clock, I say, "My flatmate is going to be home soon."

"Yep." He releases himself from my arms and stands.

He's staying on a friend's couch in south-east London tonight. His pledge to book his own place for a month has been downgraded to sofa-hopping for two weeks. But he did enter therapy before getting on the plane.

In the bathroom I look in the mirror. Get your feet under you and speak from your stomach.

We move his bags into the nun's cell, put our boots on, and plunge into the drizzly evening. As we enter the pub, I worry I've led us to the wrong place. We choose a wooden table by the fire, but the establishment is empty. He suggests a bottle, but I say nah.

"I'll drink it."

I raise my eyebrows, and he relents.

"A glass is fine. I'm jet-lagged."

At the bar I order two large house reds and some food. I place the drinks down with a sense of turning the page to a cosy, warm chapter together. But somehow during the time it took me to place our order, T's descended into his own grim and despondent story.

"I don't know, Haley. I wanted to see you. But I don't know what I'm doing here."

Agitation floods me. "See, this is what I meant about the retractions." I take a sip without saying cheers and shake my head at having found ourselves already replaying this old scene.

"It's not a retraction. I'm just telling you how I feel."

"I need you to be the solid one." I bring the edge of my hand down on the table for emphasis. "I am not convinced about you."

He hangs his head.

"You have a lot to prove."

"I'm here," he hisses. "I came to you. This is my romantic gesture."

"That's the *first* step. I told you, you need to earn my trust over time."

He looks around dejectedly.

"If you don't know if you're up for that, then you should go home."

"I've been thinking about it."

Our food arrives. The potatoes are delicious.

After about thirteen mouthfuls in silence, I say, "I don't want to be the couple arguing in the pub."

"Neither do I." He says he has a Skype session with his therapist tomorrow, which should help.

We sip and chew as the pub fills up with people clapping each other on the back and greeting one another with kisses.

"I'm so sorry I hurt you." His lip wobbles.

"It's okay, it's okay." I reach for his hand in a knee-jerk attempt to intercept tears. "Should we check what's playing at the cinema?"

"Yep." He pulls out his phone and exhales audibly.

"I wish I had a place I could host you in."

My simultaneous anger and sympathy confound me. I cross my arms during the film and I don't laugh. Neither does he. But later when I put him on the Tube with his bags, I don't want to say goodbye. We embrace passionately at the station entrance. We make plans for him to meet me after my voice job tomorrow in Soho. And he heads down to the south-east corner of the city.

Four days into T's visit, we're at a Rabbie Burns Supper Fi and her husband, Ru, are hosting. John Lewis sports a tartan jacket. Burns Night isn't technically for another week but Ru has a conference that conflicts with it, so they moved their annual dinner forward this year. Their flat smells of shortbread and

Scotch. Neither of them are Scottish but they met at a Burns Night celebration, so the day holds a special meaning for them. Fi got her period and is using gin as a balm for her disappointment. Still not pregnant after six months of trying, she's sung "Auld Lang Syne" three times and it's barely 8 p.m.

I'm tucking into a strong gin cocktail and making savouring noises. I haven't been able to get a lick of work done with T here. Even when we're apart, all I do is rewrite the same three sentences on my grant application and worry about putting a script together for my first R&D next month. Mostly I'm either lecturing T in my mind or giving myself pep talks about not shutting down.

T lifts his glass to me and says, "I'm keeping pace with you tonight."

"Okay, but don't go too far because . . ." I give him my best "we're going to get it on" eyebrows. T's house-sitting for a family friend in Maida Vale. This will be our first night alone together.

Fi sloshes between us, wrapping her arms around me and planting a juicy kiss on my cheek. "Who needs a baby anyway?" she asks. We clink glasses and sip. "Do you know, I'm probably barren."

"Let's see," I say.

"Indeed."

She dissolves into laughter and I laugh at her laughing. T looks on, annoyed.

"Sorry, I just need to say, I don't appreciate you monitoring my drinking." His voice is pointed.

Fi tsks me playfully. I pull away from her and widen my eyes, then furrow my brow at T.

"Not cool," he says.

Not caring how it looks, I turn, leave the kitchen and duck into Fi's bedroom where I crumple to the floor.

Just then I hear Milo arrive, his Scottish brogue dialled up for the occasion, followed by Fi squealing at his kilt. He strides into the master bedroom to drop off his coat. "Up off the floor McGee or you'll really get to know me."

I cover my eyes and tell him that I'm sulking.

"Get up lass! I want to meet your fella."

I stand and he hugs me. I whisper, "T is driving me bananas."

T enters just then. Milo and I let go of each other and I introduce them.

Milo says Julie wasn't feeling well enough to join and makes an excuse to leave us alone. I resume my spot on the floor and T sits down beside me.

He says he's not in the party mood. He's sad and he wants to be alone. He finds his jacket on the bed and puts it on.

As the other guests take their seats at the table, T and I squeeze behind them, wending our way to the front door. Mercifully, they're all too polite to ask what's going on. T zips up his coat and I ask if I'll see him later. He shrugs. "I don't know. I'll text you." I open the door for him, and he sets off into the night.

I explain to the group that his brother just died. Everyone understands.

The buttered leeks, swede and potatoes, haggis and black pudding are passed around as we inhale our barley broth. I get into a discussion with one of Ru's colleagues about *The Ex-Boyfriend Yard Sale*. She's a computer programmer from South Africa who moved to the UK for a relationship, which ended, but her love of London keeps her here.

A red-faced and boisterous Milo calls across the table, "Isn't Haley's project an incredible, extended joke? Talk about wringing a premise for all it's worth. I mean, that's the joke isn't it — how far can you take it?"

"Oh my god Milo, give me a break," I say, not in the mood to have my work belittled.

Fi raises her voice and tells Milo that just because he's sold himself to the corporate sector, designing the lights for trade shows, doesn't mean there aren't artists among us.

"But seriously," says Milo, looking at me with dopey eyes, "the price of anything is what someone is willing to pay for it."

The computer programmer asks how much I know about behavioural economics.

"Very little."

Milo gets distracted by encouraging John Lewis to lick sauce off his beard. And the computer programmer tells me that behavioural economics became popular when economists realised that consumer habits are not rational. Brand associations — or stories — can sway a buyer to pay more for an inferior or equal product. What Milo posited is actually just one economic theory, but unfortunately that theory is taught as gospel in Economics 101. She says she knows a guy I should talk to, an AI specialist and computer scientist who's studying how narrative and sentimentality affect the economy.

"Hook it up," I say and take her email address.

Later, Fi sees me looking at my phone and assures me I am not an asshole for staying. But, she says, if I want to see T tonight, I should simply impose myself on him.

I eat my trifle, sip a Scotch and hop in a Uber, only then texting T to let him know I'm on my way.

Once I'm inside the flat, I'm still unlacing my boots when I launch in. "I don't want to fight with you. But you're pushing me away and this *is* a repetition. I was being flirtatious with you and you fucking rejected me."

He sits down on the leather sofa. I watch him cry.

Good, I think. You should be sorry. "I thought we were going to sleep together tonight."

"You decided that," he says. "Maybe I'm not ready yet." He points at his chest when he says "I'm".

"How are you not ready? I was the one who said I needed a bit more time." I reach for the boots I've just stepped out of. "If you say you've changed your mind — I can't. That's the deal."

We go round and round, trotting out our catchphrases — "I don't know what I'm doing." "This is a lot of pressure." "I'm not going to advocate."

Until he lays down arms and says, "You're right, Haley. You shouldn't have to be the one to advocate for this." He tells me he loves me and he's sorry.

And I say it back.

Now 4 a.m., both of us cried out, we drag ourselves to bed. Crisp white sheets comfort us after all that mess.

We awake in each other's arms. He makes me come twice before saying, "I haven't been with anyone else."

"Me neither."

This is both an emblem of our devotion and permission granted to have unprotected pull-and-pray sex, something we've been engaging in for almost our entire relationship. I don't want to get pregnant, but I'm no longer worried I will. I've never been pregnant. Like Fi, I question whether I'm able. And on some level, a pregnancy would make it very clear that T and I need to figure out a way to be together — I think that compels us too.

Anyway. Permission granted. And T's inside me, and we're in this fresh bed that belongs to neither of us. Streaks of sunlight hit us through the slats of the window shutters. We shudder. I finger the sweat where his hair meets the nape of his neck. Grab his tight mannequin bum. After my non-negotiable post-coitus trip to the toilet to pee, we fold into each other, naked, bodies cooling.

It's past noon now and we decide to go for a Sunday roast. For the afternoon, we are the couple I've always wanted to be. I break my austerity rule and buy us cappuccinos at a trendy café. We sip them as we wander down the high street. T buys an *Observer* at a newsstand. We mull through it in a sunlit corner of a pub, sopping up gravy with Yorkshire puddings. He rests his hand on my shoulder as he reads, occasionally pausing to kiss the palm of my hand. Partway through the afternoon, a ten-piece brass band play a set; elderly people dance in pairs as kids hop around them. I swoon and T rolls his eyes. We debate the value of amateurism. And in the end, I win him over with the argument that these activities that once belonged to all of us — arts, music, sports — have been transformed into elite spectacles and turned us, everyday humans, into spectators.

T pays the bill. He insists on it. And tells the guy behind the bar that this is the best date he's ever been on. He fixes my scarf and, with his arm around my shoulder, we kiss in the doorway before stepping into the darkened high street.

The visit with T carries on like this, lurching from dire, stilted moments to complicity, rapture and serenity. We fight for levity in the face of his grief and my anger. And as the days stretch longer, we grow lighter. In the end, we're both glad he made the trip. But we don't make a plan to see each other again.

I accomplished nothing on *The Ex-Boyfriend Yard Sale* during T's visit. I now have two weeks until my first R&D period begins. I'm going to have to put a pin in the grant application till afterwards and focus on getting something resembling a script together and arranging for different friends and colleagues to come into the studio and give me some feedback.

But first, I go through my personal finances and catch up on the tracking I've neglected. I dread this. T and I spent way more time in restaurants than I wanted to, but the numbers tell a different story: at the end of these two weeks with T, I've spent less money than in many of the weeks prior. I wasn't aware of how often T had picked up the tab.

I intend to work on the script but I find myself lying on the living room floor reading my high school journals, growing queasy but unable to put them down. One of the unexpected costs of rummaging around for data about my old relationships is uncovering memories buried so deep in the storage locker of my mind, I've forgotten I didn't want to remember them.

Like this one: the first time I said "I love you" in a romantic way was to Mix Tape. And I told him I loved him, for the first time, in front of two of our friends. This was about six months after our first kiss. We were all standing in the front hall of Mix Tape's parents' house with our coats on, about to leave. The group of us had had some disagreement that evening and we hadn't yet resolved it.

Suddenly I felt inspired, tunnelling my vision at Mix Tape, to announce, "I just need you to know that I love you."

Silence. Mix Tape gripped the banister.

Our friends shifted self-consciously, mouths agog.

I said, "You don't have to say it back."

He said, "No. I can say it." And then he breathed out, "I love you too."

After we broke up I wrote in my journal, *He never said it again*.

And I have never said it first since.

Straight off I think, this is a disgusting project. What am I doing scrounging around, milking my life for stuff that might be entertaining? Then I think, I'm so ashamed of who I was then. And I won't be able to find the words for a long time, but later I know, I'm scared that I haven't changed at all.

Surely the horrors of uncovering parts of myself that I'd rather have kept under wraps warrants some kind of compensation — some factor in the formula. I make a note about unexpected emotional pain associated with an object, and read on.

My relationship with Mix Tape became strained. The things we both once delighted in, he began to roll his eyes at, including our mutual friends. He was no longer wearing Hawaiian shirts and basketball shorts; he'd acquired a taste for dark beer, the suggestion of shooting a horror film in the backyard caused him to cringe, and all I could talk about was the transformative power of the theatre. When I foisted myself on his new friend group, the evenings often culminated with me accusing Mix Tape of having a crush on one of the girls and him dismissing me as a jealous person.

At the end of the summer holidays he joined my family for a trip up to my aunt Harlow's. Part of the plan for the vacation was that I was going to help my aunt redecorate her sunroom. I created a schedule that allotted time for this project, but at our appointed hour, while I waited, the rest of my family had a laugh as Harlow tiptoed behind my back, with a kayak paddle in her hand.

Later she said, "I just wanted to go kayaking with Kian."

I unravelled at being the butt of a joke. "But you asked me to help," I sobbed. My family was accustomed to my unwieldy emotional side, but Mix Tape had never witnessed it. His eyes were opaque. Something has been ruined, I thought. Unlike my family, he had no obligation to remain constant. Never before had love been conditional.

I've always attributed that meltdown as the incident that ultimately tipped the scale for Mix Tape, that and the expected benefit of sex with the girl he left me for. But reading back through my journals, I see his withdrawal began earlier in the timeline, around my profession of love.

As that summer came to an end, Mix Tape claimed that the fun that once existed between us was unsalvageable. It was night-time and we were sitting side by side on the curb in front of my parents' house. We'd just entered our final year of high school and my seventeenth birthday was coming up. As we dismantled our relationship, I tugged blades of grass from the earth, pulling them apart at the base, exposing white flesh close to the roots before tossing them down the drain. I stayed focused on this as he suggested we take a break.

My pride kicked in. "What's a break going to do?"

I stared at the newly hairy knees protruding from his khaki shorts. He leaned back on his hands, looked up at the street-lamp and said, "It just doesn't work anymore."

I didn't ask if there was someone else because I didn't want to know.

Two days later, I spied Mix Tape making out with one of the girls in the student parking lot. It was as though someone had walloped my abdomen with a metal rod. But it was also vindication. I was not a jealous but an intuitive person.

Still I remained flattened by the revelation that someone could fall out of love with me. I wore pajama pants to school for several months. I listened to the mix tape on repeat. How could he have said all those loving things and then decided they were no longer true? I wondered if I shouldn't have been so rigid with my no-sex-before-seventeen rule. Were my boobs too small? Was my personality too weird? Was it because I was a theatre nerd or that I didn't smoke pot?

Later in the week at my improv gig, the suggested word is "transportation" and I do a monologue about running into Mix Tape on the bus from Toronto to our hometown, three years after we'd broken up. I tell the audience how the sight of him seized my innards. How he sat beside me, eating a bag of Cheezies, and I masked my discomfort by speaking with bubbly enthusiasm, reeling off my upcoming performances.

"I guess, I want to be a muse and amusing. It's a difficult balance," I quip. "It's like old-world femininity and new-world feminism are at war within me. Throughout that two-hour bus ride, they were head to head, but I was trying to combine them for maximum outcome. Maximum profitability?" There's a laugh there, though it's less at what I've said and more at my self-effacing delivery. But I take it and resume my place on the backline.

£ + ♥

Gemma and I squeeze each other's hands as we enter the famous Criterion Auction House in Islington. It's a relatively small storefront, cram-jammed with ornate wooden tables, uphol-stered chairs, crates of old playbills and lamps made of green blown glass, rugs and paintings and gaudy chandeliers. Behind the podium, a young auctioneer in an ill-fitting suit performs his patter to a smattering of people who raise their numbered cards from the seating area. A woman perched on a settee with a small dog bids over and over again on a hand-painted cigarette case.

As I am curious to see how the stories connected to objects and competition affect sales, I suggested we take this field trip. Of course, I also have a penchant for old stuff. We snap a few photos together and record a short video as proof of concept for the grant application I've abandoned while I prepare for the R&D in ten days.

At the front desk, we are given numbers in case we'd like to make bids and I ask if it would be possible to speak to the auctioneer at some point. After the cigarette case and several other items have been sold, another auctioneer takes the stand and we're introduced to the first auctioneer, Jimmy. He's twenty-three and this is his trade. His official job title is Valuer and his specialty is in clocks and timepieces. When it comes to valu-ation, he explains that the criteria they use are age, origin, materials, damage, special features and provenance. "Provenance" is an art-world phenomenon where the value of an object (or artwork) can increase wildly simply because it has passed through the hands of an important person.

Excited, I tell him the jewellery box I have, made by my ceramicist ex, was where he stored his pot and tobacco for years and years. "And this ex, before he lived in Finland," I hasten to explain, "lived in New York City, and he was friends with Patti Smith — well his mother was — but sometimes Patti stopped in at my ex's apartment for coffee, when his mother was visiting. And it's quite probable that Patti Smith smoked something that had been kept in that jewellery box." I want to know if that connection ramps up its value.

Jimmy patiently explains that even though a pair of trainers owned by a celebrity could be sold for £30k, since my jewellery box didn't belong to Patti and I don't have any photos or proof she ever smoked weed that had been stored in it, the story isn't credible and therefore not worth much. In his professional opinion, he says, "The only way you could affect the value of your objects is to increase your own celebrity."

Deflated, I cast my eyes over the auction house and spot the heavy bidder's dog peeing on a painting leaning against the counter. I notice as the bids slow down, but before the auction-eer brings down the gavel and yells "sold!", they say "fair warning". I jot this down: *"fair warning" — speak now or forever hold your peace.*

An hour later, in a café on Regent's Canal, Gemma and I sift through our respective research materials.

She begins by saying, "I think it would be wise to root our formula in capitalism, since we're looking for a price."

I nod. Glad to be able to placate the naysayers like Milo, banging on about "the price is whatever someone offers you".

Gemma has a couple ideas as to how we can do this. The first is use a Return on Investment (ROI) formula as the basis for our formula.

She spells it out. "So, an ROI is a widely used financial metric. It's the ratio that compares the gain or loss from an investment to its relative cost."

"It tells you how well something's paying off?"

"Correct. We'll refine as we go, but broadly speaking we'd be working with something like this for the relationship between our phrases." She turns her notebook to me:

$$ROI = (gains - costs) \div costs$$

There are different methods to gauge an ROI, but based on its elegance and simplicity, Gemma liked that one best.

The other way to firmly plant our math in capitalism is to make the first phrase in the formula our Market Value phrase, which is what we're focusing on today. And we agree that within that first phrase, the very first variable will be *current market value*. Leading with this means all the subsequent variables will modify the financial value of the object.

As we drill into the nuances of *current market value*, we realise we have two categories of objects to deal with:

1. Things that were bought brand new and could be bought repurchased.

2. Things that are handmade or vintage and therefore much harder or impossible to replace.

For items that can readily be repurchased, we decide the current market value will be determined using a depreciation formula.

In advance of our meeting, I dug up an online depreciation chart for various household objects. And in turn, Gemma found us a depreciation formula.

Depreciation is how much value an object loses over time, based on typical wear and tear. According to the chart, items lose different percentages of their value each year, and each item is given a set number of useful years. For example, suitcases lose 5 per cent per annum (pa) and have twenty useful years. Bikes lose 10 per cent and for pottery, which the jewellery box partially is, it says to use 90 per cent of the replacement cost or full value, whichever is less.

Item	Annual Dep %	Useful Years	Homemade/ Vintage (H/V) or Purchasable (R)
Mix Tape	*	*	H
Necklace	5%	20	R
Ukulele	4%	25	R
Bicycle	10%	10	V
Typewriter (home not office)	5%	20	V
Backpack (based on suitcases' 5 %)	10%	10	R
Jewellery Box	n/a	n/a	H
T-shirt ("shirts")	33.3%	3	V

*Rather than numbers, there's a note on the chart about "stereo tapes", which outlines the two factors contributing to their depreciation: obsolescence and deterioration, as a result of temperature changes and stretching of tape due to use. For these reasons, the value of a cassette tape is slashed in half immediately after the seal is broken. And with every subsequent month, it loses an additional 5 per cent of its value.

Gemma and I scrap the "useful years" component because we're interested in sentimental value, which is not timebound. And she walks me through the mechanics of the compound depreciation formula we're using. "So after one year, the necklace loses five per cent of its value. Now it's worth 95 per cent of £150, which is £142.50. Right?"

"I'll take your word for it."

"After two years, the necklace is worth 95 per cent of £142.50, which knocks it down to £135.38. We always take away the same percentage from the item, but that percentage changes slightly each year as its value decreases."

Grasping this, I feel like a million bucks.

To assess the value of vintage and handmade goods, which are not so easily replaced, I posit we take the median from the offers I receive on Gumtree. Gemma curls her fingers into an okay symbol. *"And,"* I continue, remembering Mix Tape's hours downloading, burning and recording the tunes to tape, "the *current market value* of the vintage and handmade things should also include how much time the ex expended either looking for or creating the item."

Gemma says, "We can do this, but you'll need to determine how much he was earning at the time to be able to figure out what an hour of his time was worth."

"Doable."

After some discussion we decide the Gumtree data should actually be factored into all my objects' market value as it illuminates my distinct marketplace.

With our first variable sorted, we move on to other facets directly connected to the object's monetary value.

I mention that the ukulele is missing a string.

Gemma says, "Minus the cost of repairing any damages."

"And what about improvements I've made to the items, like buying a better bike seat?"

We add both *cost of repairing any damages* and *cost of any embellishments* to the list of variables.

She asks if there's anything else we need to think about for the Market Value phrase.

I say, "You know that adage: an engagement ring should cost three months' salary?"

She doesn't.

"There was a TV commercial for a diamond warehouse when I was growing up, that said an engagement ring was the best way to spend three months' salary. I wonder if there's something about the relative sacrifice we could include?"

Gemma loves this idea. "Of course, the price of anything is relative to your financial status."

After a whack of googling we decide to embrace this concept in the Market Value phrase, and call the data point *relative generosity*. *Relative generosity* of a gift is determined by taking the purchase price of the item and dividing it by (my estimation of) my ex's monthly earnings during the relationship.

I want to add another data point for *how much thought was put into the gift*, hypothesising that the most romantic or meaningful gifts people receive are rarely the most expensive ones. "People want to be worth thought."

"And effort," adds Gemma. She suggests that we create a hierarchy for reasons for gifts.

"Gifts as an apology has to be very low."

"What about gifts for you but really for them?"

"Like sexy lingerie that you feel uncomfortable wearing?"

"Or a hoover."

She asks if any of the gifts were stolen.

"No. Though the jewellery box was technically on loan, and I ended up giving a cheque to the guy who gave me the ukulele when we broke up."

We decide unprompted gifts, such as the mix tape, take the cake, and gifts on special occasions rank high, but should be given penalties if they arrived late.

"Oh!" exclaims Gemma. "What about, 'did you want the gift'? What are the levels of wanting a gift?"

"Now that is connected to the level of thought behind the gift," I say. "It's about the gift-giver's ability to pay attention and attune to your desires."

We determine that receiving something you expressly do not want is the worst, and Gemma adds, "While something you didn't know you wanted, but when you receive it, you realise it's perfect and you wouldn't part with it for anything, is the best."

"What have you ever got from that category?"

Red blotches appear on her neck. "It's a . . . a . . . a—" She laughs. "My boyfriend created an album of music for me — wrote the songs and did the cover art. It's . . . lovely." She shuts her laptop and says, "Let me spend some time with my notes. I think we can create tables that will help us quantify the relationship between the type of gift and the amount of thought behind it."

A few days later, after some back and forth on email and a few voice notes, we have two definitive charts (according to my value system):

Level of Gift	Value	Thoughtfulness	Value
Unprompted	1.1	Didn't want the gift	0.95
Gift on occasion	1.05	Wanted it and expressed want	1
Gift to apologise	1	Wanted it, didn't express want but it was implicit	1.05
Gift for you but really for them	0.95	Wanted it but they intuited it	1.1
Something they left/forgot	0.9		

These tables will be used to work out the values of symbols in the formula. Gemma sends me a draft of the Market Value phrase a couple days later.

$$\left[\left(CMV + EM. - D \right) \times \left[\frac{P\pounds}{m\pounds} + \left(\uparrow \text{🎁} \times \uparrow \text{💭} \right) \right] \right]$$

It means: current market value plus embellishments minus the cost of repairing damages, multiplied by the purchase price divided by my ex's monthly income at the time, plus the level of gift times the level of thought put into the gift.

11. TIME INVESTED

"The beauty of time is that it can be spent on anything. This is also its ugliest feature."
Doug Zeigler, *The Currency of Time*

Fi and I clutch our coffees, hers from the kiosk, mine in a thermos from home. We let John Lewis lead us through the park, our backpacks topfull with vegetables from the Saturday farmer's market, until Fi's lower back ache lands us on a bench overlooking the Men's Pond.

I'm currently reading Annie Dillard's book *Pilgrim at Tinker Creek*. It's the text where Dillard famously wrote, "How we spend our days is, of course, how we spend our lives. What we do with this hour, and that one, is what we are doing." In the week since T's departure, I've been struggling with substantial procrastination preparing for the R&D week at the theatre. Thea recommended the book to shift my perspective and, I suspect, inspire a more rigorous work habit in me.

The murder-mystery parties stopped after Christmas, and the medical role-play gigs have slowed down too, but the catering shifts carry on. I've been donning my blacks and precariously balancing trays of champagne flutes at boutique galleries in Fitzrovia. It's demoralising but the shifts are only four hours long, which means I have the days to allegedly prepare for my R&D. I need to get a script together and gather my props. I also have to do my taxes. I completely forgot till Navid reminded me. They're due in just over a week.

Fi and I get talking about the fact that both of us spent much of our twenties completely rejecting the idea of money as a motivator — me pursuing theatre in Toronto, her as an activist in Belfast — preferring projects and experiences we perceived as unsoiled by greed. But now in our thirties we want the cheddar — me to get out of debt, she to provide for a hypothetical baby. We're puzzled, though, by how the value of our time factors into this paradigm shift.

"How could we maximise profits by exchanging the quality of our time for money?" "What bargain are we willing to strike?"

We volley the questions but don't know how to answer them. Fi's back pain has subsided and now she needs "a wee" so we get moving.

"I think of time like this," Fi says. "Every second costs a penny. There's no choice in the price, so wherever those pennies go, or however that time is spent, needs to matter."

"You're right. We are *always* spending time."

At the pavilion Fi goes to the toilet, and while John Lewis and I wait in line to buy her second latte, I text Gemma: *V. important re: formula! We need to calculate a tipping point for a waste of time.*

I'm standing with the coffee when Fi emerges. She pulls her bank card out of my teeth, her coffee from my hand and shoots me a "can I talk to you over there?" look.

A knot tightening in my gut, I follow her to the empty bandstand.

"I got my fucking period." She flings herself on the steps. "Jesus fuck!" She grabs her lower abdomen, vigorously jiggles it then lies back with an aggravated growl. John Lewis barks and she pulls him onto her chest. "I wanna know how long it's worth it to keep trying. And when to throw in the towel."

I lower myself gingerly to the bandstand floor.

Trying to conceive has turned her impeccable sex life into a calendar-driven chore. She says her husband has been tracking her irregular cycle and now stipulates they only have sex on her ovulation days. "And when we do it, he's in a lip-biting concentration mode. Doing his duty for king and country. It's turning us into bloody Victorians."

I resist the urge to offer solutions; instead I listen and nod, reflecting back what she's saying and agreeing. T taught me to do this and I'm filled with appreciation for his emotional astuteness. After Fi expels all the disappointment she can, she laughs and sighs interchangeably. I offer that I worked with an actress whose fertility issues were transformed by acupuncture.

Fi says she's afraid of needles.

I tell her I love learning new things about her. Moments like this remind me how little history Fi and I actually share, only having known each other for a short time.

"You should see someone like my guy, Riku, in Canada," I say.

She rolls her eyes.

"There are no candles or crystals, his office is very clinical," I explain. "He does Japanese acupuncture, which uses little ion balls that stick to your skin, and sometimes he presses hard on a pressure point, but no needles. He sits you in a chair and checks your chakras, organs, meridians and systems for blockages — emotional and energetic blockages. Sometimes he'll ask what was happening at a particular age in your life and if you want to, you tell him what you think of, and he clears whatever is congesting your body."

Fi sighs.

"He also gives you a full rundown on what you should and shouldn't eat. He told another actor I know to stop eating so many vegetables and drinking so much water after she'd done a juice cleanse."

The vegetable thing sells Fi. She's ready to give it a try. "But he's not here, is he?"

"We can see if he'd do you on Skype? He won't be able to stick ion balls on you, but he can check for blockages."

"Love, Skype is no way to have any real conversation."

I'm stung by this. "Agree to disagree." I call Riku's office in Toronto. It's 8 a.m. there but he works Saturdays. He answers and texts us a London recommendation.

Now impatient and keen to get an appointment, Fi uses my phone to call immediately. A parade of parents wheeling strollers and chasing after children on scooters pass by and her voice breaks as she leaves a voicemail.

At the moment she hangs up my phone, a text message from T arrives:

You are luminous.

I try to pull down the corners of my mouth to mask my joy.

"Come on now." Fi pushes herself up. "I have to go buy tampons. Give me the latest on lover-boy."

I read her his most recent texts:

My love for you only deepens

You're my most favourite person

I love the way you think

"Finally, he's wooing me."

"As he should!" Fi says this a little too adamantly. Catching my face, she adds, "I'm just saying you ought to be wooed and won over — you're an absolute prize." She contests that she has no opinion because she "barely met the man!", but if I love him, she says firmly, then she loves him too.

"I do love him."

Still, I can't help thinking, But talk is cheap. I must remember to watch how it pays out over time.

£ + ♥

"Are you aware of Sunk Cost Bias?"

"No."

I'm grossly underprepared for my meeting with Professor Albert Everett Fry, the expert on how narrative and sentimentality affect the economy; the computer programmer at the Burns Supper hooked us up. I was doing my tax return this morning and then I got into a tiff with T about how often we Skype.

I've just regaled Albert with rudimentary details of the project, saying, "My mathematician and I are going to work on the Time Invested phrase this week. Any thoughts on how we can determine a tipping point for a waste of time? Romantically, that is."

He says, "So, Sunk Cost Bias is when we keep sinking resources into an enterprise that's clearly failing, because we don't want our previous investments to have been in vain." He remarks that this happens in business investments but also in day-to-day scenarios, for instance, when we order too much food and then overeat in order to get our money's worth.

I recognise the concept from my poker days with Bicycle. In poker, it's known as being "pot committed".

Albert is from Arkansas and runs the Centre for the Study of Decision-Making Uncertainty in London, where a team of academics whose specialties range from economics to psychoanalysis, neuroscience, computer science and statistics undertake research on human responses to uncertainty. They use their research to advise big banks, corporations and govern-ments. And now, me.

Albert says, "Unfortunately, or interestingly, the value of things is often incongruous with our value systems," and asks me if I've heard of behavioural economics.

I tell him his colleague explained it a little when we met.

He says, "People are capricious. That's what behavioural economics is trying to understand. People don't buy or behave rationally. Our behaviours are predicated on a complex conflu-ence of factors, many of them unconscious and indecipherable to us. It's why we'll say things like, 'I don't know why, but I just wanted this shirt more'."

"Or, 'the heart wants what it wants'."

"Right. So, behavioural economics looks at all the factors that affect how we make decisions — social, emotional, cognitive, cultural. And how and when we consider those factors, the outcome is vastly different than what classical economic theory predicts." He continues, "Essentially, humans do not make decisions rationally. We ignore statistics. We believe that we are the exception to the stats. Like getting married, for example, is an optimistic, and some might say hubristic, act. But when it comes to the probabilities of love, we all want to believe we'll be the exception to the rule. It's an act of optimism."

"But, aren't you married?" I ask, pointing at his hand.

The algorithm worked for him. He's married to a woman he met online. "I can know the theory and the stats and still be subject to my own optimism and arrogance. The stats on divorce are not hopeful."

Later, I'll look them up and learn in 2017 there were approximately 242,000 marriages in the UK and approximately 101,000 divorces.

"However," Albert continues as a sense of doom waxes in me, "the stats also show that a much higher percentage of people believe that they are smarter, better looking and have the capability for a better-than-average romantic life and financial life on a percentile basis than is possible. Humans want to believe that we are somehow better equipped to beat the odds."

Masking my fear with wry sardonicism, I volunteer, "So it's like how everyone says, 'long-distance relationships don't work', but I believe my boyfriend and I can overcome it?"

"I don't know the exact figures, but the odds are that you won't."

"So when do I know—" I will myself to smile. "When do I know if I'm a victim of Sunk Cost Bias?"

He says he thinks of relationships in terms of how often they are bringing something positive to your life. "In my experience, relationships are endless negotiations. If it's good 51 per cent of the time, that is enough to stay."

I wonder what percentage of time T and I enjoy ourselves, as I walk from the station. Do we strike above 50 per cent? Navid's in Greece for a week, applying for jobs there. He said he's not going to take them, but Cloe needs to see some movement. At least T doesn't pretend to do what I want him to. I call his phone but no answer.

£ + ♥

My vibrator is noisy. That's a key reason I like it when Navid's away. I can spend my mornings lying in bed, masturbating to my heart's content.

What I want right now is to have sex that makes me forget myself and only see colours. Ever since I began sleeping with people, I've experienced sublime sex as colours. It's as if language leaves me and I'm bathed in sensations I can equate with shades and tones.

It wasn't like that when I lost my virginity, but by approximately the twentieth time Necklace and I slept together, I saw a colour. It was a translucent robin's egg blue. The bodily exploration was where Necklace and I really charted new waters. He picked up where Mix Tape left off.

The first time we had sex, it was physically painful for both of us. My hymen was partially intact. And the passage was so tight for him, we were both breathing through my being punctured and him strangled. It struck me as egalitarian as my plastic-coated dorm room mattress cushioned my induction into adult experience.

After a handful of slow-motion pumps, we called it quits. I was underwhelmed by losing my virginity. I expected to immediately feel like a different person. I thought going through that rite of passage would be like dunking myself in purple medical dye as the engineering students did for their freshmen initiations, that losing my virginity would transform how I saw the world and how I was seen. But it didn't. I was still the same Haley, with the same trouble waking up in the morning and the same try-hard spirit, desperate for the unforthcoming praise of my teachers. I was no longer a virgin and yet I was exactly the same.

We'd waited five months to do it. I have made most of my exes wait to sleep with me. Not as a strategic move to make them work for it, but mostly because I wasn't — and am still not — confident in my nude body to bare all immediately.

I flick on my bedside lamp and write in my notebook:

Consummation point (between confessing/having feelings & sex)
Mix Tape — never did it
Necklace — 5 months
Ukulele — couple weeks?
Bicycle — 7 weeks pining time. Space between first kiss and consummation? 1 week?
Typewriter — waited till after Christmas holidays — 3–5 weeks
Backpack — first kiss and sex all in one night
Jewellery Box — 2 dates
T-shirt — 1 year

Pining Time (between getting crush and admission/kiss)
Mix Tape — 5 months
Necklace — 0 (kissed the day we met)
Ukulele — 0 (kissed the day we met)
Bicycle — 7 weeks
Typewriter — 0 (kissed the day we met)
Backpack — couple weeks circling each other at parties
Jewellery Box — a few days between first meeting him and our first one-on-one date
T-shirt — 3 months

I wanted to be with a guy like Necklace to stick it to Mix Tape. Necklace carried himself with ease and an open chest. He was athletic, dotted with tattoos and good at fixing things. He was patient with me too. And he cried.

Fastidiously tidy, Necklace loved clothing and cleaning, and is the most macho man I've ever been with. Decidedly not an artist himself, he gave standing ovations at every one of my drama school performances while we were together. He packed a car with Tetris precision. He was generous and physically intimidating. He got in fights. Once he arrived to pick me up with a pair of bloodied jeans in the back of his car. He was especially annoyed because they were new jeans, expensive too. Some story about some strip-mall parking lot, some argument between factions of young men, probably about drugs, something about someone owing money, and then something else, words ran out and Necklace grabbed a guy by the ears, yanked the guy's head down, and raising his own knee up fast, smashed the guy's nose. Astounded, I inspected Necklace's light-washed, baggy jeans soaked with deep, thick blood that had settled and turned brown.

When we were in his car he'd frequently fart into his hand and toss it in my face, which infuriated me. He was also the first man, barring my brother and dad, that I farted in front of.

Sometime after we'd started having sex, Necklace was staying in my residence room with me; I was in agony, unable to sleep because of gas pains. When I confessed the reason for my discomfort, he was both concerned and delighted by the challenge.

"Baby, you have to fart," he said.

"I can't," I moaned.

He coaxed me until I did. The gas whooshed out of me, silent at first and then bubbling and sputtering, rounding off juicily. I keeled over and Necklace lay beside me, the two of us in hysterics.

Fart point?
Mix Tape — no farts
Necklace — farts, 3 months
Ukulele — can't recall if we did
Bicycle — farts, a couple months in
Typewriter — no farts: he was a poo prude
Backpack — farts once he moved in but mostly silent ones
Jewellery Box — no farts
T-shirt — no farts: another poo prude

My relationship with Necklace was a testing ground for intimacy and boundaries. We tried period sex, which saturated Necklace's pubic hair with my blood. Another time, I removed a blood-laden tampon in front of him. I gave him a blowjob while he was driving, spat his ejaculate out the window only to have it spray back in the car.

Despite the novelty of our bodily exploration, half a year in, it began to dawn on me that we had nothing in common. I vividly recall pulling into his driveway suddenly thinking, I don't want to be here. I don't like him anymore. The last thing I want is his penis in my mouth. So shocked by the thought and scared of its ramifications, I told myself that I was going to choose to ignore those feelings. And I did. I tried to. And I stayed with him for fourteen months longer than I wanted to.

During those months I snapped at him when he'd pull me onto his lap and stick his hands in the pockets of my flared khakis — a gesture I was once titillated by. Then I'd be exceedingly nice but only out of guilt. I blamed my increasingly crabby state on "stress" and cited both my mood and to-do list for my low libido. I prohibited myself from squirming away every time he leaned in to kiss me. All of it a ruse to not disappoint him. I'd never been the one to want out before.

I didn't know how to confess that even though I liked having a boyfriend in general, I didn't want to be with him anymore,

even to myself. I viewed my inability to get along as a poison-
ous flaw in me. I thought that if I could just get a hold of my
mood, I could make the relationship work.

But eventually, after months of withdrawing, I managed to
end it. He came to Toronto to say goodbye. My teeth chattered
uncontrollably through the conversation. I remember thinking,
oh my god, we're going here. As if break-up territory was a
place.

He left my room and after I'd showered I went to the grocery
store in my pajamas and bought seventeen dollars' worth of
cheese, and snuggled into the dorm room of a friend. We gorged
on the cheese and episodes of *The O.C.* While I grieved the relationship, my drink of choice became a bottle of Zinfandel rosé
chased with two Tylenol extra strengths, which Necklace had
bought to ease my menstrual cramps.

When my stomach gurgles, I slide out of bed and wander
naked to the kitchen to make my coffee. I should just have a
bowl of granola and get to work, but now I'm in my housecoat,
whipping up pancake batter and listening to the interview I did
with Necklace over Christmas.

I stop the recording to make a note of the timecode. There's
a moment I need to isolate, so I can play it in the show. It goes
like this:

HALEY: *Tell me what you remember about the necklace*
that you gave me for my nineteenth birthday.

NECKLACE: *I . . . I don't remember the necklace. That's so sad,*
but I don't remember the necklace.

HALEY: *You don't remember what it looked like, or*
anything like that?

NECKLACE: *No. I don't.*

HALEY: *Do you remember buying it?*

NECKLACE: *No.*

After that we laugh, and I accuse him of being high all the time. He swears that he remembers lots of other things and admits that he called his mother in advance of our conversation to ask if she had any memory of the necklace, which she didn't. For a split second, I questioned if he'd given it to me. But I know he did. He did.

My second favourite moment in the recording is when I ask him what our relationship had given him. He said that because of his experiences with me and my drama school class, he has so much time for actors. He now runs a bar at a craft brewery, and apparently he's developed a reputation for favouring actors when hiring. So much so that prospective employees slip sentences about performing in their high-school plays into their cover letters. He adds that if it hadn't been for me, he worries his homophobia would have taken a long time to be corrected and he wouldn't be living with his current roommate, his best friend, who happens to be a gay man.

We didn't talk about our break-up. And we didn't talk about the last time we saw each other — which was a couple years ago in Calgary when I was on tour there with a show. Prior to that we hadn't seen each other in over a decade. He sent flowers backstage and brought four friends to the performance, and afterwards he organised a table for a large group of us at a whiskey bar near the theatre. When he dropped me off at my accommodation, he got out of the taxi to say goodbye and we kissed on the lips, a few times. His lips were cool and soft like I remembered. It felt right to kiss him.

I tuck into my plate of pancakes with maple syrup, sitting at Navid's desk in the living room.

Even if it wasn't love between Necklace and me, we knew each other intimately for a chunk of time, and formed a bond that has withstood years of distance and silence. I glimpsed something about time, about age in that moment. There's a philosophy that souls are in sacred contracts with each other, that we arrive in each other's lives with a reciprocal agreement to help the other evolve. I'd always felt Necklace was a blip — an outlier, antithetical to my "type", chosen arbitrarily in reaction to Mix Tape, and held onto out of fear. But the sense of ease between us when we spoke made me wonder if there was something numinous between us, a power I hadn't previously given credit to. While at the time I'd logged a growing inventory of grievances about our incompatibility: he didn't like the theatre, he didn't read for pleasure, he smoked too much weed — he was exceedingly kind and generous. Necklace was — is — the only true gentleman I've been with. He taught me how I should expect to be treated.

There was no follow-up communication after our kiss. We didn't speak of that either.

I remember just then that Riku once asked what happened when I was nineteen. I told him that I'd broken up with Necklace. And Riku said, "You don't need to feel bad about that anymore. He's fine."

I start making notes on my musings about Necklace and suddenly I'm inside the project, engrossed in my writing, and many hours have passed. I emerge hungry but revitalised. I shovel a bowl of vegetables in my mouth and just as I open my tax return for the final check, Ollie calls. I ignore it, but when he calls a second time, I pick up.

"I think I did a bad."

"Oh no."

Ollie hid out in Ghent over Christmas. His divorce papers arrived via courier, but he struggled to scrawl his signature on the line. He thought that if he went back to Canada for the holidays, he'd be forced to sign before he was ready. As it turns out though, once you're served, it's over.

Breathlessly he tells me that a few days ago, he spotted a social media post about where his ex's mother was having her sixtieth birthday party, so he went to the lobby of the hotel and waited there to see his ex.

"Wait," I say, "are you back in Canada?"

"I flew back for it."

"Ollie."

"I know." There's a mischievous tinge to his voice.

"You're getting a kick out of this."

He tells me he's tried all the normal routes, and anyway, this actually kind of went okay. His ex's brother saw him and said hello. Ollie passed him a letter to give to his ex. "About twenty minutes later *he* came into the lobby, doing his low-whisper angry voice, telling me to fuck off, etcetera, but he did agree to meet with me tomorrow morning for a coffee before work."

"I mean, you definitely bulldozed him into it."

"I know. But I had no choice."

Time contracts. Ollie and I have been on the phone for nearly two hours when we hang up.

It's dark outside now. I go for a walk and lambast T in my head for his silence thus far today.

Milo texts to see when he should come in next week in a lighting-design capacity. I tell him Thursday, and head home to build a schedule around this snap decision. I slog through my list of admin and submit my tax return at 2 a.m. When T calls, for the first time, I ignore it.

£ + ♥

I crack the box open, unveiling the necklace. The pendant is an oval-shaped, dark blue sapphire with a tiny dot of a diamond sitting atop it, in a ten-karat white gold setting, strung on a snaking white gold chain.

Gemma regards the unbeloved jewel I've relocated eight times, from the university residence room where I received it to Navid's flat in the UK.

"So, the guy who gave me this was my friend's cousin — that's how we met." I tell her because it's the most expensive gift I've ever received, I felt guilty about getting rid of it.

We're in a studio at the Battersea Arts Centre and it's the middle of my R&D week. I've spent a whole day in this large, draughty, creaky-floored room, wrapping myself in bubble wrap and attempting to turn what I've learned so far into a script.

Gemma clicks her pencil. "Let's talk about Necklace in relation to Time Invested."

"Right." I'd written her to say I'd like to be able to speak about the Time Invested phrase in the work-in-progress sharing at the end of the week. This is our only afternoon together. "I hope the phrase can address the idea of the timing being right or wrong."

"He was your friend's cousin, you said?"

"Yes, but it was a friend from camp and they lived in another city."

"And he was dating another girl at the time you met?"

"Yes, but he wasn't her *boyfriend*." I explain to Gemma that though that scenario was not ideal, there were ways that the timing wasn't bad: we were the same age and had relatively the same amount of experience. Plus my friend was very cool about it. She said I blushed when I was speaking about him, so she knew my feelings were real. It's the one time I've been glad to be a blusher.

We discuss the negative side of the timing with Necklace. I was about to go off to university in Toronto while Necklace was headed to police college in another city, a two-hour bus ride away.

Gemma says, "*Long Distance* should be its own variable, separate from *timing*." And writes *LDR* at the top of a blank page, to come back to.

We dissect what makes timing apt or ill-fated and decide on two measurements: how appropriate was it for you to date that person at that precise time in your life? How high were the stakes? And we assemble a table that embodies the relationship between stakes and appropriateness, thus factoring the timing of a particular relationship into the formula.

We decide bad timing should increase value because you likely paid for it and should be compensated. As in the case with Necklace, I was in a new school situation but wasn't able to be totally present to it because I was often on the phone with him or hopping on a bus to go visit him.

Timing Stakes & Appropriateness	Value	Example
High stakes, low appropriateness	2	Getting involved with Jewellery Box. He just ended a twelve-year relationship, was much older, desperately wanted a child and lived in another country
Low stakes, low appropriateness	1.75	Backpack. Low stakes because not working together or that close friends but at a time when I wasn't keen on being in a relationship
High stakes, high appropriateness	1.5	Mix Tape. High stakes because in friend group but perfectly age and life-point appropriate
Low stakes, high appropriateness	1.25	Bicycle. Contract was coming to an end, both moving back to Toronto. Age-appropriate, both single and ready

Satisfied with our table, we turn to the *LDR* data point. To measure this, we decide to tally the amount of time spent on the phone and in transit, and any concrete expenses associated with them. For example, I racked up a thousand-dollar bill on my parents' "emergencies only" cell phone in the summer of 2003 with Necklace, equivalent to three weeks' salary, which was meant for my university tuition.

"Though," I say, "what you save in an LDR is the burden of spending time with your partner's friends and family when you don't want to." You avoid those by-proxy relationships you're obligated to nurture when you live in the same place, or together.

131

Gemma says, "Those dutiful social times need to be included as a percentage."

We name that variable *relationship admin*.

"Is there anything worse than dating someone who's close to their family?" Gemma cackles, and I like her even more.

We keep talking about time, both of us scribbling words on Post-its and sticking them to the walls. We make a big chart of my exes, looking at how long each relationship lasted and how old I was during the relationship. We examine the length of my relationships, not just in terms of months or years invested, but as a percentage of my lived experience.

BF	Age @ break-up	Rel Length in months	% of life
Mix Tape	17	8 months/.75 year	5.8%
Necklace	19	20 months	8.58%
Ukulele	20	4 months	1.67%
Bicycle	24	32 months	11.11%
Typewriter	26	6 months (over 12 months)	1.92%
Backpack	27	11 months	3.27%
Jewellery Box	28	8 months	2.29
T-shirt	31 (last time we split)	24 months (over 3 years)	9.09%

So, Mix Tape was an eight-month relationship that ended when I was seventeen, meaning it took up 5.8 per cent of my lived experience, whereas Necklace, who I was with just shy of two years and broke up with when I was nineteen, occupied 8.58 per cent, and the cumulative time of my on-off saga with T, at thirty-two, is 9.09 per cent of my lived experience. Here's how all the percentages look as pie charts:

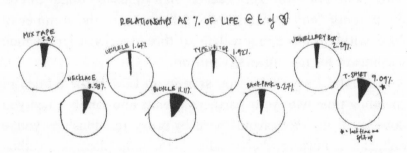

RELATIONSHIPS AS % OF LIFE @ t of ♥

MIX TAPE 5.8%   UKULELE 1.67%   TYPEWRITER 1.92%   JEWELLERY BOX 2.27%
NECKLACE 8.58%   BICYCLE 11.11%   BACKPACK 3.27%   T-SHIRT 9.09%

* = last time we split up

Gemma posits that perhaps people end up in relationships for longer durations as they age, because they have a different relationship with time.

"I actually think, until T, I've nixed things quicker and quicker as I've got older. But with Necklace I was dying to get out for most of the relationship."

"I'm going to make a timeline." Gemma draws a line and marks it into equal segments with a ruler.

"So, with Necklace, within six months I knew I wanted out. But we were together for a year and eight months."

"Okay, so for fourteen months that you were in the relationship you wanted out."

"And in the last four months, I had a crush on someone else."

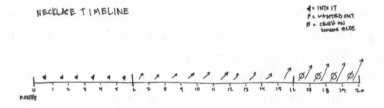

"So, the quality of the time when you want to be in the relationship is good and the time that you're in but want to be out is bad, and when you have feelings for someone else that's really bad?"

Though that seems a bit reductive, Gemma assures me that we're distilling each experience to its elemental truth in this process.

For accuracy, we're converting all time measurements into months. Zeroing in on Necklace's timeline, we discover the entire relationship lasted twenty months. At the time of our break-up I was nineteen years and five months old. Gemma calculates that's 233 months. The twenty-month relationship occupied 8.58 per cent of my lived experience at the time of our break-up, and for 70 per cent of those twenty months I wanted out of the relationship.

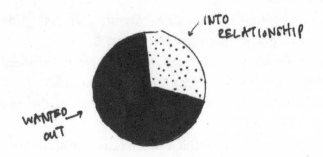

QUALITY OF TIME WITH NECKLACE

INTO RELATIONSHIP

WANTED OUT

Another way to look at it is, by the time we broke up I had spent 6.01% of my time on earth pretending I wanted to be in a relationship I didn't actually want to be in.

Gem marvels, "Aren't statistics powerful?"

Seeing that percentage, goosebumps appear on my arms. I murmur an agreement.

We label this tipping point, that only occurs in the relationships where you realise you want out but stay, the *Ew Point*.

When I was procrastinating earlier in the week, I posted a question about this phenomenon on my social media, asking what the longest period of time was that people had stayed in a relationship after realising they wanted to get out of it. From the one hundred plus replies I received, people stayed in relationships on average 4.9 months after they wanted out, while the median value was 2.3 months and the outliers were twenty-four years and no time at all.

Gemma and I don't have much time to discuss Sunk Cost Bias and my other learnings from Albert, but we come to an agreement that a tipping point for a waste of time is very different from the *Ew Point*. A tipping point for a waste of time can perhaps only be seen in retrospect. And further to that, what squanders time is trying to figure out if you should axe a relationship that you still want to be in because it's probably not going to pay out — it's predictive. Whereas the *Ew Point* is about knowing you want out and not being able to exit.

"No one teaches us how to end relationships well!" I yell.

"You should write a guide," says Gemma.

I laugh. "Okay, if this ever becomes a book, I'll include my break-up tips in an appendix*."

We leave the studio resembling a serial killer's den, and when I get on the Tube, I send a text to T saying, *I've only ever wanted you*.

When I get off the train half an hour later, I'm looking forward to a flirty reply, but there's nothing. I call him. No answer.

The rest of the R&D week unfolds rapidly. I lose the better part of one afternoon to an audition for an insurance commercial. Though it's maddening to have my studio time wasted, if I land that gig, it will pay five thousand pounds. Otherwise, the days blur with a rotation of collaborators I can't yet pay lending me their smarts. I barely talk to T — I'm rarely able to pick up when he phones, and by the time I'm able to call him back, he's often onto other things. I can't muster the energy to reply to his long text messages with more than a few words.

After a near sleepless night, I've pulled together forty-five minutes of material for the invited performance at the end of the week. Riding on adrenalin and caffeine, I get through it, barely glancing at my script. The recording of Necklace gets a big laugh and works well in introducing the audience to the

---

* Turn to page 395 to read my guide to breaking up

pricing predicament. I share some of the rudimentary math for the spreadsheet — detailing how I determined my average hourly wage in each relationship, unfurling scrolls of butcher's paper with the math written on them in black Sharpie and wrapping them around my body. There is no ending, but I can get away with that. This first outing is a chance to share material and see how an audience responds.

The performance goes better than I expect. There are about twenty people in attendance including Sam and two of his colleagues, a few of my actor friends, Milo, who helped me stage it and used his multi-tool to rig up my scrolls of math at the eleventh hour, Albert Everett Fry and the computer programmer. Sam broke into gales of laughter when I discussed the *fart point*, and we had to pause while he pulled himself together. He now wants me to come in next week to discuss next steps.

Milo huddles in a nook of the venue's café rolling cigarettes and staring into his phone. During the performance, he sat in the far corner of the audience with his eyes riveted to the lighting grid.

Once I've completed my rounds of chit chat, and I'm about to begin packing up my various papers and props, Milo approaches me and says, "So?"

"What's going on with you?" I ask.

He shrugs and begins carefully rolling up my scrolls, placing them neatly in the box I brought them in. Then he says, "Can I come over for dinner? I have booze in my car and an eight ball in my rucksack."

Scared that someone in his life has died, I say, "Of course. But I'm staying stone cold sober. Is everything okay?"

He scratches his beard. "I'll tell you at your place."

In the car, Milo switches on a Whitney Houston playlist and keeps time with his thumbs on the wheel, his mouth slightly ajar. When we encounter a traffic accident, he bangs the horn with his fist.

I laugh, desperate to make light of it. "Can't you just tell me now?"

He turns off the music and yanks his phone from the dashboard. "It makes me too upset and you're not supposed to drive when you're emotional . . . I want a curry," he grunts.

I take the phone from him and place a Deliveroo order. The driver is waiting for us when we arrive.

We enter the flat and Milo explodes. "She wants an open relationship!"

"Julie does? Please take your shoes off."

"Who else?" he exclaims, tripping over his Doc Martens. With a harrumph he plops himself down on the couch and asks me to pour him a glass of wine. "She wasn't depressed. She's miserable with *me*."

I oblige and prod him by saying, "But isn't this kind of ideal?"

"It's fucking bullshit."

"Milo, come on. You're a progressive guy."

"Theory versus practice, McGee." He guzzles wine and monologues while I unpack the feast he requested in the kitchen. When he starts in on, "Do you know how many times I could have hooked up with beautiful, I mean stunning — ten out of ten—"

I call out, "Milo! Don't talk that way."

"Sorry, but you know what I mean — I design a lot of music festivals."

He eats his way through the food, downs a bottle and a half of wine and snorts three lines of coke off Navid's TV-dinner tray.

After a couple hours of talking around the pros and cons of polyamory and open relationships, I hear myself saying, "I wish I could be open to an open relationship but I'm not, because I care about monogamy, even though in theory I understand the benefits and think an open relationship could be good for me — especially in my situation with T — but I can't undo my societal programming. And deep down, I'm pretty sure I can't undo it because I don't actually want to."

"Mate." Milo pitches forward to clink his glass with mine. "Mate. That's exactly it. I don't want to change my programming. I'm a traditional, possessive guy." He stumbles to his feet and flicks the lights on and off a few times. It's only 10 p.m. but clearly time to go home. However, when I suggest this, he starts to weep.

"Milo," I say pityingly. But my sympathy is worn thin. I'm fatigued by this one-way conversation. I've missed three calls from T. Heartbroken and newly in love people are the most tiresome company because their situation consumes them so entirely, they aren't able to listen. I worry I'm selfish — a bad friend. I hug Milo.

Clinching me hard, when I try to pull away he won't let go. "Thank you McGee." He burrows his face into my neck then kisses me three times on the cheek.

"Okay," I say, and extract myself from his arms.

He wipes his eyes with the back of his sleeve and says, "Why can't I be with someone like you?"

I tell him I'm ordering him an Uber.

"I don't know, McGee," he says, welling up again, "I think we could be great together."

I laugh and remind him he's drunk and reeling.

By the time I finagle Milo into the Uber he's resolved to give the open relationship a try, ostensibly to challenge his notions of love in the patriarchy and also because he does love Julie, so even if it is poly-under-pressure it's worth a shot.

12. NARRATIVE IMPACT

"The bigger the transformation the better the story."
T, quoting a colleague

After catering a gallery opening, I zip across town to perform in a late-night improv show with Inappropriately Attired. It's been three weeks since the R&D performance at Battersea and the pace of my life has picked up. I'm voicing a series of training videos for a major office-supplies manufacturer in America. The onslaught of recordings conflicted with one of my medical role-play jobs, so against Milo's advice I bailed on the Joe-job, which he believed would be steadier and pay more over time, but which I felt was the wrong energetic response to the universe. I've been walking around repeating the affirmation, "I love money. Money loves me" for months now, and I've been earning more. I also booked the insurance commercial gig, and if it goes to air, I'll get five thousand pounds for a clip of me gesticulating in a greenhouse.

I've been spending more time with Milo since he and Julie opened up their relationship. Maybe that's why I had a sex dream about him.

In the dream, Milo was standing on the stoop outside my flat and he was singing, "I need the answer." I knew the answer was inside, but Navid doesn't like it when I have people over without warning. I blocked the door, my arms pressing against the frame. Milo stepped forward and kissed me, very softly on the lips. A jolt of pleasure passed through my vagina. Next thing, we were in Navid's bed, making out. Me naked on top of him, asking, "Did you find it?" I woke up before he answered.

A week later I dreamt of him again. This time, we were in a speakeasy, sitting side by side. And in this dream, I told Milo about the first dream. As I was describing the kiss in the doorway, he lunged in and kissed me before I could finish my sentence. The jolt again. I woke up confused.

When I arrive at the pub for my improv show, Milo's sitting at a table near the entrance with one of his brothers. I keep my scarf wrapped around my face to hide my reddening cheeks. As we speak, I remind myself that he actually doesn't know the pale mosquito-bite colour of my nipples.

Before the show starts, our improv coach challenges us to avoid making boring choices. "In other words," he says emphatically, "be bold, make assumptions about why the other person is behaving as they are, variation between scenes — daring style and genre shifts — and A to C moves across the board — I don't want a whole show about fish fingers."

A to C is an improv term for ideas that are tangentially connected. It's the domino effect. For example, if someone talks about a lighthouse (A), your first association with that might be a fisherman (B), but rather than talking about a fisherman, which the audience can clearly see is connected, you go after an association you have with a fisherman, like sex (C).

This advice results in a zany and lusty show. In the afterglow I talk loudly, embracing my teammates in the green room. Then our coach enters and I'm in trouble because I keep doing scenes where I coerce the other player into kissing me. He chastises me playfully.

"At least I've been doing it indiscriminately!" I laugh, but shame stirs in my chest.

"Yes, Haley, you'll kiss anyone — that's marvellous. The problem is that you're in default mode."

I stop chirping and take it on the chin. "You're right." I attribute this newfound ability to eat humble pie and take the note without getting defensive to T. The great secret is, it feels so much better to eat it than to get my back up.

When I come down from the theatre, Milo's bought me a drink.

"Bloody great." His brother leans in and plants a kiss on my cheek. He wants to know how we come up with all that stuff without a script.

I find it hard to make eye contact with Milo and gulp my drink. When his brother stands to buy another round, I apologise and put my coat on.

"Don't leave me, McGee," pleads Milo.

I tell him I'm sorry and head home to digest my habitual strong-armed smooching.

While I've always been somewhat precious about consummation, I've been reckless with my kissing. I was an especially indiscriminate lip-locker in university. I honed a technique to get strangers to make out with me on the dance floor, which consisted of putting my face within kissing distance from theirs and keeping it there, unflinching, until eventually they'd catch on.

That's more or less how I seduced Ukulele. We met at a poetry salon that a friend of Ollie's was hosting — Ollie and I both attended university in Toronto. Ukulele was reading that evening. I'd never met someone my own age who was capable of wielding words with such precision and power. I decided to pounce.

The truth is, that night, I was on a mission to get laid. It was the first time I'd gone out with that mandate. The previous weekend I'd had sex with a classmate. Tension had been building between us, but it was clear neither of us would let it go farther than lifting the lid off the pot to release some steam. Still, I wanted to dilute the experience, to prove that it was a meaningless drop in the sea of sex I was having.

But it wasn't, as apart from Necklace, that was the only other sex I'd had. This had to change. After the reading, I made hash-brownie eyes at the toothsome poet and several hours later, after munching on falafels in my kitchen, we tiptoed up to my bedroom where we made out but didn't touch each other's bits. I told him I actually didn't want to go all the way. He said he felt lucky that I'd talked to him at all. I made him guess how many people I'd slept with. He was surprised it was only two. I was flattered to be perceived as a worldly woman.

The next day he called, and when I answered he read me the voicemail message he'd prepared. An architecture student with a passion for words, his speech was compacted with obscure words and self-effacing humour; it made references to the few jokes we'd created the night before. I was charmed. At last, an intellectual!

He was my first boyfriend not born in 1985, but three years before. He was also my first boyfriend who was still in love with his ex and using me to move on. He didn't watch porn, because ethically he opposed it, but he'd listen to the audio from porn videos and jerk off to that. When I handled his private parts roughly, as Necklace had taught me to do, Ukulele told me that it seemed that I didn't know how to be with a circumcised guy. That's when I understood that not all men have the same proclivities. Like with ears, which were an erogenous zone for Necklace, it took a while to understand that the reason other men didn't freak out when I nibbled their earlobes was that it just didn't do it for them, not because they were repressed.

The novelty of this literary relationship, after my primal, physical connection with Necklace, beguiled me. But Ukulele didn't walk me home or send me racy emails; socially he was shy and deferring; he didn't ingratiate himself to my classmates. From top to tail, we lasted four months. I don't remember the first time I saw him after our initial hook-up, or how the relationship built, only that I'd get drunk at Mickey Finn's, the pub my classmates were partial to, then flounder through the snow to his place on the west side of Toronto. He'd roll his eyes but always embraced me.

By the first time we had sex, we'd known each other for a few weeks. He had compiled a "sexy song list" to mask any noises his roommate might overhear. They lived in a high-ceilinged, poorly insulated apartment above a corner shop. The entire place was floored with red linoleum and lit by bare lightbulbs. His bed was pushed right up against the window where snowflakes danced in the wind-stream of a vent. I found the gesture of the playlist deeply thoughtful and our sex evoked a cool forest green.

After orgasming, he pulled out, then threw his back into the wall, despairing, "Fuck. Why does this always happen to me?"

In the dim light of the streetlamp outside the window, I could see him hitting his forehead with his palm. "What's wrong?"

His voice was low. "The condom's still inside of you."

"Get it out, get it out!" I squealed in a whisper. In the past, condoms had remained snug on the penises penetrating me. I lay flat. Arms in a goalpost shape around my head. A frog pinned for dissection.

He crawled towards me. His cool fingers scratched around my vagina until he pulled out the sopping piece of rubber. It looked like an emaciated slug.

When I heard it swack the hard plastic of the trash bin, I curled into the foetal position. "It's okay. I'll just take the morning-after pill."

He wanted to go to the pharmacy with me in the morning.

I told him I couldn't get it the next day because I was in a tech rehearsal, but I'd go on Sunday.

He snapped that the pharmacy wasn't open Sundays and the pill must be taken within seventy-two hours. His tone bruised me, but I didn't want to drop my whimsical persona.

I counted on my fingers Friday night to Saturday night (twenty-four hours), Saturday night to Sunday night (forty-eight), Sunday night to Monday night (seventy-two). "As long as I take it before Monday night, I'm within the timeframe."

He said, "That's true; however, its efficacy reduces the longer you wait. But you're on the birth control pill, right?"

I wasn't. I had been when I was with Necklace but when I ran out of pills, I wasn't having sex with anyone, so I stopped taking them.

Ukulele was morally offended. He spoke with urgency and authority about me going back on it, before returning to self-pity, saying, "I can't believe this is happening to me again."

I wrapped the towel from the back of his bedroom door around myself. "I'm not going to have a baby," I hissed. "I'm going to pee."

In his grimy bathroom, I pummelled the part of my body I thought my uterus was in. Under my breath I chanted, "I will not have a baby, I will not have a baby, I will not have a baby."

When I came back to bed he was eating leftover pizza. His demeanour now conciliatory, he explained, "My ex-girlfriend had to take the morning-after pill three times because of me and it just really sucks."

I listened to him chew for a while.

He offered to go to the pharmacy with me on Monday.

I said I'd have to go between classes, so not to worry about it.

"And if you get pregnant, I'll support whatever choice you make."

"I'd get an abortion."

"It's up to you."

"I know what I'd do."

"Then I'd go to the appointment with you. If you wanted me to."

I pulled my knees to my chest, feeling the draft from the window lick my back. Then I said, "I feel like everything is ugly now. The magic is killed."

He swallowed and looked me up and down. "Haley. You have been unbelievably cool. You haven't freaked out or blamed me. You have been magical."

I reached out and touched his knee.

On Monday I took Plan B and bled. A few weeks later I went to a doctor at the university and got a prescription for the contraceptive pill. I'd been off for six months and was back on. My boobs swelled, my bum ballooned, and my tummy chubbed. Lithe me was in new skin. I started running laps at the university track, but I wasn't consistent enough for it to return my pre-synthetic-hormone shape.

After a couple months Ukulele's sheen had worn off. When he forgot his journal at my apartment and I read passages about his undying love for his ex and bemusement with me, I wasn't desolate. To normalise our using each other to fill a void, I led a discussion about how enjoying each other's company was enough; it was okay that we didn't love each other. But once we admitted it, the hope that it might become love was dashed, and his faults became more pronounced. His narrow shoulders unsettled me. His delicate taste buds made me petulant. And I knew he was the writer, but the more he shared his poems with me, the more convinced I was that I was the better fighter for the right words.

Valentine's Day clinched it. He came over with his old ukulele and sang a song he'd written for me. He was out of tune and out of time. My long-held dream of being someone's muse, watching the man I love sing a song for me in front of a captive audience in some warm, hodge-podge café, smashed. This, him maintaining eye contact with me throughout the entire song, only breaking it to check his place in the six pages of lyrics, was the opposite of satiating. I feigned a smile and sweetness. Afterwards he gifted me the ukulele. He had a new one and he knew I wanted to learn to play.

Countless times over the next six weeks I made the trip to his place with the intention of breaking up with him, but I failed every time. On one of these trips, I brought a hundred-dollar cheque. "For the ukulele — you could have sold it instead of giving it to me."

Though he spoke about being skint constantly and his student debt governed all of his decisions, he didn't want money for the ukulele. "It was a gift," he said. "Just learn to play."

After yet another failed attempt at breaking up with him, Ollie and I prepared a script, which said, "Since neither of us view this as love and we don't see a future together, and since I don't really think I want a relationship right now, I think it's better that I focus on my studies and we break up." I called Ukulele, made it through the script, and after a four-minute, sweaty conversation I was free.

Later that evening I called Necklace. Just to say hi. It had been a year since we'd broken up. He had a new girlfriend. At the end of the call he said, "Okay baby." When I realised he was talking to her, it didn't sting. Ukulele cashed the cheque a few weeks later.

And a few months after that, I ended up in hospital, diagnosed with deep vein thrombosis. I had two blood clots, one under my collarbone and the other in my armpit. Nothing bad happened but according to the emergency room doctor, blood clots build like Lego pieces towards your heart. If I'd waited a week before seeking medical attention, I'd likely have suffered a heart attack or a stroke. I was taken off the birth control pill immediately with strict guidance never to take it again.

When I've told the story of my blood clots in the past, I've never tied them to Ukulele. It's an A to C connection at best. It could have been any boyfriend or any friend of mine or a doctor urging me to go back on the pill. Those risks weren't well known in my circles in 2004.

In my journal I write down:

Wild Cards to discuss with Gemma:

Long term impact. A — C = Ukulele's condom coming off — blood clots

Short term impact. A — B = Visiting Necklace — sitting on knife on the bus

£ + ♥

I'm in the lobby of Camden People's Theatre. Sam has just told me his theatre is committed to presenting a three-week run of *The Ex-Boyfriend Yard Sale* in their autumn programming.

We lock in the dates. The show will open mid-November and run until early December. That means beginning rehearsals in late October. Which gives me about eight months to get all the artistic, mathematical and administrative elements in shape. It sounds like a long time, it's not, but I'm elated.

I fill Sam in on all the developments on my end since the R&D week: I've got my friend Elson on board to direct — Elson is based in Canada but he'll be in the UK directing another project and will stay on to direct my show immediately afterwards. I've secured a sound designer and we've got two more R&D weeks coming up, one here at CPT in about six weeks and another one in the summer. As the meeting comes to a close, I yammer on about setting up a cost-of-love-related installation in both the theatre lobby and the windows facing the road.

Sam says the priority is getting the grant application in, because none of this can happen without that funding. Then he passes me off to the producer to hammer out a contract.

On the bus back home, I get a text from Milo.

Boogaloo?

Milo drops his cigarette when he claps eyes on me and pulls me in for a hug. I'm relieved when my cheeks don't flush. We score one of the only booths in the pub and he announces that tonight's on him. He just got paid.

"So did I!" I say, raising my arms. "Well, I got the shoot fee for the insurance advert. Three hundred pounds, less commission."

"Aw mate that's great news." But he's already up. He leans down and kisses the top of my head and pinches my shoulders. We order burgers and ciders.

He asks about my personal finances.

I tell him I owe my therapist $2,080. But otherwise, the influx of VO work, plus my solid Joe-jobbing, means I can start to make a modest dent in my debt — a big dent if the commercial money comes through, but I'm never going to bank on that again.

I tell him I've received eight messages on Gumtree from people who want to buy the ukulele. He can't understand how such a twee item would be so popular.

"People want to play."

"But not you."

"I couldn't move my fingers fast enough from chord to chord."

"And that's how we separate the wheat from the chaff."

"Or it just wasn't my medium."

He's glad to hear about the show being programmed and gives me a list of set designers to check out. He doesn't want to talk about Julie. They're about a month into their open relationship. Julie's been out with a few different people but so far, all Milo's done is trawl the dating apps.

We have more drinks.

He doesn't ask about T and I feel reticent to bring him up. What would I say? Other than complain that we don't have any plans to see each other again because he's essentially on call for a story in Chicago, so he can't leave, and he hasn't invited me to visit. I look at Milo's dating profile. "You're better looking than these photos." He gets bashful and I tell him not to be so Scottish. I itemise his attributes one by one, from his financial literacy to his massive hands, his artistic sensitivity to his veiny neck. When he objects that no one finds him attractive, the booze and exhaustion sever protocol and I hear myself saying, "I've had two sex dreams about you in the last month." I laugh and he stares at me wide-eyed and flustered. "It doesn't mean anything but — it's flattering. No?"

"Fuck it, McGee." I see he's mustering something.

Oh no.

Then he's saying it. "I like you."

"I like you too," I say with wilful enthusiasm, riding my well-trod line where friendliness and flirtation meet.

"No, I *like* you."

"I—" I smile and hold his eye. "I like you too." As soon as it's out of my mouth, I wonder, do I? Fuck. No. I have T. I love T. But Milo's here and Milo's upbeat.

Milo leans back victoriously.

"But so what?" I counter.

"You don't think it's worth paying attention to?"

"You're in a relationship."

"But it's open."

"And I'm in a relationship."

"Are you?"

I bite the inside of my cheek.

Milo leans forward, tapping the corners of the cardboard coaster on the table. "I, yeah, fuck it. I think I'm in love with you. And I don't even know what that means."

No no no.

He carries on, "I think I've been in love with you since Edinburgh — I don't even like bao. I'm sorry. I don't want to make you uncomfortable."

I tell him he's not. This isn't entirely true, but my curiosity, gall and fear are at war with each other inside me, and I can't control what's coming out of my mouth.

He says that he's kind of obsessed with me. "Not in a creepy way but in a — I just want to be around you and I could talk to you for hours and not get bored and most people really bore me and I just, obviously we're such great friends but I — And it's not just because Julie's already sleeping with other people — it's been there for a long time and . . . I wondered if I was crazy or if it was between us."

I'm silent. On one hand this is enlivening and validating and thrilling, on the other it's dangerous and uncomfortable and ill-advised.

Three Spanish women interrupt us to ask if we'll join their team. It's quiz night and the pub is filling up. There's nowhere else to sit and they'd love some English people to help them with the references. We say of course we'll join but warn them neither of us is English. The girls pile into the three-sided booth and we face the quiz master.

Milo and I sit with our thighs touching, leaning into each other to whisper our answers. During the interval he buys us all a round. I steal a look at my phone. There's a missed call from T. I text him, *Hey I'm at a pub quiz with Milo. Will call you when I'm home*.

Milo is doing some hand gesture from the bar and mouthing something.

I mouth back, "I can't read lips." He doesn't know me, I think. He doesn't love me. He doesn't know me. T knows I'm an abysmal lipreader — that it eludes me completely. I shrug and mouth, "Doesn't matter. You pick," give the OK sign with my fingers and laugh.

"You're such a great couple," says one of the women.

I tell her he's just a good friend and that we're both in relationships with other people.

One of the other women asks, "Where are they?"

"His is in Homerton and mine's in America."

"Babe. Long distance? Trust me, it never works."

Her friend says, "She's just bitter."

And the third points at Milo, adding, "But this one really likes you."

"Yeah," I say, "but he doesn't know me."

This makes her laugh. She raises her empty glass to me.

Milo arrives with pints. "What're you lot laughing about?"

"Just how the more you know someone the less you like them," I say.

He lets out a "Ha" before narrowing his eyes. "I don't think I agree."

Milo proves himself our only asset during the quiz. Thanks to his brain's capacity to hold onto old pop-culture titbits and useful facts, we win. We only had the competition of two other teams but no matter. We're awarded fifty pounds and we are elated. And drunk. We cheer and hug each other and when Milo and I begin to pull out of our hug, it just happens, like breathing; we kiss on the lips. I feel the jolt in my vagina.

"Sorry," he says, "Sorry. I hope that was okay. Sorry."

I pat his shoulder a couple times and say nothing.

The Spanish girls wink at me and scoot off to the bar.

They crank the music and Milo could use a cigarette. T doesn't smoke. I don't want to be with a smoker. Outside we shiver under a heating lamp and clumsily wade through thick silence.

Milo balances on the edge of a wooden bench. "I don't want to be pushy, I really don't, and if I've misinterpreted, I'm very sorry."

"You haven't misinterpreted . . ." I reply, standing under the heater, holding my ribs. I search for the right way to finish my sentence. I did not expect this door ever to open and suddenly we're in the vestibule. I want out of the house but I'm also fiercely curious.

He snubs his cigarette, stands up and kisses me again, fast, before the "but" he knows is coming.

I pull away and push my hands deep into my coat pockets, clutching at my keys. "You haven't misinterpreted, but so what?

Just because we feel this way doesn't mean we need to act on it."

"Because you're in love with T?"

"Yeah, I — I am. And I've invested a lot." Sunk Cost Bias flits through my mind but I bat it away. "And you're not — you live with someone — I know you've opened it up but it's not — it's just . . . not on. I'm not interested in polyamory."

He looks up at the hazy London sky of streetlights and smog. When he brings his head down, he reaches for my hand and pleads, "Just don't say no *yet*."

I bring my chin to my right shoulder and shut my eyes. "Alright. But I'm not saying yes either. And I've got to go home now."

He says he'll take it.

"No promises," I say. "There's a very low chance."

"I get it, I get it. Can I kiss you one last time?"

I nod.

Closed lips puckered hard press against mine. I feel the pressure in my teeth.

I make the short walk home in a daze and only realise I'm jangling the keys in my pocket when the person walking in front of me turns and gives me a look. I don't know what happened to my dignity.

T answers the phone saying, "Hey babe."

I love being called babe or baby. This is a new development in my relationship with T and I'm exhilarated by it. The baby gate has come down. We're in pet-name bliss.

"Hi baby," I purr. "How you doing?"

"Not great." He talks for ten minutes about the story he's working on and a conflict he's in with his editor. The progress is slow and out of his control and that's maddening. He tells me he can't cry about his brother, just for his parents, because it's the wrong order of events — is there anything more horrendous than burying a child? Without any reason to leave the house today, he reveals he's been lying on the floor listening to a podcast by a journalist he deems shallow and deplorable.

Here I have to interject. "Why are you listening to something that makes you angry? You're adding insult to injury."

He says, "You're right. You're right. You're so good to me." I keep waiting for him to ask me about my evening, but he doesn't. Instead he tells me that he can't afford therapy this month. My snogging with Milo undermines my hard line. All I get out is an "Uh huh" in response; then I ask him what he's up to this evening.

He says probably the gym.

"That's a great idea; you'll feel better."

"Yeah . . ." he first says reluctantly, and then, "Yeah," definitively. "You're right. You're so *good* to me Haley. You really are."

"No. I — No. I'm . . . just myself." I don't toy with confessing the kiss. I'd lose all my esteem, and besides, nothing is going to happen.

T says if he's going to work out, he has to get off the phone now because he's headed to a dinner later. As we're saying goodbye, he catches himself, "Oh no! I didn't hear how you're doing?"

I tell him it's fine, and we can talk about me next time.

He apologises for talking so much. We say our I love yous and goodbyes.

And with that he's off and I'm facing the wall of my nun's cell. When I masturbate, I flip flop, T/Milo/T/Milo/T.

£ + ♥

When I tell Fi about my dreams about kissing Milo and then actually kissing Milo, she fires up. "The story of you and Milo, now *that's* an origin story. Who meets in line at a food truck, become fast friends and fall in love a year and a half later?"

I tell her that we're not in love.

Through the phone I can hear Fi raise an eyebrow. She says, "Come on. It's a Nora Ephron script."

"But Fi," I protest, "I love T."

"I know you do but Milo's here, in London. And he's there for you mentally, emotionally — that guy shows up for you."

"He lives with someone."

"So?"

"So he's not available."

"He's no less available than T."

"You just don't like T."

"I don't know T. But it seems really tough with him."

"It is. But it would be tough with Milo too, eventually." I'm pacing around the flat. Navid's at the chiropractor. When Cloe discovered that he had no intention of taking any of the jobs he'd interviewed for in Greece, she broke up with him. Navid then proceeded to go on a bender that culminated with him throwing his back out at Wembley Stadium, ferociously cheering for Arsenal. Fi's put me on speakerphone now. I raise my voice over the sound of her washing dishes. "Milo just seems ideal because I don't know him. With T, at least I know what I'm dealing with — and he knows me. *He knows me.*"

"But there shouldn't be so much strife, love. It's supposed to be fun."

Fi's in a good mood today because she and Ru put an offer on a house in north-east London and her period is a couple days late.

"Does it have to hurt so much to be worth it?" she asks.

I tell her about a book I read, *Getting the Love You Want* by Harville Hendrix. In it, he describes that "I know you" feeling when you fall in love with someone quickly as being a product of our "lizard brain" recognising in the other person a similar quality to our primary caregivers when we were small. And that primitive part of us wants to return to "the scene of the crime" and fix things that went awry. It's why there is great capacity for both healing and wounding in love. Those "I know you" connections, if they're approached with consciousness and communication, hold huge potential for healing and transformation, but if not, we end up in a partnership where we damage each other by exacerbating the very wounds we're trying to mend. T and I definitely have "I know you" love and T is more willing to talk about his feelings than anyone else I know.

Fi says that no matter who you're with, they'll eventually annoy you and things will be hard, that's just the effect of time and familiarity. "Why make it harder than it needs to be?" she asks. "And what about when you don't get the healing? And all you're left with is baggage."

I agree. Carrying baggage takes a toll.

I didn't put it together until working on this project, but I'm sure part of the reason I've never been the first one to say I love you since Mix Tape — even though I was aching to say it to T for years — is because I was so mortified by how Mix Tape hesitated to say it back.

Fi has to go, but right before we hang up she says, "Ru and I have a wonderful origin story, and honestly the mythology of our relationship keeps it romantic. Good stories are important. They're what keep us together."

Part of what Harville Hendrix argues, which I didn't share with Fi, is that those relationships with a pervasive "meh" tone — where there's not a lot of fire or passion — are probably relationships that don't have the capacity for great healing. The connection isn't deep.

I don't want meh. That was the problem with Ukulele. The relationship was void of vim. It didn't feel urgent or necessary or fathomless. I want to love passionately and to be transformed by love.

But how do I have a high-stakes, healing relationship when I'm attracted to unavailable men?

I bring this to Thea in our session the following day.

"Yes, you have a thing about unavailable men." She says it's a complex, a neurotic behaviour I've developed over my life. "You're drawn to men who will keep you at arm's length because it's safe and comfortable for you." She explains that I've internalised love as being tied up with feeling rejected. Someone who is simply open and able to commit to me feels like way too much. I don't have the receptors to accept it yet.

Does that mean I should be with Milo? The dreams threw me, and his confession flattered me, and T's distance has me itching to balance the score. But Milo doesn't get it. He's reliable and good at logistics but he won't enter the weeds of creative process or unpick the nuances of human dynamics; our conversations only cover 60 per cent of the ground I want access to. T is the only guy I've ever met who I feel I can bring my whole self to, or most of myself. His willingness to delve into almost every topic with genuine interest is the quality I can't bear to lose. The cost-benefit analysis of our relationship is confusing.

Thea says I haven't signed anything with T. She also says that if T and I were able to approach our relationship, and its conflicts, with consciousness, there likely would be scope for repairing old wounds.

Suddenly indignant, I ask, "Shouldn't the success of a relationship be measured on a scale of healing versus wounding? Instead of how long it lasts? Or whether or not you own property together?"

"What do you think?" she asks in return.

£ + ♥

"My relationship with Ukulele had so little impact on my life's narrative I've been considering cutting it from the show. But that in itself settles the suffering predicament!"

"The suffering predicament?" Gemma asks, holding a piece of celery.

I've chopped up raw vegetables and laid them out in front of Navid's TV along with several varieties of hummus for our session this afternoon.

I remind her. "Does suffering increase or decrease the value of an item?"

"Right. Of course."

We're meant to be working on the Relationship Index phrase, but my thoughts on my uneventful relationship with Ukulele and discussion with Fi about the importance of a relationship's mythology have carried me to an exciting brainwave.

Brandishing a slice of red pepper, I explain that whenever I've told the story of my blood clots, I've never connected them to my relationship with Ukulele. Yet without the blood clot drama, the relationship is utterly forgettable. "But it isn't joy or suffering that makes value go up or down. It's impact."

"It's the emotional impact of a relationship that matters?"

"Yes," I say, "Impact is valuable because it incites evolution and growth. Whereas 'meh' challenges nothing and keeps us stagnant."

Gemma nods, chewing, and reaches for her notebook.

"It's the personal evolution we go through when we have an impactful experience — positive or negative — that makes for a satisfying narrative arc. A good story. The bigger the transform-ation, the better the story. And good stories are powerful currency."

"Right-right-right," says Gemma. "The objects are secondary to the play."

"Exactly. What I'm really selling, in the show, is the stories."

"What if," she muses, "there's a distinction to be made between the value of the stories you can mine a relationship for and the quality of a relationship when you're inside it?" Gemma says my point about the value of impact raises some important considerations. "Maybe we need to go back through the data we've quantified and shift numbers around to reflect impact? Or maybe this is really about the relationship between data points and how we weigh them against each other. And perhaps it might be worth adding a phrase to the formula that measures the narrative impact the item represents."

First, we refine the definition of the Relationship Index to be "a measurement of aspects of a relationship while you were inside it". Then we sort through all the data points currently under the Relationship Index and pull out any variables that have to do with the value of a relationship in retrospect, putting them into a new phrase that we name Narrative Impact. Narrative Impact measures "how a relationship contributes to, and/or affects your life, post break-up". Under Narrative Impact we'll assess:

- *Practical skills and knowledge gleaned in the relationship*
- *The big life lessons learned in the relationship*
- *Rites of passage experienced in the relationship*
- *Number of good stories the relationship contributed to your life story*
- *Baggage accrued*
- *Healing and wounding*

As we work through the data points, I tell her about how appalled Ukulele was by the holes in my knowledge of what he considered to be "foundational comedy documents", and how he set out to rectify this, insisting that I watch Monty Python's oeuvre with him.

There's a distinction between the practical skills and knowledge we gain as a result of a particular relationship versus the more ethereal life lessons we leave with.

"So, to evaluate the skills and knowledge you got from Ukulele," says Gemma, "it's not so much about how much you liked or disliked Monty Python. It's about how much of an impact their comedy made on your life."

"Tragically, I think four out of ten because I was only really watching because he wanted me to. I didn't think I'd ever do comedy, so I didn't really absorb the lessons there."

Referring to the spreadsheet, we look at the various skills and knowledge I acquired as a result of my relationships and decide, for each relationship, we'll take the top one and rank it from one to ten.

Relationship	Best Skill or Knowledge Accrued	Value
Mix Tape	Introduced me to the work of Laurie Anderson	6
Necklace	Taught me how to parallel park (10 at the time but now I never drive, and when I do, I can't remember how to park anymore)	3
Ukulele	Monty Python's oeuvre — useful in UK assimilation but not comedy career	4
Bicycle	Taught me how to make pancakes without a recipe	9
Typewriter	Made sure I never forgot how to pronounce the word "feral"	8
Backpack	Introduced me to classic books *Bleak House*, *Middlemarch* and *Breakfast at Tiffany's*	8
Jewellery Box	Finnish history	2
T-shirt	Techniques to de-escalate conflict	10

Then we look at the big life lessons gleaned in my various relationships. Trying to assess the "moral" or biggest takeaway from each one, we decide that to be considered a life lesson, the lesson must be something that's actually stuck. If I repeated the mistake in a subsequent relationship, then the lesson doesn't count because I didn't learn it.

Gemma says, "If we want to test how valuable the lessons were, I think we need to measure the amount of your life you will have to benefit from them — or in the case of baggage, when we get to it, how long you will be saddled with it."

I revel in this great idea by saying her name slowly, "Gemmmaa."

We google life expectancy. In Canada it's 82.3 for women and in the UK it's 80.96. Since we don't know where I'll retire, we consider taking the average, which is 81.63, but this number depresses me a bit, so Gemma allows me to bump it up to ninety and subtract my age at the time of the break-up from that to see how long I'll have to put the lesson into practice.

Relationship	Biggest life lesson learned	Time to use them in years
Mix Tape	Love is conditional	74
Necklace	I can't will myself into loving someone	71
Ukulele	I'm not interested in a temporary or function-ary relationship	70
Bicycle	A relationship is a third entity that needs to be attended to	66
Typewriter	If everyone warns you about a person, listen to them	64
Backpack	You don't have to stay just because you've professed love or moved in	63
Jewellery Box	I want an intellectual equal, not a teacher	62
T-shirt	Just because you love someone, doesn't mean you should be in a relationship with them/if you're not getting what you want, then walk away	59

I want the lesson for Bicycle to be, "behaviour is character". But I didn't learn it. I repeated it with Typewriter and again with T.

We knock around what constitutes *baggage accrued* and determine that baggage is something that you carry into all your subsequent relationships. My inability to say I love you first is baggage from Mix Tape that's had a direct impact on my relationship with T-shirt. I was desperate to tell T that I loved him but refused to because I was terrified to be the one to say it first. Without that baggage, I would have said it and T would have either said it back, which would have calmed me immensely, or told me he didn't feel the same way, which would have been painful but clear. Instead my baggage kept me in the grey zone for years.

Gemma asks what baggage I took away from my relationship with Ukulele.

I tell her none. "I was never fully invested. And without investment or love, it's harder to be deeply affected. From the relationship with Ukulele the only things close to baggage would be worrying my vagina tasted uniquely bad or that I was annoying in the morning."

"But after a while, those injuries proved themselves to be temporary — they stopped being reflected in your actions?"

"Yes."

"Okay, so shall we say that any hurts that linger beyond a year are baggage?"

I swirl a radish around the bowl, scooping up the last bits of the garlic hummus, and nod.

This brings us to my thought about healing versus wounding. We create two additional data points, one called *wounds*, which takes into account damage inflicted by a particular relationship that you eventually recover from, and another one called *healing*, which captures the magnitude of the healing that took place in a given relationship. For instance, through my ability to break up with T when I wasn't getting what I wanted and lay out strict criteria for getting back together, I'm learning to be less compliant, less afraid of my own aggression and more forthright, which will hopefully have a positive effect for the rest of my life.

I tell her about Dan Savage's advice to "leave a campsite better than you found it".

She pauses writing for a moment and says, "But this isn't healing *versus* wounding is it? Because if we're interested in impact, positive or negative, then we want healing plus wounding — we want to give value to both?"

"You're right!"

She makes notes and I make tea.

When I return with the pot, Gemma asks, "For our *good stories* data point, what's more important, that it's a seminal event in your life story or that it's an amusing story you share frequently?"

"Is there a difference?"

Gemma laughs.

"But is there really?" I'm thinking of all the self-help reading I've done about the power of words becoming thoughts and thoughts becoming actions and actions becoming forces that shape our lived experience. "A story becomes a part of our repertoire, whether that be something we retell to ourselves or share with others; the act of telling and retelling it shapes how we understand our own life."

Gemma says fair enough and it's decided that *good stories* will be measured by how frequently they're told to the self or to others. Then she says, "This is a good place for the dilution effect you were talking about, correct?"

She's bang on again. The impact of all these stories and experiences is diluted by the fact that I have multiple points of comparison.

Gemma suggests folding the dilution effect into the formula with a function in the Narrative Impact phrase. "Something like, frequency a good story is told divided by total number of relationships."

I give her a thumbs up and say, "Divide by eight." Then I blush. "Or . . . hmm . . ."

"What?"

"I don't really know if it is eight."

Gemma looks confused.

I consolidate all the straggling veggies on a smaller plate. "I got back together with T," I say quietly.

"Oh."

"Yeah. I haven't really told many people because, he's uh . . ." I take a sip of tea.

"Unreliable?" Gemma offers.

"Yeah." I force a laugh. "I haven't told my family yet, even."

"How long has it been?"

"A couple months." I say I'm sorry for not telling her earlier.

She says she gets it and brushes it off. "We've only known each other a short time."

"No, but we're working together on this thing about my love life." I fumble for the words. "I'm just afraid that it won't work out with him and I'll be doubly a fool, but I do also feel hopeful it will work out because a lot of changes have been made on his end. And he's on board with the things I want — no faffing around — working towards a serious relationship — family, baby stuff."

"So is he moving here?"

I wilt in the armchair. "I don't know? It's hard to know what he'll do. I don't know if I should quit or commit."

She asks why I'm inclined to stay.

I tell her, "It seems like if I leave now, the campsite will be worse than it was found. And I'm determined to clean it up." An emotional Sunk Cost Bias, if you will. I remember my aunt Harlow saying to me, "The best thing about you is that you don't give up. This is also your biggest problem."

I ask Gemma if she thinks I'm flogging a dead horse.

She doesn't answer this, skilfully bringing the conversation back to the math instead. "It's interesting, this idea of comfort with different people. I wonder if you feel the lessons, skills, baggage and so on are tainted at all by how well you get along with your exes now?"

I agree, it does colour things. Grateful to be speaking theoretically again, we dig in and create a ranking system for the level of friendship with exes post break-up.

Gemma packs her bag while I do the dishes. She tells me to just let her know whether I want to include T in the project or not. Quit or commit, she has no opinion either way.

I don't believe her, but I thank her and hug her in the doorway.

A couple days later she sends me an email with a first-draft, broad-strokes version of the formula. It looks like this:

DRAFT 1

$$\text{cost of } \heartsuit = MV \times \left[1 + \frac{NI-t}{t} \right] \times RI \times WC$$

Legend:

MV — Market Value

NI — Narrative Impact

t — Time Invested

RI — Relationship Index

WC — Wild Cards

£ + ♥

The grant went in last night. To celebrate, instead of working on the project this morning, I slept in and am indulging myself with a coffee from my favourite café in Crouch End. I savour it and amble though the neighbourhood until I end up in the health food store, staring at a wall of salt rock lamps. A woman in a crocheted sweater appears beside me and asks if I'd like a taster tarot session.

"Absolutely I would."

I follow her past the supplements and up a narrow staircase into a small room with a sloped ceiling. She motions for me to sit and enters my birth date and time into a website. "Shall we take a look then?" she asks when a chart pops up.

I nod.

She says that I'm very good with people, that I'm fascinated by their behaviour. "You could be a psychologist."

I tell her I'm an actor.

"That makes sense." She says that my career is going to be a bit slow now, but when I'm thirty-five it will take off.

I make a mental note to remember this and decide to withhold panic till then.

She tells me my sun is in Virgo, my moon is in Scorpio and my rising sign, which is how you express yourself to the world, is in Aries. "So, your front man is dynamic, doing and driven. Mercury, which is about the mind, voice and communicating, is very strong. You do have some troubling things here."

I brace myself.

"You want everything to be perfect. And it causes you great distress if it's not perfect. You want things to be useful and you want to do things that are useful. You put a lot of pressure on yourself to do everything 'just right' in your work and you want that from a mate too."

I tell her I thought I was getting better at being less of a perfectionist.

She looks at the chart then back to me and says, "Confidence is an area to work on — your sense of self is weak — belief in yourself is how you will get to the other side of worrying about being perfect."

I want to start defending my self-confidence. But the fact that it's got my back up probably means there's truth in it. I let it stew.

"You're a romantic person. But you have trouble finding the kind of love you want." She says with a Scorpio moon, there's an essence of intensity around my life and a need for passion. "But one of your problems —" she points to a cluster of symbols in the bottom right quadrant of her screen — "is that your moon is tightly involved with the planet Saturn. And Saturn restricts and holds back." She explains that Saturn and Pluto are in the seventh house of my moon, which governs relationships and significant others. She says Pluto is about power and control and Saturn adds to not wanting to be criticised and wanting to be perfect.

"So what does this mean?"

"Relationship-wise, it makes things tricky for you because you want power, control, self-sufficiency *and* you only want serious relationships."

This makes me laugh. I tell her it's true.

She says I've learned it's not safe to be vulnerable, but the only way to love is to let down the wall emotionally and make myself vulnerable.

I tell her about T, that we're sort of back together and I'm wondering if I should cut my losses and run or if it's worth investing more deeply.

She suggests we ask the tarot cards about this man.

I shuffle and cut the deck a couple times. She fans them. And I pick three.

After a moment she says, "Aha. There's a bond here, between you two. It's . . . I want to say it's ancestral. It's as though the two of you have unfinished business that belonged to your ancestors or to the two of you in a previous life."

This kind of talk doesn't faze me. Agnostic and godless as I am, I do want to believe there's something out there, in the cosmos, that has a hand in why things happen when they do.

I solemnly tell her that an ancestral bond makes sense.

She says, "He's come towards you now, and if you want to see if he's worth his salt, you will have to enter with two feet."

"I should visit him in Chicago."

Measured, she confirms, "If you can, yes."

Time suspends sitting with her. I ask if I can pay her and she declines, reiterating this was a taster. I sign up to her mailing list and leave without the shampoo I came in for. On my way back to the flat, I call T. It's 5 a.m. for him. He's groggy but in a sweet mood.

"I want to come visit you," I coo.

"What?" I hear the grin in his voice.

"I want to come visit you in Chicago. Soon. I had an epiphany."

He says, "Okay. Okay. Of course, I'd love you to come here. Of course. Come."

I squeal. "Is this fun?"

"It really is."

I tell him I'm going to book a flight today.

He says, "Good. I'm going to go back to sleep now, baby."

That evening, under Navid's critical eye, I book my direct flight to Chicago.

£ + ♥

Tonight is Milo's birthday drinks. I haven't seen him for a couple of weeks. I've now applied and wiped off my red lipstick three times. I can't figure out which look best says "I don't care". I've been avoiding him since our kiss, claiming work's been busy. It has been busy, but the truth is I've been avoiding him because I don't know how to navigate the situation, and I've capitalised on the fact that Milo's too repressed to talk about his emotions.

I shouldn't be nervous. I have T.

When I get to the pub Milo is outside, hugging a man I don't know while balancing a pint in each hand.

"Hi," I say under my breath, waving at him.

"Hey!" He moves out of the tight embrace with his pal into a loose one with me. Only our shoulders touch and he taps me on the back.

I charge myself not to blush as we pull back, but the moment we make eye contact my cheeks get hot. As do his. At least we're in the same boat.

Milo holds the door open for me. "Is it really weird that I'm here?" I whisper.

"No. It's great. What are you drinking?"

"Water."

"Come on."

"White wine? No, cider. Wait! No. I should be getting you a drink!" I call out as he moves towards the barman.

Leaning over the bar, he orders me a large white wine. When they present him with the contactless payment, he pushes me out of the way and taps his card.

"Milo! It's your birthday. I should be treating you."

His mates are in the snug, but when my drink arrives, he doesn't move to join them.

"So, how are you?"

"I'm good," I chirp. "How are you?"

"I broke up with Julie. I didn't want to tell you on the phone." He's smiling but speaking into his pint.

"Oh shit. I'm — shit. Sorry."

He raises his glass to me. I clink mine to his and we lock eyes for a moment. I sip first. I don't know what to ask. Did he end it because of me? Should I tell him I'm going to Chicago in a week's time? Why haven't I told him I'm going to Chicago? It's been eight days since I booked the flights and now it seems too late. I'm only going for a week. When more of his friends arrive and barge between us to wish him well, I'm relieved.

As the receiving line dies off, Milo turns to me. "This is crazy — please feel free to say no or tell me to fuck off."

"What?" There's a clenching in my solar plexus.

"Well, my brother's wedding is in a week and . . . I need a date."

I'm so relieved he's not professing his love, it makes me laugh. "Do you *need* a date?"

He makes a grim expression.

"I'm just saying it might be a little weird to bring someone they don't know, and what? Explain that you're freshly broken up, or—?" I'm speaking glibly, attempting to jolly him along.

He says, "It can be platonic."

I want to raise an eyebrow but instead I flare my nostrils.

"Look, it's a resort in the Maldives. All inclusive, all paid for. You're great with people. All my siblings are married, there will be tons of kids running around and my family loves to dance." Then he says, "I just don't want to do it alone. I've got a double room — there will be empty chairs and extra meals everywhere I go."

Thankfully, one of his mates noses in between us to introduce himself. When they begin catching up, I turn away, find a spot in the snug and worm out of my pea coat.

Before long, Milo slides in beside me again, passing me another glass of wine. "Forget about the wedding. I'm all over the shop."

I take a sip. "The trip sounds good, really good, but—"

"I get it."

"I mean, it's probably a lot at this point and—"

"Yeah. No. Yeah. I knew it was a long shot. I just figured it was my birthday and maybe . . . Never mind."

Our knees touch and I have the urge to throw my arms around him. I want to sit on his lap. I want to feel the weight of him above me.

Someone asks, "So Haley, how do you know Milo?"

Milo talks about the bao truck but all I hear is Thea's voice in my head, reminding me that I haven't signed anything with T. He hasn't held up his end of the bargain entirely and historically he's let me down.

Sitting next to Milo in the pub, surrounded by his friends, I'm the girlfriend I've always wanted to be, instantly accepted by his tribe, admired by my beloved, simultaneously safe and free.

As Milo shimmies out from behind the table to get another round, I look at my phone. There's a message from T. *Babe, when are you going to be home?*

I text him back. *At the pub, home in 45 min.*

When I come up behind Milo at the bar, he turns to pass me a third glass of wine, but I don't take it. "I have to go."

His face turns broody. "You do?"

"Yeah. I just hit the wall and—" Fishing around for my wallet, I pull out a ten-pound note and press it into his hand. "Here. I'm sorry I can't drink it. I have a voice job in the morning," I lie, "and I just realised what time it is."

"Okay. What about—"

"I'll think about the wedding. But probably no. I think it's a bit—"

"Much?"

"Yeah."

He walks me out of the pub. He seems totally sober suddenly. We step towards each other and stand a couple inches apart with our foreheads touching. I run my fingers over his beard, he stifles a hiccup. He smells like laundry detergent and hops.

I say, "Happy birthday," squeeze his hand and back away.

"I meant what I said, McGee. And I will wait."

I smile and turn away from him. When I turn the corner, the cold evening thwacks me on the back. I am unleashed back to myself. I stop in at the World's End pub, push through the students and tourists to get to the disgusting loo. I hover and spray the contents of my bladder into the toilet. Empty now. Northern line. Home.

T is delighted that I'm a little drunk.

I purge my mind. "Milo asked me to go to a wedding with him." Then I perjure myself with a half-truth. "He and Julie opened up their relationship and I think he has a crush on me."

"He definitely has a crush on you."

"Well, he asked me platonically."

T chuckles. "Oh boy."

"I'm not going to go."

"I almost feel bad for you that you can't have an affair with that rock star."

"Ew no. No. God no." I laugh. "Tell me what you've been doing."

He lists the various things that he's been worrying about. I put the phone on speaker, on low volume so as not to wake up Navid. While T unloads, I unscrew my jar of coconut oil and wipe away my attempt at glamour. With my fingers still slippery with oil, I touch myself while he talks. Silently I make myself come.

T asks, "Why are you out of breath?"

"I'm not," I say, gaining control of my voice. "How's therapy?" After a month off, he returned last week. During one of our honeyed moments he agreed it was important and sent an email to his therapist while we were on the phone.

"Good. Hard. I had it yesterday." He speaks about the difficulty of understanding his role in life now that his sibling is dead. He's thinking of writing about it, but he fears that doing so would objectify his brother. When my yawns obscure my words, he urges me to sleep.

I put on his T-shirt and get under the covers. It's after 1 a.m. I ask him if he's excited to see me. He responds with a terse, "Yep", but I'm too tired to confront him about it. I'll let it slide till tomorrow. We hang up and I turn on my white-noise sleep app to the city rain setting.

Milo texts. *No pressure about wedding. Don't write me off completely. x P.S. You looked gorgeous tonight. I'm not objectifying you just speaking objectively. xx*

THE LEDGER

Love	Milo likes me, or is in love with me
	I kissed Milo
	I don't feel that guilty, but I like T better
	T doesn't suspect
	I'm going to Chicago
	I hid Chicago from Milo
Money	Flight to Chicago cost £350
	R&D week, VO work & travel to Chicago made it harder to maintain Joe-jobs
	– £8,968.13 in debt
	£930.03 in bank
Career	Filmed TV commercial for insurance company — fingers crossed it goes to air
	The Ex-Boyfriend Yard Sale is going to have a three-week run!
	Grant submitted to Arts Council — waiting to hear back
Total	*?? Not the worst.*

13. RELATIONSHIP INDEX

*"That's love: Two lonely persons keep each other safe
and touch each other and talk to each other."*
Rainer Maria Rilke

After some prodding, T agreed to meet me at the airport. He's late. I lean against a large concrete pillar and watch other travellers hop into cars. I don't want to feel annoyed, but I do. Milo's always early. I coach myself not to compare and contrast all week, remind myself what the astrologer said about going in with two feet. T had his normal pre-emptive freak out. After calling me less over the past week, he responded to my *I can't wait to see you* message this morning with an underwhelming, *Oh yeah?* Not the enthused *Me too* I was hoping for.

I spot T walking towards me, squinting, scanning. I step away from the pillar and wave. He quickens his pace, wraps his arms around my waist and kisses me before we speak. He shaved this morning. I instantly forgive him and run my hands through his hair.

"I wanted to make you a welcome sign but—" He removes my backpack and takes hold of my wheelie suitcase. "Can you walk for twenty minutes?"

I raise my eyebrows.

"This is the trick to getting a cheap Uber fast."

I nod, determined to be a good sport.

He walks ahead of me as we move through the mass of travellers waiting for slower, more expensive rides. I follow him along the sidewalk, past the four, six, eight lanes that funnel into O'Hare International. The sun is high and the sky is wide. I behold the billboards and hold out for the promise of sky-scrapers and Lake Michigan.

It's early afternoon by the time we get to T's place and I've been awake for over twenty hours. He's subletting a semi-famous politician's apartment — a one-bedroom with floor to ceiling bookshelves and a wood-burning stove. French doors open onto a patio framed by Edison lightbulbs, furnished with a gigantic wooden dining table. The March weather is too cool to enjoy it, but I can't wait to snuggle up in front of the fire.

"It's perfect," I say, stretching out on the worn leather sofa.

"It's okay." T gestures to a Buddha shrine in the corner. He offers to make me a tea but then joins me and holds my feet to his chest. I want to close the space between us, but he seems to need me at my legs' length. I fill the silence with gossip: Ollie's mediation sessions with his ex aren't yielding the dividends he'd hoped for, and his ex now has a new partner. T hums his responses till he starts to doze. I gently extricate myself and start rummaging through the kitchen.

Suddenly beside me, he asks, "What are you looking for?"

"Tea."

"Oh right. Sorry." He pushes me out of the way with a stiff arm and opens a pantry cupboard. "Here are the dates you wanted. Not cheap." He points to the counter. "And the bananas. The spinach is in the fridge."

I thank him and ask where he keeps the blender.

Water hits the back of the metal kettle. He turns off the tap, puts the kettle on the hob and leans over to watch it ignite.

"Where's the blender?" I repeat.

"What?"

"Where. Is. The. Blender?"

He turns to face me. "I don't know if she has one." And with that he sits at the table and opens his laptop.

I'm trying to laugh. "So you got these ingredients for a smoothie without knowing if you have a blender?"

"Take a look in the cupboards."

"Wow," I mutter and open them one by one.

"What's that?" he says reflexively, gazing into his screen.

I stop. "T."

"Yep."

"Can you just be with me?"

He sucks in air through pursed lips. "Yep. Just — I have to reply to this email."

I finish my search. No blender.

I retrieve my laptop from my backpack and lie down on the sofa with it on my stomach. I'm going to request an interview with Bicycle. Midway through entering the Wi-Fi code the kettle whistles. T doesn't flinch. Silently I count down from five before swinging my legs to the floor. As I pour water into a clay mug, I see he's now on Instagram. My jaw tightens as irritation mounts in me.

While I blow on my tea, we have a back and forth that includes all our go-to sentiments. He wonders why it can't be light and easy between us and I am tired of advocating for his attention. "I'm scared," he says. "All I do is disappoint you." I hear myself exclaiming, "Everyone's scared! Love is scary." The scene culminates with me clutching the now tepid tea, sagging into the bookcase, threatening to leave, and him apologising, enveloping me in his arms, drawing me to the sofa.

"I don't want to be this woman."

He strokes my hair till I run out of things to say. Then we hold each other for a long time, not talking, until our comforting turns sensual and we're kissing and clothes are coming off.

Post-coitus and slack-jawed, he tells me that sex with me feels like coming home. I kiss the scar on his cheekbone and hold his torso tight. I love his ribs. He wants to take me out to dinner, even though I said no restaurants. His treat. I relent. T has top-notch taste in dining out. My only stipulation is that I don't want to walk more than thirty minutes.

On the walk to the restaurant, T traces his fingers around my back, tugs lightly at the ends of my hair and massages my neck. His hands transmit a wholesome quality. Chicago is cold, but fresh buds embroider the trees planted in the boulevards. And though the sidewalks are empty, the traffic hurtling past us is distracting, making for an unpleasant pedestrian experience. Too bad, because, as T says, we're best when we're walking. After a while, the weight of his arm pressing down on my shoulder bugs me. I look at my phone and discover we've been walking for thirty-eight minutes.

"I thought you said this was no more than a thirty-minute walk."

T says we can get an Uber. He thumbs his phone and steps out into a multi-lane road.

I look left and right and left and jog to catch up to him. My instincts are discombobulated from living in the UK. I sigh when he says we have sixteen minutes to go, but insist it's fine; I don't need a taxi.

At the restaurant, T strides in ahead of me. When we're asked if we have a reservation, I widen my eyes at T. He chucks me a look that says, "Cool it."

We're told it's a twenty-five-minute wait, but we can sit at the bar and have a drink.

My eyes bulge. Milo *always* has a reservation.

"That's great," says T, and moves through the crowded dining room with ease, sliding onto a bar stool. I follow. When I get my jacket off and my purse hung up he says, "This is okay, right?"

"It's not ideal," I retort. What should be a pleasurable evening, basking in each other's presence, has been flattened and frayed through our inability to fall in step together.

"We can go somewhere else."

"What're you drinking?" A raspy-voiced, tattooed bartender intercepts our tiff. Her ease elicits deep envy in me. I wish I were a nonchalant Chicagoan instead of an uptight worry wart who gets hangry.

"Negroni?" I ask, switching gears.

She says they're primarily known for their wines, but happy to serve me whatever I want.

I ask for a brutally dry white wine.

T winces at me trotting out a phrase he knows I've picked up in London and orders a Sangiovese.

As the bartender turns, I raise my voice, "And could I get some bread? I just flew in today and I haven't eaten since the flight, and I'm scared to drink on an empty stomach."

"Cool."

I swivel, satisfied, to see a chagrined T.

I lean in. "Am I embarrassing you?"

"No." He looks around. "Don't watch me so closely — you're giving me the scrutzs." That's our short form for feeling scrutinised.

I lower my voice and ask, "Have you eaten here before?" I'm grasping for some innocuous conversation. Something to lift us out of this stilted hell.

"We came here after we sold the story to the *Times*." My senior by a decade, T's leagues ahead of me professionally. To his credit, I often forget how accomplished he is — he always asks my opinion and will often amend pieces he's writing based on it.

"Oh, wow," I say as softly as I can. "This is great."

"I don't know," he says, pointing to the speaker behind the bar. "The music's . . . meh . . . and it's . . . trendy." He crinkles his nose as though a bad smell had wafted under it. In actuality, it smells of browned butter, sage and oregano. "The food's really good. Expensive but good."

"I'm paying for whatever I order."

"Nope," says T. "I invited you."

"Yeah, but I'm hungry and I don't want to be inhibited or indebted. I want to feel free to order exactly what I want."

By the time they move us to our table he's had two glasses of wine to my one and a half, and I've eaten all the bread. I shouldn't try to keep pace with him, but I want the edges sanded right down.

In silence, I slurp up the most divine bolognese. T starts sputtering. "I don't know why this isn't easier for me."

I wipe sauce off my chin.

He gestures to the other people in the restaurant. "What are all these people talking about? We're going to spend *six* days together?"

"Is the blank page freaking you out?"

"Yes," he says with a sense of relief.

The fact that we now have this shorthand gives me hope — a symbol of progress. The blank page terrifies T. He doesn't like to plan things far in advance, but rudderless days together also propel him into existential terror. I crave a lot of solitude and he bops around doing something and seeing someone different hour by hour. These visits, where we essentially lock ourselves in a room and stare each other down, challenge our natural rhythms.

I pull out my notebook and we create our schedule for the week. I'm getting a yoga pass; he'll spend time at the office; I will see my few pals who live in the city. We decide that we'll go on a hike together and I book us tickets to two comedy shows from my phone. It's a good plan. We both lean back, satisfied.

In the comfort of my wine mind, jet lag and tomato tongue, it falls out. "Aren't you glad I'm here?"

T hesitates. "Yes. Yes. I—" He refolds his napkin. "I have to be careful here."

Icicles shoot up my spine and I begin to steam. Why can't he let us rest in a nice moment? Why does he have to torque everything?

He continues. "It seems like, when you decided to come to Chicago, you made some decision about our relationship without telling me."

I furrow my brow and then realise he's right. "I guess I did. I decided to enter." I venture, "I thought you were already in, waiting for me."

"I'm figuring this out too."

"See, no. You're not. You're not. You're in." Zero to sixty, I'm fighting to keep from projecting my voice, to keep from hissing, to keep from letting on to our fellow diners that I want to strangle my boyfriend. "I told you, you need to be solid. No more ground shifting—"

"The ground isn't shifting — I just — I'm not a solid person."

"You need to be the champion of us this time. You put me in this role and it's — I'm so tired of repeating myself. We agreed we weren't going to repeat anything."

"Yep. No, yep. You're right."

My elbows are on the table and my face is in my hands.

"Hey." He pulls my hands away from my face, cups my cheeks. Curling over the table, he says, "I love you. I'm really glad you're here. I'm sorry. I'm so bad at this. You're the best person I know and I'm so goddamn lucky you have been so patient and generous with me. I don't deserve it. I admire you Haley."

I apologise in turn but refrain from giving a compliment.

We fall into a tranquil way with each other, tender, a bubble all to our own, gazing at each other over the tealight. I insist on paying my share of the bill but my card's denied and I don't have any juice on my phone to call the number on the back of the card to let them know I'm travelling.

T says, "Haley, I wanted to pay for this. I'm glad you can't."

I sit in the middle back seat of the Uber and nestle into T. He kisses my forehead and holds me as the driver zips around corners. I wish the ride home was longer.

The next morning I sleep till the sun comes up, kiss T and scour the cupboards for coffee. He doesn't have any. He curbs his caffeine affliction by only ever drinking it in cafés. I throw on my yoga gear, grab his mat and start walking. When I get to the studio the class has been cancelled. It seems important that I not return immediately, to give T this time to himself. In the coffee shop next door I buy what I first judge to be a wildly overpriced cappuccino, until I realise that actually it's on par with London prices, it's just that I've been off the coffee-buying habit for eight months now. Using the Wi-Fi code on the menu, I send the interview request email to Bicycle. My table in the window grows warmer as the sun rises. I want to make some notes but I'm without a pen or notebook. I head back to the counter and bite it, $33.90 for a Coptic-bound journal and a hefty pen, and I resume my seat with the good view. Got to get my money's worth, after all.

Fi calls. "Can you imagine," she rails, "my in-laws, over a dinner in Mayfair, asking me if the consistency of my vaginal discharge was like egg whites?" The more she emotes, the more John Lewis yaps. Ru mentioned to his doctor parents that he and Fi are trying to conceive, and she's been bearing the brunt of their "advice".

I say, "Well at least they actually know what they're talking about — medically."

She says that gaining more parental surveillance is her least favourite thing about being married. Her parents may drink too much but they're "live and let live" people. "Now I have drunks *and* overbearing parents to contend with."

"But they're crazy about you," I say, thinking of Bicycle's mother's disdain for me. I ask Fi whether it's more important that she like her partner's family or that they like her.

She guesses that it's more important that they like her because it means there's no drama about her behind her back.

I tell her I don't really care what my people think.

"Hold on," she says, "if you don't care, why haven't you told your brother about T?"

Unmasked, I hem and haw, telling her that he's protective and I'm scared he'll be mad at me for going back to a place I've been hurt before. "I know where he's coming from. I'm more forgiving of people who've hurt me personally and atoned for it than I am of people who've hurt people who are close to me."

"Right. Because the lines are clear when you're at a distance, and up close it's pointillism."

I tell her that's good and make a note to talk to Gemma about relationships with our exes' friends and family.

"And ultimately," I say, "a relationship exists between two people."

"Well it should, but unfortunately a relationship exists within the context of two individuals' social contexts and personal ecosystems. Every person comes with a whole village lined up behind them."

"And in their head."

"Exactly. That's my problem. I'm now trying to have a baby with my husband and his parents. He's hearing them in his head while we're fucking." Ru got tested and his sperm count was low. They're viewing this as a positive piece of information because there are simple things he can do, like stop taking so many hot baths and wear loose-fitting underwear.

Suddenly I'm desperate for the toilet. "Fi — I think the caffeine has taken effect." I say.

She laughs. "One last thing — our offer on the house was accepted. We're moving to Walthamstow."

I tell her that's great and she says, "Go, go!"

The washroom at the café is out of order, so I use the yoga studio's instead. When I return to keep writing, my table's been occupied by someone else.

Wandering through the neighbourhood, I consider Fi's point about not wanting drama outside the relationship, but how I *feel* about their village — their people — is more important to me than what my friends or family might feel about them. It's annoying when my people disapprove, but I value my own feelings over my family's judgements. I nip under an American elm tree to quickly write in my notebook:

> *My feelings are of greater value than my family's judgement.*
> *What about how much your people like your partner? And*
> *how your partner feels about your people?*

I think about Fi's life unfolding in the right order, a timeline progressing in line with convention. I don't want conventional, but I do want progress. I remind myself that my measuring stick isn't whether you own property together, it's how much you're able to heal old wounds. Plus, T kisses me exactly how I need. Our physical chemistry is effortless and we can talk forever — that's what has kept us going on the phone for months at a time. I resolve to go toward T with kindness, and accept him as he is. The wind ushers me along as I take the side streets back to the apartment. But T's out. When my phone connects to the Wi-Fi, messages from him pop up.

I'm waiting outside yoga for you.

At the café next door. What can I get you?

Haley?

Anxiously, I call him as I hurry back to the coffee shop. And we try. We attempt to meet each other in the middle. Moments of bliss are fleeting and as I claw at them, they wither and turn laboured.

Later in the week, our hike through Harms Woods, a lush and mossy woodland trail, is undercut by an argument about the comedy show we saw the night before. No matter how much time I spend with T, I can't understand his changeable nature. How could he have been laughing the night before, careening into me, delighted at the show, only to wake up claiming it was hack, gross-out humour, lowest common denominator?

I try to address this. "How can something you obviously enjoyed be negated by a thought process?"

He says something fast and impressive and I am steamrolled by his intellect.

"You know." I shake my head and stop on the path. "You know, you have so many opinions about solo shows and comedy but—" I shake my head again and continue walking.

Now he stops. "Say it."

"You don't do it. All you do is criticise. I'm the one who actually does this kind of work."

"Now we're talking." He's almost happy egging me on.

"You did comedy for a hot minute in university. You're not an expert. You're a critic."

He says, "That really fucking stings."

I shrug and keep walking.

"But you're right."

I smile when I hear him say this but it's thin. I'm tired out by these loop-de-loop conversations. "I don't like arguing for sport." It makes my heart beat fast and skull feel tight.

He says he loves it.

He does. His whole life has been dedicated to assiduously interrogating systems and people from all possible angles.

"I know you do; that's where you get your kicks."

We laugh. We don't laugh that often. Our sense of humour is not aligned, but we never use humour to deflect, and that's got to be to the greater good.

It seems as though we're on the precipice of equilibrium, until he says that he worries that we're too different.

"T," I warn, "I don't want to know about your worries about me."

"I'm just being honest."

"It's too honest. You need to say that stuff to your friends or your therapist. It injects too much doubt in this for us to move forward. We have to lay down a stone so we can step forward."

"Got it."

"I'm tire—"

"Of advocating. Got it. I'll stuff it down."

"You don't have to stuff it down. Just don't tell *me*."

The crushed limestone path leads us over a bridge crossing the North Branch of the Chicago River. For a moment we stand side by side, appreciating the scores of trees and shrubs that frame the frigid water, and our animosity evaporates. T takes a picture of me.

Our calm, quiet closeness as we exit the trail is one of the hard-won jewels, mined in pig shit, lined up in the crown of this relationship.

I peer at a shattered ceramic mug that's been glued back together. One side reads, "love you" the other side, "fuck you". I'm at a pop-up gallery in Wicker Park. The Museum of Broken Relationships has taken their collection on the road and at Fi's counsel, I've made the pilgrimage. I'm reading every single placard.

It's chock full of objects like mine, donated anonymously by the public. There's a wedding dress in a pickle jar, the only thing that a woman left behind when she divorced her ex-military husband because he never sought treatment for PTSD. A gigantic Marry Me sign from a failed proposal occupies the entire back wall. And on a rotating display case is a wooden crate of mix tapes, made for each other by a couple who broke up after eighteen years.

When I arrived, I tried to pay the student admission price, lying that I'd forgotten my student card at home. But the woman working the door called my bluff, saying, "You can show me a college email."

I said, "Oh, never mind," poking at my phone screen, "it's only two dollars more."

My attempt to play the system goes directly against the ideology I've been learning in my money-attracting meditations. I should joyfully pay the full admission fee, sending a message of abundance to the universe, rather than a message of scarcity and lack. I vow to give two dollars to the next homeless person I see, to appease the gods of money.

After two hours combing through the entire space, it dawns on me that I should speak to the curator about what kind of patterns they notice in the break-up stories and how they select which objects to display. I return to the admission desk and ask to speak to them. It turns out I'm not able to tell anyone at the museum about *The Ex-Boyfriend Yard Sale* because the curator isn't in today, and the museum is a small enterprise where the assistant curator also works the door.

Though she knows I'm a liar, she graciously chats with me about the collection. She says, "More often than not, the objects that carry the most emotional angst are souvenirs of relationships cut short, where there was unexplored potential."

A little while later, I write that down along with some other thoughts on why relationships with unexplored potential are excruciating to recover from.

I think this is because the imagined relationship was never proved wrong, it still exists. These relationships with unexplored potential are all promise, no pay-off, like unopened gifts.

That's the difference between Bicycle and T. Bicycle and I
unwrapped and saw what was there. T and I circumambulated a
gift still in paper for years and have only just started to peel it open.

I'm giving T some space today. When I said, "Absence makes the heart grow fonder," he came back with, "And familiarity breeds contempt."

I have a message from Navid. He hooked up with a colleague from the Iceland office last night and he's hoping she can use my shampoo. I tell him I want more details and sure, she can use any of my toiletries.

Then I shift gears and respond to a series of administrative emails about *The Ex-Boyfriend Yard Sale*. We have another R&D week in a studio at Sam's theatre next month and I'm arranging for the sound designer and scenic designer to join us. We'll receive the grant results from the Arts Council application in about three weeks. Elson, my director, has written to me that my next task is to find an ending for the show. I type back, *How can I find an ending when we haven't figured out the whole formula yet? The formula is my framing device.*

He fires back an email almost instantaneously saying:

Yeah, it's a device. You don't actually need it to be textbook complete to write to the end of the show. You know how it's going to go: You are in debt. You decide to sell things — ooops they're all things from your exes. You don't know how to price them. It occurs to you to make a formula. You try to make a formula. It's really hard to make a formula because there are all these considerations to take into account because of all the ways you've paid for and profited from love in the past. Eventually you'll make the formula and you'll be able to get a price. And then you'll tell us what you think about the price. See it through to completion.

This simplification of my show's structure irks me, but I concede he's right. I reply: *Okay okay, I'll write to the end of a draft.*

He shoots back: *Write an ending.*

[Sigh] Yes, I'll write an ending.

Both excited and daunted by the prospect of this assignment, I make a list of all the chunks I've already created and all the chunks I need and want to create for the show. My phone rings. It's my voice agent, Agnes. She wants to know if I'm really in Chicago.

"There's a job tomorrow — has to be tomorrow — for an advert, £30k buyout. They love your voice and want to book you."

Stunned, chuffed, panicked, I ask her if I can record it in a studio in Chicago.

She already asked them that, and for indiscernible American actor union rules, it's not an option.

My stomach flips. I google flights as we speak, but nothing will get me back to London in time, even if I wanted to spend $5,000 on the ticket. "Is there any way they can record another day?"

She says no. Apparently the voiceover artist they had cancelled and they have a tight turn around on the roll out.

"This is torturous."

Agnes says, "Murphy's Law isn't it? Aw well, not to worry, hon. There will be more to come."

I tell her I'm really sorry.

Never one to stick on the phone for long, she's gone.

I write:

Cost of Love = £30k and counting.

Supremely dejected, I'm unable to take another bite of my cookie when my phone rings again. I buzz with glee. They've changed their minds. Then I see it's Ollie.

506 miles away, Ollie's pacing and speaking rapidly. He got a strongly worded email from his ex's sister — who is a family lawyer — saying that if Ollie doesn't back off, they will apply for a restraining order against him.

"What do I do? What do I do? It means I can't ever show him how I've changed and all I've learned and . . . Best sex of both of our lives and yeah, when I was anxious we fought a lot, but no one makes him laugh more than I do. And that's — that's — I was making him laugh in the mediation sessions. He wants to be *right* instead of fighting for a love that is so fucking rare, the fucking, self-centred twat." He rages for a while; I hear traffic whizzing past him. He's just outside our hometown, at a highway rest stop. His brother's friend is a lawyer and he's going to see her.

I ask him about the last mediation session.

When it came out that Ollie's ex was seeing someone new, Ollie "reached out" to this person and this person broke up with Ollie's ex.

"Ollie," I say.

"Yeah. I know."

"You've been split up for two years—"

"I know how long it's been."

"You have to respect people's boundaries."

"I KNOW." There's more swearing and I can hear him kicking something. "Ow!" he exclaims and quiets down.

I listen to him breathe for a bit then say, "Ollie?"

"I'm still here."

"You're going to love again."

"You don't know that. I didn't love anyone before him, and I don't ever want to do this again. Loving someone is like handing them your heart on a plate along with a butcher's knife and then hoping they don't hack it up."

I tell him that with someone else it might be better. "A computer scientist told me, the next one's always better."

"You don't believe that. If you did you wouldn't be battling to make it work with T after all the bullshit."

I stay on the phone trying to talk him down, but no amount of reassurance or tough love penetrates his forcefield of woe. While we're on the phone, T calls me on the other line three times.

"Ollie, Ollie," I interrupt. "I've got to go." I promise him I'll call right back.

He says not to bother, he's got to meet the lawyer anyway.

When I call T's phone, a voice I don't recognise answers and asks me if I'm T's wife.

My initial thought is this is a joke by his pals. But when the voice repeats, "Are you the partner of T?" my smile dissolves. "I'm phoning from the hospital. He asked us to get in touch with you."

"Yes —I —yes," I stammer. "Is everything alright?"

The voice tells me that T was in a traffic accident. He was hit while riding his bike.

"Oh my god." I hurriedly shove my laptop into my backpack. My knees tremble as I crawl under the café table to unplug the cable.

The voice on the phone tells me the name of the hospital and its address.

"Hold on!" I yelp, now rifling through my packed bag for pen and paper to write down the name of the hospital, so I don't forget.

"Okay and when I get there?"

"He may be in surgery or having tests. Does your husband have insurance?"

"He's Canadian."

"Does he have US medical insurance?"

"I don't know."

"You don't know?"

"He's here for work and I'm just visiting."

In an Uber, I frantically google medical insurance. Traffic is horrendous. What should have been a forty-minute ride takes nearly two hours. I lie down on the back seat, alternately weeping and instructing myself to think positive thoughts. A nurse calls me. They're concerned about internal bleeding and possible swelling in his brain, so they're going to send T in for some scans. The driver tells me his younger brother, who worked as a coder for Google, was hit while skateboarding, suffered permanent neurological damage and lives in their mother's basement.

At that moment, I pray to god, to the universe, to my grandpa — patron saint of the yard sale — let T be okay. I bargain with the Uber driver and the voiceover overlords. I'll never talk to Milo again. I'll stop being so angry with T, stop punishing him for not delivering on what he promised when we got back together.

When I get to the hospital, I'm told T has a fractured rib, a concussion and a broken arm. No internal bleeding but they did have to put him under to perform minor surgery on his radius. The anaesthetic should be wearing off soon. They'll let me know when I can see him. They keep referring to him as my husband.

I perch on a blue vinyl chair in the waiting area. The tiled floor is covered in a grey film, thick dust collects in the corners. Curled notices about handwashing and cell phone usage cling to the pale yellow walls. I notice everyone is using their phone, so I call my mum. I cry and tell her everything, that I'm in Chicago, that I'm back with T, that he's in the hospital. She says if we need her credit card number use it. This makes me cry harder. She says she loves me. She says everything's going to be fine. She says she's always liked T. She says don't forget to eat.

A nurse comes and tells me T's awake. The bandage wrapped around his head, slightly askew, makes him look like a soldier on a TV series about WWI. The corner of his right eye is pulled down. My first thought when I see him is, his beautiful face . . . I worry he's been disfigured and I'm immediately ashamed of my vanity. Later I realise that the bandage has been pulled so tight, it's smushing his eye closed. The architecture of his face remains unchanged.

"Hi baby." He reaches out and then draws his hand back, clutching at his rib. His other arm is in a sling. "My bike's totalled," he whispers.

I sit beside him. Press my fingertips ever so lightly against his cheekbones.

"It's a scratch — a scratch, Haley." He tells me he has nine stitches under the bandage. Another scar for his big bad face. He was cycling down Michigan Avenue with a blender in one hand — he was going to surprise me with it. It was a guy driving a grocery delivery truck who didn't see him. T got wedged between parked cars, recycling bins and the truck, and the truck veered a bit to the right, squeezed T and flipped him over the hood. The driver begged him not to sue.

"I hope you got his details," I say.

He assures me the police have. "Could have been much worse."

I say, "I know," and kiss the fingers on the hand of his good arm.

In the Uber home I realise we are ravenous and dehydrated. He says he doesn't care what we eat so I order pho to be delivered to the apartment. He keeps his hand in my hair the whole ride there. We breathe in the same rhythm.

When our soup arrives, T hoovers his up but I've lost my appetite. When I go to text my mum, I see there's a message from Milo. I delete it without reading it. I put on a fire and we watch it sitting side by side. T rests his head on mine. Later he'll tell me all he wanted to do was inhale my scent.

Jarred by suggestion of life's fragility, I'm overcome with desire to do something that would bind us — like get married or have a baby. I think, I'd move here if he wanted this to be the place, sure. I want to invest in us.

In bed, T passes out, but I can't sleep, so I go to the living room and call my brother.

Kian says, first of all, he's sorry that T was in an accident. And second of all, he's sorry I felt scared to tell him we were back together.

I tell him it's my fears of judgement. "I don't want to be the boy who cried wolf."

To this he says, "Hales, I just want to know, what is actually different this time?"

"See, you judge me instead of supporting me."

Sensing my exasperation, my brother stays calm. "I do support you. But this guy treated you like shit and I don't want to see you get hurt again."

I poke at the embers.

"I know. But I love him."

Kian says, "Okay. Here's the deal then — no complaining about T to me. Because when most of what I've heard about him is negative stuff, I'm gonna want you to stay away."

I tell him I've got it.

I pull out my notebook and make some notes. It feels trivial but I don't know what else to do.

- *We need to consider how much they like my people vs how much I like their people AND how much my people like them vs how much their people like me.*
- *Me liking their people is more important than their people liking me. But if their people don't like me, and it's their parents and it's for no apparent reason other than my personality (or they're not going to like anyone their child dates) — that's hard.*

On my final night, we watch another comedy show, this one in the backroom of a mariachi bar. The stage is framed by curtains pulled back with such precision they look like seashells. T orders us mojitos in Spanish and I nab two seats near the front of the stage. We laugh hard and whoop, never losing physical contact with each other, all the rigidity between us at last relaxed. T has spritzed himself with cologne tonight and his musk transports me to the high school gymnasium dances of my teenage years. My guts flutter whenever I catch a whiff.

After the show, we stay in our seats as the venue empties out, finishing our drinks and quietly discussing how best to get to the airport tomorrow. I wrap my arms around his neck and kiss his bandage.

On the walk back to the apartment, T asks if we can take sex off the table for the night. He just wants to cuddle. Somewhat drunk and exasperated, I lose it by the Chicago River. All day I'd been anticipating a beautiful final evening together, making love and talking low. I interpret this request as abject rejection and find myself crouching in my dress holding myself in a tiny ball, sobbing, "How could you not want to sleep with me on our last night?"

He says he hates the pressure of these final evenings to be romantic.

"You should be so lucky," I bark at him.

Looking down at me, he shrugs.

And then I say, "I've been taking care of you — this whole trip has been co-opted by your accident and I've lost £30k being here."

He doesn't know what I'm talking about.

I know I should be ashamed for throwing that in his face, but right now it's a relief to feel the fullness of my anger's release.

Rather than retaliate, T squats down beside me. "Say more," he says.

I tell him about the voice job I lost.

"Oh Haley." He rubs circles on my back. "That's a shit ton of money."

Now thoroughly embarrassed, I apologise. "I want to take care of you."

"But we just can't get along, can we?"

"Why would you say that?"

He sighs. "I can't say anything right." We sit in silence for a while, until, without any bite, he asks, "If it's so disappointing, why do you even want to be with me?"

"Because I love you. And . . ." I touch my nose to my knees. "And I have this sense that on the other side of all this struggle there's a beautiful relationship waiting for us. And I'm holding out for it. I don't know?"

He says, "Me too. I feel that too."

He helps me up off the ground with his good arm. We make our way back to the apartment, and eventually we do have sex.

In the morning, we have sex one more time and then he wheels my suitcase with his good arm as we walk to his favourite breakfast place. We snag a booth. Eating poached eggs and drinking coffee, his shoulders relax. He stretches his legs out and rests his good elbow on the table. He looks good – well loved, well fed, well rested. My flight leaves in the afternoon.

After boarding the plane, I see that T has posted a slew of photos of me on Instagram along with a beautiful caption about his bike accident and my grace. Wind in my sails, I balance my laptop on the tray table and I begin to write the story of my relationship with Bicycle. Puffed up, I scrape for all the details I can. I still haven't heard back from Bicycle for an interview.

Bicycle, clearly, gave me a bicycle, but our relationship began and ended with a sculpture. He was the first person I met on my first day at my first job out of drama school, which was perform-ing outdoor theatre on a farm in rural Canada. It wasn't kismet, but it was idyllic.

I was twenty-one. I liked him immediately.

For the next six weeks we circled each other. He invited me to go second-hand clothes shopping with him — he only wore second-hand clothes. On dinner break, he'd heat up his pork chops in the microwave and talk to me about art. Along with being a theatre director, he carved sculptures, led survivalist skills workshops, painted landscapes, read books and made dumplings. During one of our chats, I'd flirted, "Well, I really love words. Words are very valuable to me." A couple days later, I found in my dressing room a hand-carved wooden sculpture, wrapped in a piece of paper. And on the paper he'd written this poem:

> *a few odd lines of rhyme and pace*
> *for me seem roughly out of place*
> *a word, a line, they cannot show*
> *the way you set my heart aglow*
> *but I have something up my sleeve*
> *that holds more truth I do believe*
> *I can't express in words so good*
> *but I can carve a poem in wood*

By far the most romantic way I've ever been asked out. We spent the remainder of the summer entangled in each other's limbs, drinking wine on the banks of Otter Lake, doubling on bikes to the farmers' market and dancing to live music in small-town British Columbia. We'd say to each other, "I can't believe I met someone who wants to do all the same things I do. We're the same we're the same we're the same."

Shy, soft-spoken and strapping, he was the farm heartthrob. All the young women vied for his affection and I was flabbergasted that he 'chose' me. And we laughed a lot. When I was self-conscious of my small boobs, he held me to his chest and sang me a Stan Rogers song.

It was the most joyous beginning to a relationship I've ever had. If I could bottle its bliss and ration it, I would.

The first time we slept together he stayed over at the shared house I was lodging in. Not wanting to be separated for a moment longer than necessary, we brushed our teeth together in the morning. We admired our image framed in the bathroom mirror, discovering how we would be perceived as a couple. We were bloody pleased.

The bristles of the toothbrush he kept in his saddle bag were worn flat. When I passed him the tube of toothpaste, he dragged the remnants of my squeeze along his brush.

He said the amount they show you in the commercials was a marketing ploy to get you to use more than you need and spend more money. "It adds up."

I laughed and spent exponentially longer spitting and rinsing than he did before we could make out again.

When our contracts at the summer theatre ended, Bicycle and I both moved back to Toronto. I was no longer a working actor but a struggling actor, and he landed a prestigious, all-consuming job at a major cultural institution. Nonetheless, we began knitting our lives together. He introduced me to his friends, and they taught me how to play poker; on Saturdays he'd make us pancakes without a recipe; we started calling ourselves "the dream team".

At twenty-four, Bicycle seemed set with a repertoire of tastes and skills. He drank strong coffee with honey, played the fiddle and gripped his purse strings tight. He was uncompromisingly committed to his own bicycle and proud of the hard bum it gave him. He'd never worked in the service industry; I was always adding more to tips or shaming him into ponying up 20 per cent. He held a pessimistic view on the world. His belief was that the planet was fucked, we fucked it and there was nothing we could do because humanity was selfish and people were rotten. But his calloused hands and sturdy frame dazzled me.

Our kisses weren't soft and deep and our sex wasn't adventurous, but if anyone else ever hit on me during that time, I'd scoff, thinking, do you know who my boyfriend is? I wrote in my journal, *I like everything about him, except he's NOT FUNNY.* But I made him laugh really hard, and that was almost satisfying enough.

Bicycle told me he loved me three months into the relationship, on the patio of a beloved Toronto haunt, which has since burned down. The sun had set and before we embarked on the city's annual all-night art exhibit and party, we both needed to take care of a bit of business on our jalopy phones.

He flipped his open and then closed, saying, "No — wait — no."

Sensing his seriousness, I followed suit. I'd seen him bashful before but never flustered.

His voice was low and nervous. "I just want to tell you that I love you." He smiled and shrugged in a tiny way, as if to say, "So you have me."

Colour drained from my face, then a rush from my loins to the pit of my gut. My chest, neck, cheeks flushed and out of my mouth, a whisper, "I love you too." This blessed admission charged us with a fortitude, soaring through those first six months with arrogance and ease. Convinced of our infallible power as a duo, we were unwrapping the gift.

Bike theft was something of an epidemic in Toronto during the noughties. Igor Kenk, the "world's most prolific bike thief", commanded an army of petty criminals who helped him amass and hoard over 3,000 stolen bikes in warehouses. My own blue Raleigh Linton cruiser, a family heirloom with a wicker basket and red saddle bags, had been stolen, but I was out of town on a job when the police cracked the case and opened up the warehouses to the public. Bicycle went to look for my bike. But the police said that the photo of me riding ahead of him was not detailed enough to prove what bike had been mine.

On my next birthday, Bicycle presented me with a new vintage bike. On its low crossbeam, in orange and cream, bold letters spelled out FREE SPIRIT. I felt known and seen. And he gave me a copy of *A Wheel Within a Wheel*, a book by Frances Willard, 1895 feminist icon and champion of the bicycle. Her words on cycling are advice for life:

> *Strange as the paradox may seem, you will do this best by not trying to do it at all. You must make up . . . your mind – make it up speedily, or you will be cast into yonder mud-puddle . . . It is the curse of life that nearly everyone looks down, but the microscope will never set you free. You must glue your eyes to the telescope. Look up and off and on and out.*

I proposed — invited myself? — to visit Bicycle in his hometown over the Christmas holidays. He was delighted to have me to his family home in the Prairies for a week. I had understood that Bicycle was the prodigal son. His sister had gone to Australia for a year and ended up eloping with a born-again Christian Aussie, who didn't work but home-schooled their kids and forbade them from eating sugar, including fruit. Certain that Bicycle and I were in it for keeps, I decided I would be the antithesis to this guy, the perfect in-law. Charming parents was my specialty. Both Mix Tape's and Necklace's mothers adored me, their fathers doted on me. I had no doubt it would be any different with his parents.

But after I failed to join in the sung grace canon at dinner, and my teasing of their son fell flat, I called Ollie for help. He said, "They're the kind of parents who think their kid's shit don't stink. Nothing you can do."

If only I'd been able to take heed. My tactics — joking around with his dad, sucking up to his mum — got me nothing but bewildered looks and head scratching. I was constipated for three days. Even my GI tract was on "best behaviour".

Bicycle and I borrowed his parents' car and set out on a day trip. We had waded through umpteen suggestions from them of places to go and things to do, until, desperate to escape the stodgy, oppressive and stale air of his childhood home, I randomly agreed to one, affirming, "That sounds great. Let's go there." With mouthfuls of driving instructions at our backs, I swung open the car door.

At the end of the block I asked, "What are we really going to do today?"

Bicycle was confused.

"I'm not okay."

He pulled over.

"Your parents don't like me. I can't poo. And I'm sick of classical music."

He instantly turned off the tape deck that was blasting some ghastly eighteenth-century dirge. He didn't try to convince me that they liked me, but he did admit they weren't the "easiest company" and suggested we see some friends from Toronto who were also back home for the holidays. We spent the day singing to each other and rummaging through the best second-hand clothing store in the nation. We dove into a photobooth. In the pictures, I'm radiant, sitting on his lap in a red beret, laughing.

About a year later, however, our early days being our best selves — me not giving into floods of emotion and him doing his damnedest to stay open and express his feelings — had ebbed. I resorted to my irascible, weepy self to get his attention and he clammed up in response. He proved to be stingy: not only a bad tipper and a lacklustre gift-giver (the sculpture and poem set a precedent never met again) but with his time and affection.

An older actress I once met in Germany told me that the versions of ourselves we present early on in romance aren't lies, but they are the best versions of ourselves. New love awakens us to our own potential, and we exist at its peak for a time. However, it's tough to exist in the best version of ourselves unless we've done a lot of therapy. Thea says there's a lot of projection going on in the early days. You don't know the whole story, so you fill in the blanks with details that suit your taste. Then the wrapping comes off the gift, all your ideations about what it could have been are dispelled and you're left with a tangible, limited object.

About a year and half in, Bicycle said to me, "I hate money. I hate that you have to make it." He hated his prestigious, all-consuming job. He said if he didn't have to make money he'd wander around the woods and carve sculptures.

"But you can!" I said.

"No, I can't."

Around the same time, we went tobogganing and had a fight because I wanted to go for brunch afterwards and he didn't.

He said, "Just because I make more money doesn't mean I should spend more on this relationship."

I said, "I don't want you to."

But I did want to eat in all the nice restaurants and go travelling. He did not want to be my travel companion. He'd been to Italy on an exchange during university and was done travelling. He wanted to save for a down payment on a property.

He said, "I'm tired of paying for half of your expensive taste."

After that, every coffee not made at home, every vegetable not purchased in Chinatown became a tiny battleground where our values rivalled each other. When he finally quit his job, I wanted to move into an apartment just the two of us and get a cat. He replied with jokey emails when I sent him links to Toronto cat-rescue pages. But when I pressed the move-in timeline, he said, "I can't talk about moving in until you get your finances under control."

I witnessed the evolution of the hair on his chest, from a thin line at the top of his sternum and delicate circles around his nipples to a fuzzy, speckled coating. And my image grew tarnished in his eyes. Once perceived as "full of wonder" and "admirably positive", I was now "endlessly emotional", "continually dissatisfied" and "emotionally manipulative". I nagged Bicycle about inconsequential details, like where he hung his coat. I expressed my displeasure when he didn't want to sleep over. I picked fights about our sex life, saying, "I'm twenty-four. Sex once a week is not enough!"

He'd say:

"You forget every nice thing I've ever done for you."

"You make me feel like the worst person ever."

"Don't fucking cry."

I was crying all the time.

He said, "You're not the person I fell in love with."

I countered with, "You don't love me the way you used to." Baffled by this and desperate for it to be untrue, I stayed in the relationship, hoping to be disproved. But for months all we did was argue.

My dad came to Toronto and insisted I meet him for lunch. He said, "If you're not getting what you want, Haley, end it. Do it on your terms." Dignity.

So, I said to Bicycle, "Maybe we should break up."

And he said, "That would be a relief."

So we did. Sitting in the pickup truck he'd inherited.

"I can't believe it's not going to be you."

"I can't believe it's not you."

"If it's not you, then who?"

I catalogued the ways I'd be absent from his life. When I got to, ". . . and not going to be at poker anymore", I saw him cry for the first time. Small victory.

I spent the following weeks wandering around Toronto in a green ski jacket with chapped eyes, lying on picnic tables, not trying to not cry. I started personifying our relationship as a starving dog, emaciated, ignored, kicked for whining. I'd think, but you *know* when a dog is dead. How do you know when a relationship — an invisible bond between two people — has been neglected or damaged beyond repair?

I stopped eating. I subsisted on a diet of Jack Daniel's and ice. I got strep throat and kept going. I got scarlet fever and kept going. I brought home men I was bartending with, only to leap out of bed to go cry in the bathroom — classic stuff. I couldn't figure out how to get a new dream for my future life.

A month later, at our requisite material-goods exchange, Bicycle unlocked the door to my apartment, entered without knocking, then handed over his key. I handed him a bag, which he inspected. Then without saying a word, he nipped into my bathroom and came out holding his red toothbrush.

"No need for it to go to waste."

We had a dry kiss on the lips when we said goodbye.

The shape of our relationship is a shape I can understand. It looks like this:

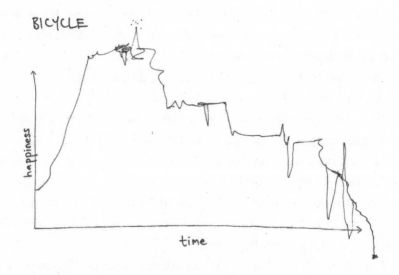

It's a satisfying, classical trajectory. It was sad but kind.

Six months after Bicycle and I broke up, he called to wish me a happy birthday and ended up telling me he was sleeping with a stage manager I'd worked and lodged with the previous summer. I leaned on a trash can and said, "I can't talk to you for two to five years." I don't know why that timeframe came out of my mouth, but it made him laugh. And that in turn brought me to the brink of vomiting. I hung up on him. Then I went home, ripped up the pair of his underwear I still had and rearranged all the furniture in my apartment. When I lamented to our mutual friends, "I don't even want to want to not want this," they'd scowl, "But Haley, you broke up with him."

"On his behalf!" I'd cry. "I broke up with him on his behalf."

His new love unlocked the rage I'd suppressed at his unwillingness to fight for our relationship. He'd called my bluff to some degree and I felt like a fool. I took his moving on as a betrayal and a negation of the love that existed between us.

After several months as the person in pain, drawing every conversation back to how I was hurting, Kian blatantly told me that everyone wanted me to get over Bicycle and stop talking about him. I understood. I had exhausted my friends and family talking about my break-up. I also understood I was nowhere near done ranting about it. I needed to pay someone to listen to me. I needed to go to therapy. Within a week I was on Thea's couch.

Partway through my relationship with Bicycle, to support his artistic side, my parents commissioned him to create a sculpture for my aunt Harlow's birthday, the equivalent of one hundred and forty-eight pounds. A year after our break-up, I was talking with my mum, and I suddenly remembered this. I wondered what he did with the half-built sculpture before leaving Toronto to live in the Northwest Territories with his new girlfriend.

My mum confessed that after Bicycle called and told me he was sleeping with my former stage manager, he reached out to my parents to let them know he'd finally completed the sculpture. Unbeknownst to me, they corresponded with him. My dad secretly drove two hours to Bicycle's house in Toronto, picked up the sculpture and gave him a cheque — which he cashed. Then my parents secretly drove the sculpture five hours north to my aunt's house, and hid it on her property.

My family has since apologised, over and over, and asked me how they could make it right. My aunt even offered to host a ceremonial burning. I said, "If you want to burn it, then burn it. But I don't want anything to do with the sculpture at all." Short of a time machine, no solutions satisfied me. In fact, I'm still bothered by it, so it may be a mistake to include the anecdote in the show. When I mentioned this to Elson in our last conversation, he told me to cut it. But I want to keep it, because I'm creating a show about value, and how we arrive at values for objects, and how we express our values, how we learn our values — our value.

Thea once told me that forgiveness is a place you arrive at. It takes time. It took five years, but I arrived there with Bicycle. I don't often think of him. It didn't last with the new girlfriend. She left the NWT within several months. From what I know, he lives with another woman there now. She's a teacher. I check her Twitter once or twice a year. Bicycle doesn't have social media.

Eight hours later, the plane touches down at Heathrow. There's a WhatsApp message from Milo, inviting me to a gallery opening next Thursday. Absolutely not, I think to myself, and put my phone away. But on the Piccadilly line towards Cockfosters, I see that T has deleted all the photos he posted of me. When I ask him why, he justifies it by telling me, "You mean more to me than some pictures on social media." But the gesture rips the wind from my sails. While I still have signal on the Tube, I reply to Milo:

Just off plane from Chicago. Haven't slept. I can make it Thurs . . . x

He responds immediately: *Chicago?????? What? Great about Thurs. Hope you get some rest today. X.*

£ + ♥

Navid and his Icelandic love interest have taken over the flat. (She gifted me a high-end body "soufflé" (lotion) as thanks for using my shampoo.) So today Gemma and I are working on the Relationship Index phrase in the Wellcome Collection's reading room. Housed in a science museum, its walls are lined with books, and at the far end there's a grand staircase strewn with pillows for people to lounge and read. The steps lead up to a wraparound balcony filled with bookshelves. We're at a table in the corner, looking out over Euston Road. As of yet, no one's told us to stop whispering.

The RI is all the quintessential stuff that you can assess for just about every relationship. It captures the quality of a particular relationship while you were inside of it.

So far, the data points are:

- *Key highs/lows*
- *Ratio of fun to misery*
- *Calibre of the poetry/romance*
- *Quality of sex*
- *How much you like their people vs how much your people like them*
- *Who broke up with who*
- *How much you laughed*
- *How often you fought*
- *Intensity of the love/were you in love?*

Gemma wants to know how I differentiate *key highs* from *the ratio of fun to misery*, and from *how much you laughed*.

To me, key highs and key lows are stand-out moments in a relationship, seminal moments emblematic of the dynamic — moments that defined the polarities or the parameters with another person. Key highs with Bicycle were kissing him for the first time in the attic room of the house I was lodging in, skinny dipping together in northern Ontario on a camping trip and him playing his fiddle for me in front of my friends on my birthday.

Gemma says, "So for *key highs/lows*, let's take the highest three and lowest three, and rate them on a scale of one to ten."

Key lows include begging him to love me, literally on my knees, being angry at him for saying that he wanted to "get my orgasm over with" so we could actually have sex, and an incident at a Moroccan restaurant where his mother said flippantly, "I realise my son is much more of a free spirit than you are." Without a flicker of dissent from Bicycle, like the good WASPs before me, I amicably nodded along to her passive aggressive bile about my identity, scared setting her straight would be perceived as kicking up a fuss. Later I whispered my impassioned defence to the bathroom stall, "Your son is the one who stays in the secure job that he hates. I'm the one chasing a dream, living on a wing and a prayer."

The *ratio of fun to misery* is about the general tone of the relationship. And *how hard they made me laugh* is, on a scale of one to ten, the quality of the laughs with that person.

I did a little research and learned that laughing is scientifically proven to be important for our health. When you laugh your nervous system resets itself. And as a performer I know that when audiences laugh, their defences give way and then they're more receptive to complicated ideas, darker subjects and more likely to cry.

"So," asks Gemma, "it's more about the quality of the laughs and severity of the fights, rather than frequency?"

I nod and explain that I have long listed sense of humour as my number-one priority in a prospective relationship but rarely fallen for anyone who slays me.

She asks if T's not funny.

"Not to me. But that's because he performs his jokes rather than building them with me."

Gemma says if her boyfriend wasn't so hilarious, they probably would have split up by now. "But he is actually the funniest person I've ever met and he's funny when he performs, yes, but he's also deeply silly at home."

I tell her I'm deeply jealous.

She laughs.

I ask her how bad the fights are when they fight.

She says they don't really fight.

I don't trust people who say they don't fight. There needs to be some amount of friction to keep things dynamic.

"And for *calibre of the poetry/romance*," I say, "I want to reflect that romantic gestures are only valuable if they're preceded and followed by reliable actions. If not, romantic gestures are selfish." I share that I've thought extensively about romantic gestures — I made a whole solo show about them. My take is that the gestures are more meaningful to, and reflective of, the person performing them than the person receiving them, unless the person performing them has been consistently loving, attentive and generally reliable.

"Such as?"

"You know, calling when they say they're going to, showing up on time, and so on."

"And presumably in a consistent mood. Not playing hot and cold," adds Gemma.

"Absolutely."

She says she'll figure out a way to express this mathematically.

Gemma goes to order another coffee. I've got a text from my bank warning me about a low account balance. There's also, serendipitously, an email from the medical role-play bosses asking for women who'd be willing to have doctors practise pap smears on them for three days — double the day rate and you have to sign a waiver. That's your penance, I think, frivolously running off to Chicago and ending up back at zero. I respond rashly, *I'm in.*

When Gemma returns, we talk about *quality of sex*, and it quickly becomes clear we need to measure a few things for this variable. At the beginning of my relationship with Bicycle the quality of the sex was an eight (out of ten) because we were falling in love and the tone was so sweet between us. By the end it was a four because he'd lost interest in my pleasure and would barrel through getting me off so he could get inside me, and we'd begun to bicker about our approaches to sex and its frequency.

"Right. So frequency is important too." Gemma writes that down.

"Yeah. Early days we had lots, but it dwindled to once a week which is not enough for me."

I've often had a higher libido than the men I was with (Bicycle, Backpack, Typewriter, T); intervening trysts helped with the complex I was beginning to develop around that, serving as a counterpoint to my worry that I was repulsive.

Gemma cocks her head to the side and then says, "Let's capture the data at beginning and end of relationship."

"Also, at the time of the relationship with Bicycle I'd only slept with five people, so I thought the quality was eight but it was actually five in retrospect. And he didn't really expand my repertoire, but he did get me comfortable with cunnilingus, which has revolutionised my sex life since. So—"

Gemma interrupts me saying, "I think we should keep it an eight because this is about the quality of the relationship at that time." But she suggests we add a qualifier connected to how useful the new sexual territory they introduced me to was in the future. "Technically it's an NI factor, but I think it works here."

I agree.

We create a table to help weight those measurements appropriately.

Value	Quality of Sex	Quantity of Sex
Best	High	High
Second Best	High	Low
Second Worst	Low	Low
Worst	Low	High

The worst scenario is lots of bad sex, because though not having much sex is annoying, we concur there is nothing worse than lots of bad sex. When we get to *their people versus your people*, we land on a decision to measure two things: How much I liked their people and how much my people liked them, because those things directly affected me. How much their people liked me no doubt had an effect on how I felt about them in return — case in point, Bicycle's parents — but it's a once-removed relationship. Same with how much my ex liked my people, which seems to be more their domain and measurement than something I have access to. We agree both those things *can* have an extreme impact, but if they did have an extreme impact then they belong in the formula as a Wild Card.

Gemma has an addition to the RI: *How well you took care of them/how well they took care of you.* It never occurred to me to measure the level of care we showed to each other. I notice Gemma marks down the variable by drawing little cups of tea. I imagine her and her boyfriend asking each other if they want a cup of tea, rubbing each other's backs, carefully passing off a hot mug, blowing on it, cuddling on the sofa together watching TV.

"We definitely need to include care."

And finally Gem and I hash out the *who broke up with who* data point by creating a ranking system for *how* a relationship ended, from least to most brutal.

This chart excludes extreme situations such as death, illness, addictions, gender or sexuality changes, abuse, massive betrayals — even being left for someone else, and so on. But in a straightforward break-up situation, here's how it breaks down:

HALEY McGEE

Rank	How brutal?	Who broke up with who?	Want to?	Math	Justification
1	Least	You	Yes	1 ÷ 20	You wanted it to end and you ended it. This is the best-case scenario because you were in charge and it's the outcome you wanted.
2	Second Least	Them	Yes	1 ÷ 10	You wanted it to end but they ended it. It hurts your pride, but it's ultimately the outcome you wanted.
3	Second Most	Them	No	1 ÷ -10	You didn't want it to end and they ended it. This is painful; it can take you by surprise; you might feel rejected. But at least the other person took responsibility for their feelings and acted with integrity.
4	Most	You	No	1 ÷ -20	You didn't want it to end but you ended it. This is the most brutal, because it means you've realised that you're dating a coward and that you will be strung along and dissatisfied. You realise they're so determined to not be the "bad one" you become responsible for ending a relationship with someone you want to be with who doesn't want to be with you anymore.

The quality of the component parts of a relationship are far less valuable if I wasn't in love. We vote to add one exponent to the entire formula. A power, also known as an exponent, refers to the number of times a number is multiplied by itself. For example, two to the three (written like this: 2^3) means: 2 x 2 x 2 = 8. Our exponent is *the power of love* and it's applied to the RI phrase. Once each part of a relationship has been assessed, the whole thing is multiplied to the power of whether or not I was in love. If the relationship was one in which I was *not* in love, nothing changes, but if I was in love, then the RI is to the power of two, which means whatever number the RI spits out, it will then be multiplied by itself. For example, if it spits out a 78 it will be multiplied by 78, equalling 6,084, to account for how love makes everything more potent.

210

A few days later Gemma sends me a draft of the RI phrase. Note that it's all to the power of love.

$$\text{RELATIONSHIP INDEX}$$

$$\left[\frac{K\uparrow}{K\downarrow} + \odot + \frac{\text{LoL}}{\langle \text{fun} \rangle} + \left(\uparrow\!\heartsuit \times \text{rel} \right) + \left(\uparrow\!? \times y? \right) + \frac{\uparrow\text{SEX}}{\oslash} + \left(xxx \vee \text{USE} \right) + \left(\oplus y \times \ominus\uparrow \right) + \frac{?\heartsuit}{\frac{\text{WANT}}{2}} \right]^{\heartsuit}$$

$$£ + ♥$$

I'd been feeling increasingly wounded by Bicycle's non-response to my interview appeal until he wrote to say he'd be glad to talk, at once overthrowing my animosity, replacing it with endearment at his request for help with the technology.

Our call begins with a celebration of said technology complying with our wishes.

"It worked."

"It worked!"

"It totally worked."

He speaks quickly, sometimes breathlessly, and he laughs a lot. I'd forgotten these details about him.

He says his biggest gain from our relationship was "a sense of humour and how to be friendly with people". I ask him about the cost of being with me.

"I think I became a little bit more callous throughout our relationship because I felt kind of bombarded with a lot of emotions. And I wasn't ready — I've never been a very emotional person — so having to deal with them, I think I probably — my skin got, well, calloused. I probably became desensitised and a little bit angrier, or forlorn about it all, you know what I mean? I could never figure out how to match that amount of emotion. I never could. And I don't think I ever will." He says it almost apologetically.

"Yeah. I remember you saying, 'I want off the rollercoaster'." I play up the desperation in my impression of him.

He laughs. "Have you found another person who has been a better match, emotionally?"

"Mm hmm. But an artistic temperament, you know? So that's been a challenging saga, but yeah. He's probably more emotional than I am. He's so up for the big talk. He's like, 'Bring it on!'" I growl in a mock pro-wrestler voice. "But he—"

"More!" Bicycle interrupts, adopting my tone, building on the joke.

"Yeah, yeah." I laugh. "He actually said, 'I like this cry-y part of you'. Early on, I apologised for getting weepy and he said, 'Nah, I like it. It's real.'"

"Wow." He thinks for a moment. "Isn't it tiring though? Talking out every emotion?"

"Yes."

After we hang up, I listen back to the recording of our interview and make notes. I'm startled by the warmth between us. I'm not angry or hurt anymore. I'm not trying to settle a score. Time *has* healed the wounds. What remains, I realise, when I hear myself lying about how much I meditate, how often I swim in the Ladies' Pond, about the state of my finances, is that Bicycle is still an impressive person who I desire to impress.

It's not so much that I want to sleep with him again — I'm aware of our mediocre physical relationship, having just catalogued it in the RI — it's that he holds a distinction. A Wild Card should be applied.

I want to call it The Martha Card after the subject of the Tom Waits song "Martha". In the song, a man in his sixties calls an old flame, Martha, who he hasn't spoken to in forty years. Both of them have married other people. He asks her to meet him for coffee where they can "talk about it all". In hindsight, he sees that what existed between them was singular and precious and all that remains now is a good feeling.

Whether that's the correct interpretation or not, The Martha Card represents an effect a few people may have on us in our lives, which is that no matter what does or doesn't happen with them, they will occupy a space in us that no one else can touch. And that is somehow divine. Gemma and I agree that it will increase the overall worth of any object it's applied to by 10 per cent.

I want to give it to both Bicycle and T-shirt but Gemma raises a good point: this kind of effect can't truly be assessed until you've been split up for at least ten years. So it's pending for T.

T's been calling and texting a dizzying amount. In the wake of our visits, Herculean good goodbyes warrant rhapsodic phone-time in the subsequent weeks. I relish T's attention and attachment to me. This is how it should always be, I think. This level of engagement and interest. It's like a bank account. Getting together fills it up and then it gets depleted. Without seeing each other we can't make deposits, especially because he won't have phone sex.

14. WILD CARDS

A wild card is something unpredictable
and outside the normal rules, or something
whose influence is unpredictable or
whose qualities are uncertain.

"Clap your hands if you worry about money!" I shout to an audience at the pub theatre, then lower my voice and wink. "I'm testing the market."

Elson isn't convinced about the market-testing audience participation bit I want to include in the show, so while I host this improv night, I'm workshopping it between sets. It begins with me setting up a metronome to keep the beat. Speaking in rhythm, I lead the audience:

"Clap your hands if you've had your heart broken." I demonstrate that they should clap four times on the beat, if the statement applies to them. *Clap. Clap. Clap. Clap.*

They catch on to the pattern. It tickles me to watch people begin to clap and then realise they have to sit that round out because "Clap your hands if you have an ex that you'd definitely get back together with" doesn't apply to them. We work our way through my list:

"Clap your hands if you've ever felt worthless

"Clap your hands if you've done long distance

"Clap your hands if you have an ex you dread running into

"Clap your hands if you've loved someone who didn't love you back

"Clap your hands if you're never the first one to say I love you

"Clap your hands if you've ever been betrayed

"Clap your hands if you've broken someone's heart

"Clap your hands if you're scared of commitment

"Clap your hands if your parents' relationship freaked you out about being in relationships!"

"There was a real sense of solidarity," I report to my brother on Skype the following day. I've already sent Elson an email telling him it was a gigantic success and we have to keep it. "Now, how do I measure those responses?"

My brother utters a prolonged "uhhhh" and then, "Not sure you can measure that Hales. I mean you could create a real survey perhaps?" He's eating a leftover curry from his favourite Indian joint while he chats with me.

I tell him I'm not a moron. I know it's not a controlled blind study.

I'm riding a line between wanting the show to be intellectually sound while also being entertaining *and* a cathartic, relatable experience. My market research has been slipshod so far, though the typewriter did receive one incredible response. A woman wanted to give it to her partner for his birthday, she wrote:

Hi Haley,

I'm looking for something special to gift my partner for his birthday, I think this will be a perfect gift! I would love to buy it from you and would be able to pay £100 and collect it whenever is convenient for you (pre-27th of April). I hope to hear from you soon.

Kind Regards,
XXX

PS. I'm sorry to hear that the typewriter has such a negative association for you, I hope that we can give it a good home.

PPS. It will be used a lot if you decide to sell it to us :)

I share this with my brother, who says, "That's a nice email", and attempts to assuage my guilt about neglecting my Gumtree homework. "Ultimately the market research doesn't matter, so don't stress about it. It seems like you're more interested in stories and anomalies than numbers."

"But I want to do this right, Kian."

He says, "The point is to make art, not sell the data or use the data to maximise profits. Don't worry about it. I think looking at the prices for similar ones online will be a good gauge. Look at five, take the median."

"But it looks like people do give a shit about my pain."

He laughs. "Fair." Then he says, "I guess your project is about trying to put math in a place it can't go."

I don't understand.

"Well, sure," he says, pinching a piece of potato with naan, "you can go there, but it's never going to be *definitive*. It's always going to be amorphous — a performance of math."

"Why?" I don't mean for it to come out as a desperate plea, but it does.

"Because math can't know emotion. Emotional spectrums are not quantifiably comparable. Sure, there's talk about assessing EQ but there's no definitive test for it, the way there is for IQ."

"But couldn't the math in the formula be specific to my individual emotion?"

Kian considers this for a moment. "But what's a seven of heartbreak?"

"Bad but not the worst."

216

"So right there —" Kian swallows. "That's a flaw, because there's nothing clear-cut about that measurement."

"But is it a flaw, or does it mean our formula has strength of character?"

My brother says formulas can't have personalities. "They're meant to be cold, distant and objective."

The idea coalesces as I speak. "But don't divorce lawyers have standard formulas for turning pain into money?" I tell him Ollie's lawyer told him that she wouldn't represent him unless he also hired a therapist.

"Sure, but a lot more than feelings are taken into account, because assets are wrapped up in it too."

He tells me about a colleague of his who is going through a noxious divorce. While at a conference with Kian, her wife violated their agreement and introduced their child to her new girlfriend. The colleague broke down over lunch, saying, "But it's me. It's me. How could she do this to *me*?" To which another colleague said, "But it's not you anymore. You have no emotional sway over her. You have to hit her where she still feels it." She asked where that was. "Wallet," the other colleague replied, simply. "Don't give her half the house."

Beyond the customary material goods exchange, I have no idea what it would be like to pick apart shared finances or DNA. I text Gemma: *Divorced people should be able to use the formula. Yes?*

When Kian asks what's up in the rest of my life, I gripe about Milo having a crush on me.

My brother has no sympathy for me. He says I've always kept these "pseudo-boyfriends" around for entertainment and then complain about them liking me.

"No, I think we're friends, and then they transgress a boundary."

He says, "You don't behave like someone in a committed relationship — they think a window's open. There are people

217

you know are off the market, and you don't come across that way."

I'm about to protest when I remember what I've learned from T and shut up. And I see it. I'm irritable because he's caught me out. "You're right." The common denominator is me.

But when Milo suggests we meet at the gallery, I say yes.

£ + ♥

The noise of Dalston recedes as I step into the repurposed industrial space. Vast sandblasted brick walls and a cathedralesque ceiling dwarf us. It smells like fresh paint. Milo hugs me lightly and we talk over each other. I ask how he's doing. He asks about Chicago.

I say, "Good," in a high-pitched voice, nodding to close the topic. He tells me that he and Julie have started sleeping together again.

Keen to avoid talking about our love lives, I move towards the free food and booze. "Let's look at the spread."

"Aha. The starving actress has arrived."

"That's the best part of these things."

"Be sure to tell that to the artist."

Just then the artist in question, an affable loaf sporting white overalls and cherry Docs, flops over to welcome us. He's a friend of Milo's.

"Some of them aren't even dry yet."

I take in his giant oil paintings, bold strokes, glumps of paint clinging to canvas. The artist laughs and so we join in. He tells us all the work is about his parents' divorce settlement. "I pitched it before I painted it. Turned out to be more painful to paint than I anticipated."

Milo explains that he's designing the lights for my show, which is about love and money.

The artist nods, saying, "It's brutal isn't it? Like behind the curtain, it's all just shite, isn't it? Isn't it all façade?" before his eyes dart to the door and he bounds off.

We weave through the growing crowd to the drinks table. When we clink glasses, Milo exhales and a waft of stale cigarettes and smoked mackerel infiltrates my nostrils. Uneasy, I drift towards a piece called *The Settlement* — a large, old-timey balancing scale piled high on both sides with flesh and gold-coloured specks and something that resembles intestines.

"Entrails," Milo mumbles. Then jeers at the price, "£7,500?"

"Half goes to the gallery," I remind him.

"Still."

"And then you have to factor in the cost of the supplies, plus the time to make it, plus studio rental and utilities, plus website hosting, plus admin time organising the show and the cost of publicising the show, plus all the paintings that don't sell."

Milo says he's proud of my business acumen. Given that list of expenses, the artist's probably working at a loss.

I tell him, "Everything I've created for myself has pretty much operated at a loss."

"An expensive hobby," Milo replies nonchalantly.

The sting of this label blindsides me like a jellyfish sting when floating in the ocean. "It's not a hobby."

"Just technically." He grins. "Isn't the definition of work being paid?"

"I think the definition of work is the pursuit of a purpose." He's about to retort, but I lean in and say, "Would you claim raising children or taking care of a sick relative is a hobby? If we follow your definition, I think that's where we'll end up. And that is incredibly sexist."

Later, with *l'esprit de l'escalier*, I'll formulate a more clinical response. Many businesses operate at a loss before turning a profit. Does that render their work a hobby? But for now we linger in the awkwardness, moving towards the next piece.

The evening carries on in this vein. Me putting him in his place with a pithy phrase, then guiltily patting his arm, whispering some joke and blaming jet lag. After an hour like this, I hug him hard and thank him. He's disappointed I can't go for a drink just the two of us.

"I have some work to do in the morning."

"But it's the weekend."

"But I am in a flow with my research and writing, and rehearsing—" Changing tactics, I say, "You know we have another R&D in a few weeks and we're sharing stuff with a paying audience at the end."

I watch him decide not to try to convince me. When he offers to walk me to the Tube, I can't bring myself to decline.

Except for my deep breathing, it's silent as we stroll to the Hackney Central Overground. I use my enjoyment of the air to try to keep the mood light.

When the station comes into sight he says, "So the wedding was okay in the end." He took a friend from university and they had a super time. He describes the food and a dance party with loads of kids doing rhythmic gymnastics. "It would have been better with you though."

I give him a playful warning glance.

"Sorry, sorry, I know you're with T. I'm just saying it."

I sigh. "Milo." I search for the words to convey what I want to without eviscerating him or causing him to quit the show. Behind us, my train arrives and leaves the station. The next one won't be here for fifteen minutes. He comes up to the platform with me.

I tell him I'm confused. I don't understand how his feelings for me could be real when he's started sleeping with Julie again.

He says, "Love and affection for someone isn't a tap you turn off. And besides, you were in America with T, I guess?"

"Mm hmm."

He asks why I didn't tell him I was going.

I don't know. "I always feel weird telling you about T."

"Because there *is* something between us."

"I don't know, Milo. But T got hit by a truck in Chicago and it made a lot of things clear." I tell him about the accident.

He's sympathetic and says the most important thing is that we can stay friends.

"Yes," I exhale as I reach out and grip his shoulder, grateful to return to the friend zone. "Good."

He says, "And in that case, I can also tell you I ended up hooking up with someone at the wedding — not my date — a . . ."

"A bridesmaid?" I ask. We watch my train arrive and leave the station again.

He scrubs his face with his hands. "Unbelievable, I know."

When the next train comes, he says, "Ciao." I wave merrily as it pulls out of the station, amazed by how straightforward it was to quell that issue.

£ + ♥

The grant application was rejected. I worry it's because I don't have a track record of work in the UK. Sam tells me to simplify my ask and resubmit. Incorporating my lack of notoriety in the UK, I argue that the show itself will also help to raise my profile, allowing me to build a self-sustaining career with longevity. I spend two days on the rewrites and re-jigging the budget. I put it in the first person and remove any loftiness about the world-changing potential of the project. I focus on its value to my career and the potential for conversations that applying math to heartbreak could engender. I send the application off again.

In preparation for our second R&D next week, I've written as much of the script as possible without having completed the formula. I'm considering including some of my recent correspondence with Typewriter. He responded to my interview request with the following:

221

Oh jeeze. Alright. Here's an idea – write me a part in your show!? Write us riding off into a big old sunset together!? Make it a two-hander. In any case, I'd like to read what you've written so far. Particularly what you say about me. Then we can talk.

I sent him my current draft yesterday. I'm developing a method for wrapping my body in bubble wrap, rehearsing on my own in between the few voice jobs that the gods have bestowed on me and my patchwork Joe-jobs.

I've now had thirty-six pap smears. Not to toot my own horn, but I was a bit of a hit with the supervising GPs because of my "sense of humour". This has nothing to do with my wit and all to do with my Canadian sensibility. I still seize up about my labia, bracing myself when the student has to plough through it to slip the duck lips inside. At least they're BPA-free plastic, not cold metal.

I've been talking about fertility a lot recently. Fi was considering freezing her eggs. The best time to do it is before you turn thirty-five, but it costs tens of thousands of pounds to do. Fortunately, thanks to a combination of Fi's husband taking fewer baths and wearing looser underwear, Japanese acupuncture and dietary changes, Fi is pregnant. It's too early in the pregnancy to be a sure thing, but I offer to throw them a housewarming party as a celebratory gesture. Last week they took possession of their house in Walthamstow, a neighbourhood in north-east London. I invite their friends, colleagues and siblings and tell them it's a potluck. The house has three bedrooms and a garden.

"It's all happening," I say as I dance through the living room with Fi.

The house fills up with well-turned out, accomplished people. I keep my arm tight to my side to hide the hole in the armpit of my top. I reduce my job description to "I do voiceovers" and cling to Milo, grateful to have a comrade to hide out with in the corner of the front room.

In the last couple weeks, he's gone hell for leather with the dating apps, yielding some juicy stories.

Two cocktails in, he's describing his struggles reintegrating condoms and erectile strife. First, he tried MDMA, and when that didn't work, he tried Viagra. He's been on seven first dates in ten days.

I ask him how he is able to come up with plans for each of the dates.

He's figured out a system. The system involves meeting at the same café in central London, then walking through St James's Park. If it's going well, depending on the time of day, he either suggests they grab an artisanal doughnut and check out the free exhibition at the Royal Academy or go for a cocktail at a bar south of the river. He sticks to a budget and he wears the same thing every time.

"Do you have your opening lines in a note on your phone?"

He admits he does, but swiftly adds that all he can control is the opening, the rest is banter. "Though, there are a few vetting questions I like to ask."

"Such as?"

He says mostly stuff about politics. And whether or not they're in credit card debt.

"For a one-night stand?" I ask sardonically.

"McGee. I'm always looking for the real deal."

"Do you follow up on the dates by sending them the same songs and poems? Do you have a compliment mad-lib that you pull from?" My voice is cutting.

He asks why I'm getting hostile.

"I'm not, it's just shitty to know women who think they're precious gemstones are actually just garden variety rocks."

That's how I felt when I discovered I'd been played by Typewriter, after being put through his elaborate pattern of wooing, pursuing, withdrawing, gaslighting and dismissal. I'm about to explain this to Milo when he reaches out for my knee.

"It's hard because I don't like anyone as much as . . ." We both stare at his hulking hand cupping my joint.

"Julie?" I guess.

"No. You."

"Milo." I'm stern.

He jostles me. "I know, McGee. I know. I'm accepting my place on the friend-ship."

Milo has to leave early to return Julie's computer charger. Left to fend for myself, one of Fi's husband's mates takes a shine to me. He's around my age but has three small children who are at home with his wife. We talk about Edna St. Vincent Millay and I recite some of Leonard Cohen's essay 'How to Speak Poetry'. He isn't bad company, but I mention T early on to avoid any crossed wires.

He asks what my boyfriend is up to this evening.

I explain he's in the States at the moment.

"Do you guys have an open relationship?" he asks.

"Not anymore." I don't ask if his marriage is an open relationship. I don't want to know.

He tests how ajar the door is with a bumbling, "Why? When? How did that change?"

I tell him initially we were not monogamous, so I got involved with a few people in my vicinity, but with each one, I just thought about T the whole time.

"And what about him?"

"He's extremely loyal," I say with finality and begin looking around for an escape.

"Don't be so sure about that." He goes on to tell me that everyone is dubious, that even the purest people have a shadow, that we can never really know another person. "People will get away with whatever they think they can."

"T's not a cheater," I say. "I've been with a cheater. I know the difference."

Typewriter not only funnelled me through a system, but repeatedly cheated on me throughout our time together. On

224

some level I knew something was up with Mix Tape, and with Typewriter, but I chose to believe their lies instead. T is very intuitive. I sometimes wonder if he senses something between me and Milo. This is why I cannot act on it. Because I don't want to be caught? No, because I don't know if T and I could recover from a betrayal, and I couldn't lie to him. Do I need to tell him about the kisses? No. I should carry the burden of that meaning-less misstep. And besides, Milo is still living with Julie. He has no plans to move out. Okay he's sleeping in the spare room and is on the dating apps, but he's nowhere close to being in good working order, and besides, Milo's not my guy. He's not my guy.

Ru's friend pulls me from these thoughts, asking where I've zoned out to.

"I just remembered something," I apologise, and scoot towards Fi.

Ru has burned the pie I'd baked for the event. He's also royally aggravating Fi because while she can't drink during the pregnancy, he's been imbibing more than ever. "He's already pissed. I'm not speaking to him for the rest of the night," she huffs in my ear. And then, referring to my now-charred pie, "Can we salvage it?"

"Leave it to me," I say, as Fi's sister sashays in and swoops her away.

As I scrape off the burnt crust, I stew. It's all a sham. No one's happy. No one's got it figured out — certainly not the married people. It might not be perfect with T, but at least we have honesty.

Several hours later, the flat empties out; just Fi, her sister, Ru and I remain. While I methodically fill up their dishwasher, they corner me.

"Babes. Milo is fit." Fi's sister is drunk.

"No." I tell them we're just friends and I'm with T.

They know that, says Fi, but it just seems obvious that Milo and I have a connection.

I laugh to mask my irritation. "You know advice is only useful when asked for."

She says it's just an observation that the price of admission with T is very steep.

I say maybe before the accident, but things are really changing. "And besides," I add, "you're not inside my relationship."

Ru steps in, saying I'm right. It's none of their business. They just want me to be happy. But it does seem like Milo would be a good fit.

I recoil. "I don't want to have sex with Milo!"

Playing the older sister, Fi reminds me, "Love, there's so much more to a relationship than sex."

"And there's so much more to a life than—" I stop myself. Our values are different. "I'm not telling you how to live."

"What's wrong with how we live?"

"Nothing. But just because the life I want is different doesn't mean it's wrong." I feel myself about to cry.

It's late, I wish I could walk home but it'll take two hours. I spend fifty-five minutes on the Tube instead. I haven't heard from T today. When I get off at Highgate station I call him, but no answer. Telling him off in my mind before writing him a winsome text, I then chastise myself for my hypocrisy. The whole enterprise of marriage is doomed. I can see that, but I'm jealous too. Part of me wants to own a house and have a baby with T, and let the dog out into the garden to pee before we sleep in our king-sized bed after an evening of hosting our friends. Even Navid's going for it with Ísleif, the Icelandic financier. She's thirty-nine, wants a family and he's ready to commit. They subsist on video calls and when he hangs up, he assures me she's the one.

I know this is primarily projection. And while I'm jealous of his abandon to love, I see the futility in it too. Most couples I witness are playing idealised versions of who they are, squashing themselves into a well-known script and assuring each

226

other it's the mature thing to do. I wonder if it's arrogant to think T and I could have something truer, better? Or if that's the optimism Albert was describing — this human propensity to believe we are the exception to the rule.

T returns my call as I'm getting into bed. I answer even though it's 2 a.m. Our back and forth devolves into an argument. I want him to tell me he misses me. I want him to tell me when he's next going to visit the UK. Our bank account is depleted and we need a top up. He says money is tight and so is time. I ask him where he's at in the passport process, something I haven't inquired about in ages. He says that's a bigger question. I say everyone else lives a life that moves in a forward trajectory and all he and I do is tread water. He reminds me that I've always moved faster than him. At 3.30 a.m. I am delirious, and he has a deadline to write towards.

The next day in therapy, I begin with a series of questions I've prepared, pertaining to the show. I want to know:

1. *Are some people better built to love than others?*
2. *Are some people better built to have relationships than others?*
3. *Can you explain neuropathways created via modelling by parents and treatment in childhood?*
4. *Is there hope if you're a person who is less well-built for love? Where is the hope? How long does it take?*

Thea says we can use these questions for my own therapy, but she can't give me one-sentence answers to them. These things are more complex. She does admit, though, that some people have better receptors for love than others based on attachment patterns and wounds formed in childhood.

"Aha!" I say self-righteously. "So, what can I do?" As she begins to speak, I cut her off, "Don't tell me nothing — it can't be nothing."

She asks why I say that.

"Because if it's nothing then it means the world is cruel or indifferent or random." The word "random" is imbued with the meaning of a colossal curse. "I'd rather be at fault. I'd rather have made a whole bunch of errors and be a perpetrator rather than a victim of the universe — the butt of some horrible cosmic joke."

She asks me what I think the "right" course of action is. I don't know. And the more I rack my brain the more agitated I become. White noise fills my head. My voice quakes and I start to beg her, "Tell me what to do. Just tell me, please. I don't know what to do. Why am I so fucked in love? How can I fix myself, so I just find something that works?" But when she replies, I don't hear what she says. I can't. It's all wrong and I'm attacking her, poking holes in her "psychobabble". When she goes silent, I lash out. "Why aren't you answering?"

She speaks very calmly and with warmth. "Everything I say seems to be dissatisfying to you, so I thought it would be better for me to back off."

I continue on the offence. "What's the point of all my positive thinking and manifesting and meditating? What's the point of all that if all it is, is a placebo? I got into therapy because I needed to fix my relationships with men, and now I'm paying all this money and spending all this time 'working on it' and it's not fucking doing anything!"

"Tell me more," she says.

"I need to know the truth. The truth. The truth. I want an answer."

She remains silent.

"If I'm such a great person, why can't I find it? Why have I failed so egregiously in my relationships? What's wrong with me? And don't tell me you find it when you're not looking for it or thinking about it. I don't know how to not think about it. It's all I want, and I am ready for it. I'm so ready to love someone. I'm ready to build a life with someone."

She says, "I know you are."

"And I want to have a baby," I whimper. "When — how am I going to have a baby? And I don't want to do it alone. I want to do it with someone I love. That I was friends with first, then fell in love, then had years together just the two of us and I'm running out of time!"

After an extended pause, she delicately says, "You know Haley, every time you say 'I wanna have a baby' it comes out in this whiney voice. It clangs in my ear."

I cry harder at her impersonation of my tone. Confirmation that the most annoying, childish, insufferable part of me very much lives on eviscerates me. I am ashamed of my lack of growth. I am ashamed of my ineptitude, and conduct, and inability to figure shit out for myself. But I don't say that. I lie just outside a swatch of sun on the carpet and sob. She listens.

When I speak again, I'm calm. "You're right," I say. "I don't know if I want to have a baby. That's just something I say to make T feel bad. You're right."

"And I would argue, there's an element of masochism in it."

"Yes." It's as though the two halves of my brain have been pulled apart and in between them is clear, fresh, open space. Breathing room. I do not want a baby, now, or soon. A baby would destroy the life I am only just beginning to create. I may not want a baby ever. But I use the worry about not having a baby as a way to make myself feel bad.

Later in the day I call T. This revelation makes it easier to want less from him, to strike a few items off my list of grievances and be okay with what our relationship is. I tell him about my epiphany.

He says, "I'm the same. I really like kids, but I do not want my own now."

"They're a huge imposition."

We laugh.

"But it's true," he says, "most of my friends who have babies have had really hard times in their relationships. It really puts a strain." He says he needs to deal with his own crap before he can help a little human navigate the world.

I want to ask if he's still doing regular therapy. But I close that pop-up and keep the conversation in a state of complicity. Us versus everyone we know, bound through mutual aversion to the status quo. This revolutionary call culminates with him booking a ticket to come and see me. He'll arrive several days after my next performance.

£ + ♥

Alright. I just gave your script a quick read. I like it. I have a few issues, but we can work them out. Drugs were a major issue for me. I know I'm not supposed to make excuses, but it's the truth. Also, quite frankly, I reject that you can say what was love and what wasn't. Or is and isn't. I continue to carry you in my heart and think of you like no other. It's just a fact. We can argue Wednesday 11 my time.

That's what Typewriter sent last night.

Typewriter was the lead singer of a popular Canadian indie outfit. He wrote most of their lyrics, played guitar, sang with perfect pitch and delivered the most hilarious commentary between melancholy, heart-wrenching tunes. Narrow-hipped with a floppy mop of curls, I was enthralled by his small quizzical eyes, which always gave the impression he wasn't quite convinced of whatever had just been said.

He was one of those svelte men who ate like a garbage can till his early thirties and then found himself struggling with a metabolism come to a grinding halt. When I met him, he'd developed a tiny paunch. He'd say, "My garburator is clogged," and made jokes on stage about wearing his belt on the last loop.

In an attempt to cut down on calories he only drank white wine, but he ate every meal in a restaurant, favouring greasy spoons and 24-hour diners. He was nostalgic about Boston and Italy even though he'd never visited either place for more than a couple days on tour.

Bicycle and I had seen Typewriter perform several times while we were still together. We shared a copy of his latest record and repeated lines from his interstitial joshing as inside jokes. Through the factory town that is the Canadian arts scene, I was aware of Typewriter's reputation as a scoundrel. But nine months after Bicycle and I broke up, after one of Typewriter's gigs in Kensington Market, he caught my eye across the bar, pointed at me and made a beeline.

"Who, are you?" he asked, swirling his white wine in a cognac glass.

He bought me a drink and grilled me about myself. I told him my first solo show was about to open at a theatre around the corner the following month. He found that ridiculously impressive. We bantered, by turns cavilling about the stodginess of Canadian art and crafting grandiose schemes for a nation-wide artistic revolution. His sharp nasal inhales, quick turns of his head and emphatic finger-pointing, all while managing to keep a grip on his drink, made for an intoxicating comedic performance.

After the many double G&Ts that he kept flowing in my direction, he suggested we go make out in the alleyway. I raced him there. We smooched against the vinyl siding and he bellowed, "Haley McGee!" to the lame echo of Baldwin Street. I giggled too much for us to kiss again. He told me he was going to write songs about me and then quoted Irish poet Patrick Kavanagh, "I met her first and knew/That her dark hair would weave a snare that I might one day rue", insisting that if he got involved with me, I'd eat him alive. All this was catnip for me.

When I told him I had to go home because I had rehearsal in the morning, he was dramatic and fervent. "Meet me for breakfast."

"Before rehearsal?"

"I've just met the One and I'm going home for Christmas in nine days! We don't have much time!" His family lived in Prince Edward Island.

By the time I got home he'd sent me a link to Bob Dylan singing "Make You Feel My Love", proposing it be "our song". I met him on College Street the following morning. His unbuttoned trench coat flapped as he approached and pulled me into a kiss.

Over our greasy spoon breakfast, he lunged into the table, exclaiming, "Marry me!"

I laughed and declined.

"Okay!" he said, slamming his hand down. "First time, she said, 'No'. That's one."

As he walked me to the theatre, I repeatedly tripped off the curb, my cheeks aching from laughing.

Later on, I questioned him about his terrible reputation with women. "I've got your number," I said. He insisted it was different with me, playing right into my long-held fantasy to find a wicked man and reform him. When I suggested that we hold off on sleeping together until after he returned from Christmas in PEI, he was gung-ho. The restriction had him kissing me with desperation, groping me hungrily over my clothes, playing the chaperoned romantic and thwarted lover with great panache.

After Christmas, my show opened. The first reviews to come out in the national papers were two-star heartbreakers. The artistic director consoled me, calling them "the final gasps of a dying breed". Mercifully, the alternative weekly magazine heralded the show with the headline "Hail Haley!" and four stars. Still, I floated through those weeks in a stupor, believing I'd been publicly shamed.

"You're joining me," Typewriter said, and trotted out a list of artists who'd also received negative reviews. In the lobby, after seeing the show, he told me I was a genius, and begged me to let him fly me out to see him while he was on tour.

I said I had to think about it.

He sent me love poems by Rumi, Rilke, Anaïs Nin and Edna St. Vincent Millay.

The first alarm bells rang on New Year's Eve, when after dinner at Coracao in Little Portugal, we went to a party at one of my friends' apartments.

Typewriter wanted to leave before midnight, to celebrate the new year in a private romantic moment. We colluded to leave without saying goodbye to anyone. Real rascals. I slipped out the door, assuming he was directly behind me. Waiting in the hallway, I expected a passionate embrace, but instead he blew past me, pressing the elevator call button repeatedly. In the taxi I held him while he sniffled and gulped for air. "We're supposed to make each other look cool." Someone had laughed in his face and said that I ditched him. How could someone so funny, I wondered, be so humourless about this misunderstanding.

Perhaps a more potent life lesson from this relationship is that, as with good looks or searing intelligence, you can't date the sense of humour or the talent.

The more we slept together, the more distant he became. The less he texted and called. The less he answered his phone. The less he called when he said he would. But I was enveloped in the exhaustion of performing my show and the pain of not being adored by the city at large.

One morning after sex, I got out of bed and returned with two cups of coffee. His face transformed to a mixture of crestfallen and caged. He didn't want his coffee.

I made a lame, humiliating joke. "Coffee and a blowjob, isn't that the classic combo?"

His skin had gone cold and he rolled away, pulling his shirt over his head.

"Kiss me," I pouted.

He sighed and laid a sloppy, perfunctory kiss on me. Mashing his lips into mine — an approximation of a kiss, the way kids do when they're making fun of grown-ups, the way improvisers do when they mock make-out on stage.

He was out the door, and my apartment suddenly looked dingy and was eerily silent. I made the bed and drank the tepid coffees. I missed Bicycle.

Typewriter left again for several months on tour. His tsunami of attention slowed to a drip. Plans to Skype were broken. I went on a date with a guy who'd seen my show several times. This date didn't elicit guilt in me. Typewriter and I had no label, but I found myself wanting to want to be with someone in a committed way. I pinned this desire on Typewriter, who blamed his gruelling schedule for his aloof behaviour. Frustrated, in the wee hours of the morning, I booked my first solo trip abroad, three weeks in London, Paris and Berlin. I'd stay with pals in London and Berlin and I'd spend two nights in Paris in between. Typewriter was thrilled for me. I was thrilled for me too.

From a café in London Fields I wrote to Typewriter that I'd decided, yes, he could fly me to meet him on his tour after my trip. His response obliquely evaded his initial offer. Consumed with indignation at having been demoted, I was also grappling with the difference between his grand romantic declarations of the past and this behaviour. When I spoke to Thea about it, she introduced me to the idea of behaviour as character, shown not in what people say, but what they *do*. But I elected to disregard this at the time. I'd been waiting to have one of these blown out, whirlwind romances since I learned to read. I'd been hankering after this kind of instant, kismet chemistry and fervour since childhood. I didn't want to accept that fireworks could turn to ash. I wanted to believe there was an epic love story written in the stars for me.

Back in Toronto, enduring the bleakness of the mid-March slush, the first anniversary of my break-up with Bicycle rolled around. I had not heard from Typewriter for several days. I called him and left a message indicting him for failing to send me a poem in recent weeks, and asking him when was he ever going to write a song for me? Typewriter wrote that the pitch we began this at wasn't sustainable. And we ended whatever "this" was via email. I wasn't heartbroken, more pride-sore and ashamed.

Six months later, having nursed my pride, I was in a rural town performing summer stock theatre when Typewriter started phoning me incessantly. After several weeks of ignoring his calls, I answered. He'd been on a meditation retreat, and apparently, when he got very still, what was important to him bubbled to the surface: "It's you." He apologised for "misprizing me" and asked if he could see me again. Within days of that, he rented a car and drove to the tiny town I was in to meet me for dinner. He slopped on the same thick icing he'd used the last time.

"The best indication of someone's future behaviour is their past behaviour," Thea said. "Do you want to take another spin on the dance floor?" I knew it would likely end badly, but I did. So with open eyes, weary as I was, we danced hot and increasingly cold again for another three-ish months. He sent me transcripts from his journal about me and sang me songs. We'd go out for lavish dinners where he ordered willy-nilly, waving me off when I expressed concern, and then revealing, on more than one occasion, that he'd forgotten his wallet. A poo prude, Typewriter forbade me from discussing my gas pains with him. He went down on me less and less and only kissed me when he wanted sex. Genuinely helpless in the kitchen, he destroyed a paring knife my father had given me when I asked him to slice a peach. Looking for an escape hatch, I struck up a flirtation with an actor I was working with.

I was planning on ending it when I saw Typewriter before he went home for the holidays, but he showed up with the type-writer for me, and I couldn't figure out how to dump him after accepting the gift.

I kissed the actor in a park a couple days later. Typewriter was back in PEI and missed our Skype date because he was allegedly "buying icicle lights at the mall" with his mother.

I texted, *Should we talk about ending our relationship?*

And he replied, *I'm afraid so.*

It was Christmas Eve and it was an easy call. He apologised and cried a lot. I kept reassuring him, "It's okay." Neither of us said there was anyone else. The actor and I only lasted a few months, but he pulled me out of Typewriter's orbit and for that I'm grateful.

Soon after my prosaic break-up with Typewriter, not only did I learn that he'd been chasing and seducing other women, many of them artists, almost the entire time we'd been together, but he baited and caught those other women using the exact same box of lures he'd used on me. He had a pattern.

The pattern included the Facebook message proposing "Make You Feel My Love" as "our song" followed by the same poems sent in the same sequence, calling me "the one!", jokily proposing marriage, journal transcripts, dinner at Coracao, promising but never following through on writing a song about me, withdrawing his affections after sleeping together, ending the relationship in writing and then attempting to win me back, but not being able to sustain sexual or romantic interest.

I was mortified when I started meeting women who'd also been put through the pattern. But the more I compared stories and emails with them, the better I felt. Typewriter had terrific taste; it was oddly nice company to be included in. And as the numbers amassed — today I'm aware of twelve women in Toronto he pulled the pattern on — the less personally I took it. Clearly, it was a pathology and had nothing to do with me.

I'm pretty sure this has something to do with the law of diminishing returns, because each time he repeats the pattern it becomes less special. At the same time, the more he repeats it, the less offensive it becomes because the repetitions indicate a flaw in him, not me.

I write to Gemma, *It's time to tackle a Wild Card.*

Of all my exes, Typewriter is probably the only one I would consider an actual friend now. I see him when he's playing in the UK. I hear from him on my birthday. He still makes me laugh, really hard. Before we reached our current truce, there was a period of silence that lasted several years. It ended when he wrote to inform me he was going through a twelve-step program and asked if I'd meet with him after performing in my latest show. Over a cup of tea, he told me about his newfound sobriety. It was a different story to the one he'd told my now-friend, who he'd dated simultaneously, but I appreciated the apology.

I asked if he'd also quit women.

He blushed.

I asked why he went after women so hard. Why he never let women come to him.

He said, "If I did that, no one would come."

That is the only vulnerable moment I've ever witnessed from him. Usually our interactions consist of him vaguely attempting to win me back, which makes me howl. It's hard to know if there's any truth in his feigned disappointment.

Now I'm shutting the door of my nun's cell and getting my notes in order to convene with Typewriter on Skype. Our call is much the same as many of our recent conversations. Except rather than vying to get back together with me, he's now fixated on being featured in the show somehow, perhaps as a musician on stage with me, or a fellow actor. This cracks me up. He insists he's serious, only he doesn't like that I want to use our actual story in the project. He thinks we should fictionalise it.

Midway through our call, with a smirk I say, "I want you to openly admit that you were playing some kind of a game, and that you knew what you were doing—"

"No, no—"

I carry on, "— and that you knew that I didn't know what you were doing."

"No."

"You disagree?"

"No. I won't admit that."

"Because it's not true?"

"It wasn't a game." He frowns. "I mean, I don't want to make it suddenly really serious."

I drop my interrogation. "No, you definitely need to have a serious response."

"It was about the drugs, you know. I was fast asleep."

I can't help but dig. "What do you think about the adage, ask not why the addiction, ask why the pain?"

Typewriter sighs. "Well that's huge. I don't know that there was underlying pain. I was using because it was fun and it had been romanticised in the music industry and I was an addict. All my days went into trying to feel better and then at 6 p.m. I'd start again. And I hid it from you — I hid it from everyone. People knew I liked to party, but they didn't know the extent." He takes a sip of lemon balm tea — pointing out he's also quit caffeine. "I remember you, but a lot of the events you're asking me about are really foggy. They feel like glimmers of a dream."

We talk more about his addiction. I keep probing for the why, determined to uncover the root, but he isn't having it. I turn my attention to the typewriter itself. "What do you think that typewriter was worth, given what you paid for it, and all the ways you lost and gained by being romantically involved with me? You told me you paid a hundred bucks for it and on Etsy—"

"I didn't," he interjects softly.

"How much did you pay?"

"It was three hundred and something. Three-sixty or something like that. Yeah. It might have been four hundred bucks."

Impressed, I say, "It was top, top drawer. And it had all the little brushes."

Typewriter groans.

"Do you want to tell me why you'd rather do a fictional scene together than have me use this recording in the show? Do you want to tell me about the value of story?"

Perking up, he points at the camera. "Yeah, yeah, I fucking do because it's fault-line pretentious first of all. You're on a fault-line of self-indulgence with this project. So it's gotta be . . . you gotta have a spoonful of sugar, you know?"

"What does spoonful of sugar mean?"

"A spoonful of sugar helps the medicine go down, Haley," he replies surlily.

I break into hysterics and he looks pleased with himself.

Speaking more seriously, he says, "It's dangerous to make it just about you. The idea of ex-boyfriend, one-person shows — if I had a fucking dollar — you know what I mean? At the fringe."

"Oh yeah." He's not wrong.

"Yeah. That's why having me in it, it's like . . ." he raises his mug to his lips.

"Is what?"

"It's just more interesting, I think."

£ + ♥

Gemma yowls when I play her the recording.

Confirmation: the interview is entertaining and earns Typewriter airtime in the show. At our fast-approaching work-in-progress performance I plan to experiment with playing some of it to the audience.

Gemma clarifies, "So that's the guy you dated after Bicycle?"

"Yes," I say. "Every person I date seems to be an antidote to the last." And I show her the graph I made of my time with Typewriter.

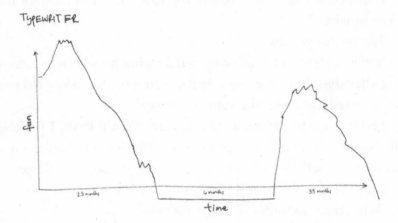

Things are kicking into high gear for *The Ex-Boyfriend Yard Sale*. We've just headed into our second week-long R&D workshop process. Elson is now tied up with a large-scale show in Canada, so we'll have a few sessions over Skype, but mostly it will be me flying solo with a few visits from my collaborators, Sam, Milo, who will swing by and design some lights for our work-in-progress presentation, and the sound and scenic designers, who will pop in for an afternoon to see where I'm at and talk ideas. I've been inviting VIPs from fancy theatre institutions, trying to drum up more support for the project. For late-night kicks I wrote to my handful of acquaintances who program festivals and theatre seasons around the world, offering to send them a video — I'd love to take this show on the road. And I've invited everyone I know in London to the performance. Today Gemma and I are tackling a Wild Card to share with the audience at the end of the week.

"So I was thinking this Wild Card is about betrayal and being put through a pattern."

"Bad shit," says Gemma.

240

"That's good. The 'Bad Shit Happened To Me' Wild Card."

To figure out the math, we break down the efficacy and injury of Typewriter's pattern. First we identify the variables, then discuss how they're related to each other, and finally I assign each data point a numeric value (1–10). After a couple hours, this is what the "Bad Shit Happened To Me" Wild Card looks like.

$$\left[\left(\left(\odot \times \uparrow cR\right) \times \left(\frac{\text{PAIN NOW}}{\text{THEN}}\right) + \left(\uparrow resp. - \underline{!}\right)\right) \times \left(\sum_{i=1}^{\infty} \frac{1}{2^{i-1}} \times \text{👻} \right)\right]$$

And this is how it works. The first thing assessed is:

– *How much fun I was having while he was enacting his pattern with me.*
  (8/10. It was a riot to have someone slamming his hand on tables begging me to marry him.)

That is multiplied by:

– *How creative the elements of the pattern were.*
  (6/10. I'd already read a lot of Rilke at that point in my life.)
  That number is then added to:
– *The amount of pain I feel NOW about being put through the pattern.*
  (2/10. It wasn't about me, he had great taste in women so it's pretty nice company to be in, and we're now pals.)

And that is divided by:

– *The level of pain I experienced upon discovering his betrayal.*
  (5/10. At the time I was embarrassed and angry, but I never loved him, so I wasn't heartbroken.)

Then we add:

- *How well he's taken responsibility for his actions since.*
  (2/10. I know he's apologised for his narcotics use, but I want
  him to own up to the womanising.)

Minus:

- *How much I ignored the red flags.*
  (9/10. At least eight people warned me about him. But when I'd
  confront him about it, he'd insist it was different with me, and I
  wanted to believe I possessed the power to convert a notorious
  cad.)

That is all then multiplied by:

- *How many times he repeated the pattern.*
  (We employ the law of diminishing returns to temper this, where
  x equals the number of times that he repeated the pattern with
  other women [twelve, as far as I know]).

The law of diminishing returns is an economic theory that says that you can, in fact, have too much of a good thing. It forecasts that after an ideal level of capacity is achieved, trying to do more will actually start to result in smaller outputs.

Gemma explains that there are various ways of including this theory, and shows me a special summation she's adapted to best capture the law of diminishing returns as it applies to bad shit (LODBS).

$$\text{LOD} \,\text{☺} = \sum_{i=1}^{x} \frac{1}{2^{i-1}}$$

The Greek letter is called "sigma". Gemma's summation alters the math so that the more Typewriter repeats the pattern the less offensive each betrayal becomes. Essentially, the first time the pattern is repeated it has an impact of 1, the second time .5, the third time .25, the ninth time .111, the fourteenth time .071 and so on. In other words, three times is bad, but the difference between nine and fourteen times is almost immaterial. But although each additional betrayal has less impact, we'll never reach a number of betrayals that have an impact of 0.

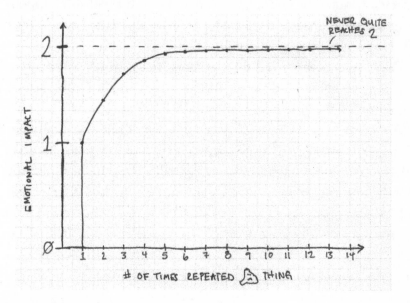

We multiply the LODBS summation by:

– *What percentage of the relationship he was pursuing and wooing other women.*

(92 per cent to give him the benefit of the doubt.)

As with all our Wild Cards, which are like taxes or credits, this will be applied to the overall price the formula gives us. With the numbers plugged in it spits out a 22.

'BAD SHIT HAPPENED TO ME' WILD CARD WITH #s

$$\left[\left((8\times6)\times\left(\frac{2}{5}\right)+(2-9)\right)\times\left(\sum_{i=1}^{12}\frac{1}{2^{i-1}}\times92\right)\right]=22$$

This number becomes a percentage — a 22 per cent tax — that is applied to the base equation for the typewriter. With the litigious precedent of "suing for damages" in mind, Gemma and I decide I should be financially compensated for bad shit happening to me, because the impact of bad shit can become our baggage. And baggage costs us.

Having accomplished this, we can't resist turning our attention to the other Wild Cards and how they might be connected to some of my other items for sale. The "short term impact" Wild Card, which we quickly rename the "Collateral Damage" Wild Card, makes up for physical items I had to replace because they were direct casualties in a specific relationship, like the jeans that tore when I sat on the knife on the bus ride to visit Necklace.

It's a straightforward formula that creates a tax. It looks at the repair or replacement cost of the item, divided by my monthly earnings at the time of the relationship.

COLLATERAL DAMAGE WILD CARD

$$\left(1+\frac{\text{Repair Cost}}{\text{monthly £ during ♥}}\right)$$

With the figures plugged in, we get a 1.06 per cent increase.

COLLATERAL DAMAGE WILD CARD WITH #s

$$\left(1 + \frac{£84.95}{£1378.17}\right) = 1.06$$

We use the A to C concept from my improv life to craft the "long term impact" Wild Card. The goal is to reflect how a seemingly singular event can result in unforeseen consequences down the line, as in the case of the morning-after pill incident with Ukulele, leading to my going back on the contraceptive pill and ultimately resulting in the blood clot medical fiasco.

This Wild Card measures the A to C impact on my emotional state, headspace, and body at the time of the inciting event through its long term implications (i.e. worry about getting more blood clots, not being able to take the contraceptive pill, never being able to smoke cigarettes). It also captures the financial impact for me (lost waitressing work, hours spent cycling to get my weekly blood test for a year, as well as the cost of these blood tests and my hospital visits as a Canadian taxpayer (approximately $11, 183 ÷ a population of 32M) in relation to how many words from Ukulele set the whole sequence in motion (eight: "But you're on the birth control pill, right?").

Since the ripple effect on my body is the key feature, we weight the physically connected variables more heavily, and once complete, we christen it the "Bodily Harm" Wild Card.

BODILY HARM WILD CARD

$$\left(\sqrt{\left(\text{😦}-\text{😁}\right)^2 + \left(\text{🫀}-\left(\%\text{🫀}\times t\right)\right)^2 + \left(\text{💀}-\text{🧍}\right)^2 + \left(T\$-\text{🎯}\right)^2} \right) \div 100$$

With all the data input, it spits out a 2.57 per cent tax.

BODILY HARM WILD CARD WITH #s

$$\left(\sqrt{\left(69.3-4\right)^2 + \left(105.12-86.4\right)^2 + \left(254-8\right)^2 + \left(43-8\right)^2} \right) \div 100 = 2.57$$

Gemma asks if those percentages feel right.

22 per cent tax certainly feels vindicating. 1.06 per cent feels about right for the flesh wound, given how little Necklace had to do with that scenario. And the 2.57 per cent seems fair. It wasn't Ukulele's fault, but that first domino led to substantial consequences for me. Mostly I'm buoyed by the fact that hard numbers are emerging at all. "It's adding up to something," I say to Gemma as I admire the math covering the walls of the studio. Chuffed herself, she raises her palm and I give her a high five.

"Oh!" I exclaim. "We have to do Crying Tax."

Gemma has to run off to teach, so we work hurriedly. She writes × .95 on a piece of A4 paper. "Okay, how about this: if the item was given to you before 2012, the price is docked five per cent?"

"To compensate for all the garbage I dumped in those relationships that actually belonged in therapy? That's good."

And we decide The Martha Card, which is applied to objects, like the bicycle, from people who — whatever the outcome

— occupy a place in you that no one else can touch, adds 10 per cent to the overall value of those objects. After Gemma skedaddles, I have a call with Elson, during which he kyboshes an idea I spent an hour practising yesterday, a performance-art-esque sequence in which I say, "I object. I, object", over and over.

The week in the studio exhausts me in a deeply gratifying way.

£ + ♥

The effects of my insomnia eclipsed by adrenalin, I'm on stage in the crumbling and dusty Camden People's Theatre — a space that was once a pub and has been converted into a black box. There's a pole that blocks part of the audience's view, sirens can be heard outside and the air conditioner whirrs and rattles when it restarts every fifteen minutes. The vibe is scrappy and edgy. I'm surrounded by my items from my exes, bubble wrap, and scrolls of brown paper covered in math.

In this second work-in-progress performance I'm trying out my current draft of the script. We haven't completed the formula yet, and I still have no idea how to end the show, but it doesn't matter. This is a chance for me to test out staging ideas and gauge how people respond to the concept and stories.

Right now, on stage, clad in white cotton underpants and T's T-shirt, I take a big sip of water while my recording with Typewriter plays. When he makes his bid to be included in the show, I give the audience a look and they laugh. Someone slaps their knee. I pull a retractable pointer out of my ponytail and open it, circling the typewriter.

I tell them how, in the aftermath of my break-up with Typewriter, not only did I learn that he'd been pursuing and wooing other women almost the entire time we'd been together, but he pursued and wooed them using the same tools and tactics he'd used on me. The Bob Dylan song plays, and I bounce, taking them through his pattern, then explaining, "So Gem and I have done some aftermath math, to figure out the cost of being put through the pattern and how that relates to the value of the type-writer he gave me." *Pièce de résistance*, I throw open what was once a concession window to reveal a big piece of cardboard with a title that reads, "The Bad Shit Happened To Me" Wild Card, under which is the math. I use orange Post-it notes to replace the math functions with my data, demonstrating how we arrive at 22 per cent. The audience is delighted, and I glide into my non-ending ending effervescent and rinsed.

In the dressing room afterwards, I'm surfing an endorphin high. I pull off my white underpants and wipe the sweat between my breasts. Catching a glimpse of my lithe, naked body in the mirror, I realise I've lost weight — not intentionally, the anxiety of putting a show together often has this effect. My boobs have never been smaller, but my cheeks are rosy. I catapult into the dress I brought with me and step into the lobby, where I am surrounded and embraced.

Ru pats me on the back. "Bloody good," he says, and demands my drink order.

I see Gemma and her boyfriend together for the first time. She hasn't seen me perform until now. "I'm in it more than I thought I would be," she says, amused.

"It's a work-in-progress," I say, mostly to reassure myself. "It'll get better." It will. My self-assessment is that it was a competent outing, but I have about forty thousand nit-picky acting and writing notes for myself. However, for tonight, I opt to drop into the relief of it being relatively well received.

Fi hugs me and begins to weep, yanking me to a quieter spot by the toilets. "I loved it Haley. It's your best thing yet. But love, please. Listen to me: T is never going to change." In the show, I'd made a parallel between Euler's Identity and T's feelings on LDRs, describing a crushing moment of being rejected by him a couple years ago. Her voice is resolute. "There's only one way a relationship works and that's if the man likes the woman a little bit more than she likes him." She's laughing at herself, but weeping nonetheless.

My defensive instinct is thrown by her tears. "Oh Fi," I say, "you're so protective of me."

"I don't want you to waste your life." She swallows and then says, "I'm emotional because I had a miscarriage." She won't let me hug her but allows me to wrap my hand around her forearm. She says, "It's common and it happens all the time. Thank god I have John Lewis." She hiccups, "He's such a good pup," which makes her both laugh and cry harder. Sam taps me on the shoulder. He wants to introduce me to one of the theatre's board members. "Go, go," says Fi, dabbing at her eyes. "Go!"

Taking me aside, Sam says, "That was very good. Let's meet soon to discuss next steps with the script," before leading me into the crowd of people again. I beam.

Audience members who I don't know form a queue to tell me what parts of the piece resonated with them. A couple of artistic programmers give me their cards. Milo says he feels inspired to date more people for shorter periods of time, and that this is the only piece of theatre he's liked in the last seven years.

Oh my god, I think. It's going to be a show. It's going to be a good show.

Just then a woman I don't know drapes an arm around me and says, "That was surreal." I clock that she has a Canadian accent as I hear her asking me if Typewriter is actually — and then she says his real name.

My mouth gapes.

On her phone, she shows me an email from Typewriter sent years ago, with an excerpt of a Rilke poem.

I want to unfold . . . I don't want to stay folded anywhere,
because where I am folded, there I am a lie.

Quite an ironic poem for a master manipulator to send, we agree.

"Though, to be fair," she says, "he got into recovery when we were together. So then I had a very different experience with him."

"Right," I say, erasing the smile from my face.

She says I might want to add something redemptive about him into the show. To indicate that he's not a sociopath, but an addict, and that that was guiding his duplicitous behaviour.

Sobered by this thought, I agree, "Good point."

"Still wouldn't recommend dating him though." She laughs and I join her.

On the bus home I wonder, Does the reason for Typewriter's shitty behaviour matter? Does it matter why someone treats us badly? Or is our experience with a person, how we felt in their company, the most important consideration? I think the reason why does matter, but only insofar as it's good to know that you weren't crazy; it was them behaving in an irrational way, their misprizing of you had nothing to do with your value as a person.

As the bus chugs up Archway Road, I think more. If I'm wrong about that, then certainly knowing why someone has treated you badly is not a reason to stay or forgive them. A relic from primary school pops into my head. "Forgiveness is earned and has to be asked for." I wonder if it holds water. I think I could only forgive someone who *hasn't* admitted their guilt and offered an apology if they're no longer in my life. My thoughts take on a judicious tenor. If they're still in my life — or want to be — then they have to take responsibility and make amends. And then say what they're going to do differently. And follow through on it.

As I descend the bus's stairs, my body is tossed into the railing. Once I regain my balance, I get it: forgiveness is earned through repeated actions over time. As I walk home, I refine this position; unless the other person is dead or completely out of my life, then it's up to me to forgive them or relinquish my anger.

This justifies the irritation I'm feeling towards T. True to form, as our next visit has approached, he's withdrawn. He'll be on an airplane in a matter of days. And face to face I can tell him what I really think, and he can prove to me why I should stay.

£ + ♥

On the sunny day T arrives we swim in the Hampstead Heath Mixed Pond and then head up to the lookout, where we lounge on our damp towels, devour blueberries and take pleasure in interlacing our fingers, silently exploring all the ways we might hold hands. His arm is healed, though still a bit weak, and he has a fresh scar above his right eye from where the stitches were.

Later, we attend the drop-in pottery session in Hackney City Farms. Sitting in tiny blue plastic chairs, we share a bottle of rosé and hand-mould cups out of clay. I experience total immersion in this creative task, a sensation I've scarcely felt since childhood. The man who runs the studio tells us to come back in a week to glaze our pots.

At the last minute, Navid has run off to Iceland to save his new relationship from perishing. There had been an opening at the Reykjavik office, but Navid neglected to apply for it. I only know this because I heard a play-by-play through the wall of the nun's cell. Ísleif schooled him about her reproductive odds.

Since getting real with myself and T about my desire, or lack thereof, to have a baby, I've been noticing that a lot of people want to procreate because they believe being a parent will give their life meaning. I guess it would, but it seems like a selfish reason to bring a person into the world. I'm stumped by this.

What then is the right reason to have a child? The world doesn't need us to increase its population.

Navid shouted, "What's the point of having a child if you can't afford to give them a good life?"

She screamed, "A good life isn't about money! It's about time together and love."

He said it's not so simple.

And she said, "It would be if you loved me."

With Navid gone, T and I don't have to be quiet when we have sex. T sleeps on the trundle bed that pulls out from beneath mine, which he affectionately calls "the shelf". Having him close but not on the same mattress is epiphanic: I am pro separate beds. We're close but I have my own zone to turn and kick blankets off my feet as regularly as suits me. The result is that we are both better rested. This is tremendous progress, we say to each other in a rowboat in Finsbury Park.

I don't touch the formula and I pause my rigorous self-imposed work schedule. There's a break in my medical role-play bookings. And I blow off my Inappropriately Attired improv rehearsal for cervix-knocking, spiritual, touching-of-god sex with T.

Four days into his visit I have a voice job. While I dash through Soho to the studio, T calls to tell me he's been offered a contract on a Canadian panel show that would pay $10k — but he'd have to cut his visit short by a week and leave tomorrow.

I'm in a flap. Blissed out by the sex we'd had this morning, I went the wrong direction on the Tube and I'm now running to make my gig. "When can you come back?" I ask.

He doesn't know. I hang up to get to the recording studio on time.

After my voiceover I call him. His speech is clipped. He's turned down the position.

"But I didn't ask you to do that!"

"You made it seem like it was that job or us. Not cool."

When I get back to the flat, I say, "You know I lost out on £30k when I came to Chicago."

"Great, so together we've lost 40k."

"Well, actually, yours is in Canadian dollars so it's more like £36.5k."

He doesn't find this funny. And good, because it was meant to be an insult.

I tell him I can't be punished for an assumption he made.

He says I'm right and that he's letting it go.

In an attempt to get the sweetness back, we return to the pottery studio. Our pots have been fired and are ready to be glazed, but the studio is an absolute stye and we can't locate T's creations. The towers of trays rammed with janky pottery overwhelm him.

"They're gone, Haley. Leave it," T commands as I search for his missing pots.

I lie on my stomach, reaching into tray after tray of baked clay, turning over little receptacles to search for T's initials. And, "Ta-da!"

Something about me doggedly hunting for his pots softens him. And his own handiwork makes him giddy. Surprised and grinning, studying his wares and holding them close to his face, I see the little boy in him. I love that kid.

Afterwards we share a romantic dinner at the farm's restaurant. When we almost slip into a disagreement because I feel he's hogging the booze, I manage to say, "You know what? I don't need to die on this hill," and we retrieve the warmth between us in the nick of time.

He reaches over the table, caresses my neck and kisses me. He tells me he loves me and looks up to me. "Your wisdom carries us."

We walk to the Tube, clutching each other, my arms around his waist and his around my shoulders.

On T's final day in London, I awake with hope.

Sleepy-faced and groggy, he reaches for me, "Come here, baby."

I roll off my tiny bed onto the shelf.

T blows his morning breath over my head and kisses me as passionately as possible with firmly closed lips.

"Let's make pancakes!" I say.

He agrees, but his response is less spirited than I would have liked.

He grabs a towel from the back of the door and heads to the shower. I throw on my housecoat and open the blind. Sun hits the cheese plant T carried back from the Columbia Road Flower Market the last time he visited. The mattress bounces under my feet as I spritz my face with rose water and dig the crust out of the corners of my eyes. In the kitchen I agonise over which podcast T will approve of and scoop coffee grinds into Navid's cafetière as the kettle boils.

When T tiptoes into the kitchen, towel wrapped snugly around his waist, I sense his impatience at my lack of progress.

"Hi hi," I say, eager to lift the mood, tapping his shoulders. "Coffee?"

"Uh . . . not right now." He gingerly touches my back then leaves to get dressed.

I get out a bowl and debate. If I do healthy pancakes I'll have to look up a recipe, or I can improvise traditional ones as Bicycle taught me to do (1 cup flour, 1 cup milk, then some oil, an egg, some lemon juice, bit of sugar, baking powder, pinch of salt). When T returns, I ask him what he'd prefer. He inspects the stove and sink and plunges the coffee but doesn't reply. When I ask him again, he uses his social-worker voice to tell me that either pancake is fine.

"Traditional then." I whirl around to pull open the fridge. Taking out the ingredients, I say, "Do you want to chop up some fruit and fry this bacon?"

"Sure," he says curtly.

I place my wet ingredients on the counter and track down the dry. "Maybe we can throw some ground flax in too, just for — you know — healthy."

T sets himself up at a cutting board. I hug him from behind and he pats my hand.

"Do you want water?" I ask reaching for the tap.

"I'm okay." It comes out in the tone of congenial finality that is so typically Canadian.

"Are you in a bad mood?" I ask.

"No." He turns to me. "But you have some image, some idea of how this morning goes and you're trying to . . ." He looks out the window ". . . force me into it."

My chipper demeanour disintegrates and I lean my forehead into the cupboard door. "I wanted to cook breakfast with you."

He abandons the kiwi he was slicing, jumping to make a point. "That's what I mean, you have this fantasy of us, happily making breakfast together and it's—"

"What's wrong with that?"

"You're annoyed, or disappointed with me, because I can't live up to this fantasy you have."

My voice gets shrill. "How is wanting to make breakfast with my boyfriend a fantasy?"

He reminds me he's not really a breakfast person.

"What would you rather do then?" It comes out as a challenge.

He says he doesn't know.

I deflate. "I just want to have a nice Sunday morning with you."

He says I give him too much power, he doesn't want to have this much control over how I feel.

I tell him I don't know how not to be affected by his moods.

Very softly he says, "I don't want you to be different. But I think you want a different guy."

"I don't want a different guy, I just want you to be happier."

"You want me to be different. I'm moody."

"Well, do you not want to eat these?" I hold up the wooden spoon, letting the batter gloop back into the bowl.

"Look, I'm doing the breakfast, but you can't dictate how I feel."

My heart hangs heavy between my ribs, my shoulders curl at its weight. I sigh. I want to argue that my request isn't unreasonable. But he got me. I did have a fantasy of making breakfast with my boyfriend. I did have an expectation that this would be loving and intimate and cosy, rather than stilted and cold, with him refusing coffee and trying to abdicate his participation. I want a judge to tell us who's right. By the time we eat we reach a muted okay-ness. We decide to spend the afternoon separately. I hate the idea of him not wanting to be around me, but the space that surrounds my thoughts when he's not in my vicinity calms me.

Within a couple hours, he texts me to say he misses me, but when we come back together the warm reunion is fleeting. I tell him about the law of diminishing returns. "When the profits or benefits gained are less than the amount of money or energy invested."

He chuckles and says he finally understands what my show is. We kiss until we're ravenous.

Over dinner at a Turkish restaurant, we argue about whether we're going to have sex later, until the argument becomes much bigger than sex. "You wanted this," I remind him.

"You can't hold me to something I said months ago, at the height of grief."

Yet by the time we walk back to Navid's, we've returned to "I love you and I'm sorry". And the sex is all mauve for me.

Afterwards he asks, "Why do we have to go through all this pain to come together?"

You tell me, I want to say, but I keep the blame to myself and look down on him on the shelf.

T leaves at 4 a.m. He texts, thanking me for a beautiful visit, before his plane takes off. I want to sleep in, but Pina arrives to clean the place before Navid's return. She met T when she was here last week. She drops her purse on the sofa and tells me that T is not the man for me. She says her sister had a man like him and now she's forty, the man has left her and she's very sad because she can never have a baby.

I nod slowly and say, "Yeah, it's hard to know what the right compromises are." And then I ask Pina if she likes being a mother.

She chuckles and says she liked it from when her son was three to five, and only again now that he's eighteen.

That afternoon I sit down with Sam in the theatre lobby.

His main notes are to stop adding threads and go for depth over breadth. "You're very charming, so an audience will follow you anywhere. But that's dangerous because you can get away with anything."

I clap my hands over my cheeks. "I know, I know — curse and a gift."

"The show is good as is, but it has the potential to be excellent." His directness once would have scalded me, but now I find it refreshing. He also thinks it's important that I write everything I need to, to get it all out. "Write to the end Haley — you need an ending. Then see what you have and begin the ruthless cull."

I ask if he has any instincts as to how I should end the piece.

He thinks for a bit and then says, "Maybe there's something in your own social currency — that idea of sitting too long on the shelf."

"Oh, ageing," I laugh.

"And growing up. Perhaps you're willing to renegotiate what you're prepared to settle for, given a shift in priorities." He also adds that no matter what happens with the grant, the theatre's committed to the project.

On the bus home I begin writing an ending for the show based on Sam's suggestion:

The formula works. We get a price for each of the objects. Haley puts a price tag on each of the objects and she tells us the sum total of all her assets. She says:

"So that's what all that is worth . . . that's the total value of my assets.

That's the answer."

Haley puts price stickers on herself with a price gun. This evolves into her ripping off her bubble wrap packaging. As she struggles:

"The entire time I've been working on this project, people have been asking me why dive into something so futile, so impossible, immeasurable and subjective?

I started this project needing money.

I had these objects, wondered about their worth.

When I started to take stock, I got scared that I'd invested all this time and emotion and the outcome is that I've become an expert in breaking up and the balance on the ledger was zero pounds.

I'm thirty-two.

I've had eight failed relationships, not including the myriad flings in between.

I'm tired of breaking up.

I'm tired of being poor.

I'm tired of shopping/selling/trading.

My values are changing, and I'm aware that, in broad cultural terms, my value is beginning to diminish.

So in this recalibration, I find myself ready to negotiate what I'm willing to pay for steady love and more money, for the kind of life that reflects my current values.

But to figure out what that is exactly, I'll need another formula."

I read it to Thea that evening. An unsettling pause follows.

"I hate this ending," I roar. "Never mind that it ends with a cheesy wink and groaner joke, it's not what I believe. It holds no hope. I don't want to hop on the cultural bandwagon and encourage people to resign themselves to a lacklustre, utilitarian relationship. I don't want this for myself."

Thea says, "Yes. I must admit, it didn't ring true to me."

When I tell her about the visit with T, she asks, "But how does it feel to be with him, Haley?"

"The opposite of fun."

She challenges me to interrogate why I withstand this painful dynamic. We talk and talk, and it becomes clear that the only way to transform what I have with T into the kind of relationship I want is to risk gunning for it — to truly ask for all that I desire from him, and let the chips fall where they may.

15. ROSE TINT CORRECTOR

*"Cynicism is the only tool that can scrape
away the tint off rose-coloured glasses."*
Taona Dumisani Chiveneko

I'm up at 6.30 a.m., hard at it. *The Ex-Boyfriend Yard Sale* has a premiere date. Tickets go on sale at the end of the month. The last ten weeks have been a rapturous affair with the project. Milo helped me put together a fundraising plan and shoot a video soliciting potential donors. A colleague who I met in Finland and runs a performance venue in the Netherlands has programmed the show for his next season and it looks like I'll be taking it to a festival in Toronto in the new year too. Milo and I will celebrate these favourable turns over pizza later. The second grant application was successful, which is a huge boon, and most miraculously, a voice job that I did for a bank months ago is now set to go on air and the buyout is £18,860 *after* the commission to my agent. This money will clear my credit card debt in one fell swoop, pay Thea the funds she's owed (the equivalent of £2,176.06), allow me to quit my Joe-jobs for the next three months through the run of the show, and invest in hiring a more robust team (£4k).

Once I received the money for the bank advert, I wondered if I should cancel the fundraising campaign. I felt guilty asking people for money to support my art when I had this influx of cash myself. Milo was appalled that I would use any of my own income towards my business. When I tried to explain that it was investment in a new venture — the UK expansion of Haley McGee Industries — he said that that was plain bad sense. I'd told the Arts Council that I'd fundraise a portion of my budget and I was well within my rights to do so. Moreover, I suspect he couldn't stand the thought of having spent several days shooting and editing my fundraising video only to have it shelved.

Still, after I prepared the crowdfunding page, I hesitated to go live with it. Thea came at me with questions about my self-worth and my limiting beliefs around money until eventually, worn down and exasperated, I told her, "Nobody likes a comfortable artist. It delegitimises. People like me because I'm scrappy and industrious."

Once we bashed through the many stories I tell myself about money and my value, and she convinced me that this was a narrative I was imposing on myself, I summoned the confidence to press 'publish' on my crowdfunding campaign and began sending emails and posting chipper videos inviting people to donate.

Otherwise, I took Sam's advice and in a few feverish weeks I wrote "the draft I needed to", ending up with a sixty-thousand-word tome. It took six hours to read aloud. Elson patiently sat on Skype with me while I plodded through it during our third R&D week.

Now I should be prioritising the script and the math. But when Navid comes in, cologned and buttoned up in a freshly ironed shirt and holding a protein shake, paper, string, tape and bubble wrap have exploded over the living room. I'm creating one of the key props for the show so I can begin to work with it and understand how it'll shape the text.

"You're up early."

"I feel crazy," I laugh.

I'm sipping coffee and sitting on the floor in my housecoat, careful to keep my legs together. I don't wear underwear with my loose-fitting pajama shorts. I'm tying short bits of string to another string on a spool.

"Getting crafty," he says. "I like it."

"Yeah. It's — it's a timeline of my relationship with T."

"Oh my days." He surveys the mess I've made of his living room. "Early doors for this?"

"I want to stretch it across the stage in my show."

I carefully follow the sketch I've done in my notebook. Each arm's length of the string — my wingspan — represents a year of my life. I then divide each wingspan into twelve equal sections, each representing a specific month. Periods of time when T and I were in the same city are marked by short pieces of white string tied to the big, long string. They dangle vertically. The longer the dangling string, the better the sex we were having during that time. Periods of time when we were in touch but not in the same city are denoted by orange electrical tape wrapped around the horizontal string. And when there was nothing — silence between us — the string is bare.

We begin rehearsal in two months, not the long runway I'd like. I have to slash and burn the script into a ninety-minute show; Gem and I have to complete the formula; we've got to film a video trailer, flyers need to be printed, Facebook ads need to be designed and scheduled. In lieu of paying myself the salary I allocated in the budget, I've chosen to heave as much money as possible at hiring people who will save me time and stress. I've hired a 21-year-old to oversee all the social media marketing, and a PR company to write and distribute the media release and drum up preview press and reviews. I've got a graphic designer on board. A stage manager is on board, and so are designers for lights and sound, and a scenic design consultant who is going to make beautiful my janky ideas. I have interviews lined up with three potential producers, so I can outsource the business side of putting this show up. A producer's job is to oversee the administration of a project

— contracting, liaising with the venue, organising a tour, buying insurance, managing the marketing and publicity campaigns.

Navid, still in the doorway, sips his shake. "So Haley, I wanted to talk to you about your plans for next year." He's shifting his weight from one foot to the other as he speaks. "I'm going to move up to Reykjavik." He says Ísleif put her foot down and since she's the most extraordinary person he's ever met, he's going to go next March. At that point they will have been together for a year. "Fuck it. You know?"

I'm holding the orange electrical tape taut with my teeth while I use my hands to measure and cut it. I snip and the tape floats down to my bare leg. Navid watches me, waiting for a reply.

"Okay. Wow," I say. "Big changes." The impact of this barely registers. It's only August now. March is a long way off and I'm too engrossed with the task at hand to give much credence to what his move will mean for me.

Navid nods. "So here's what I'm thinking. Ideally T comes and you two have the place. You could use your room for guests, or Airbnb it, if you need cash."

"That would be ideal," I say, fiddling with tape that's stuck in the wrong place.

Navid asks what the plan is with T at the moment.

Smoothing out this rogue piece of tape, I tell him I don't know. "It's hard for T to make plans far in advance because of how journalism works."

"Not good. You need a plan."

I make a guttural noise and tilt my neck back, resting my head on the seat of the armchair behind me. "I know."

Navid wipes his mouth.

"Look." I hold up the string. "It's been almost four years since I met him."

"That's why people can never go back." He shakes his head, knowingly. "I told you, things end for a *reason*."

"I know!" I cry. "If only I listened to my love guru."

Navid raises his shake to me and polishes it off with a slurp before tossing the plastic cup into the sink. "So I shouldn't bank on him living here with you then," he calls from the kitchen.

"No."

Navid hovers in the doorway of the living room as he pulls on his shiny shoes. "I thought he was going to get a passport?"

I shrug at this and keep tying 'better sex' strings to year three.

"When you know, you know. These things should be easy decisions." At that he throws his laptop bag over his shoulder. "Peace." And he's out the door.

With some effort I stand up. My right foot is asleep. I limp a little as I attach the string to the expensive lamp and the door frame.

Nearly four years of increasingly good sex punctuated with time on the phone and swathes of silence. Or maybe a better way to look at it is, four years of time on the phone or no talking at all, punctuated by sex that incrementally improved. It's still my favourite sex. And I'm not sick of it yet.

Later Fi calls and tells me she and Ru are going away for ten days. She got pregnant again after her miscarriage, only to have another miscarriage three weeks later. They're going to Santorini on what she calls "a self-directed fertility retreat" because they have to do something about the stress they're under. She wants to know if I can stay in their house, take care of John Lewis and water their plants.

"Happily," I say.

When we hang up, I call T and tell him I'll have Fi's house for ten days and he should come to London.

His voice is weary as he apologises. He's sorry he can't afford the time or money right now. He asks what I've been up to.

I tell him I've been making props for the show.

"You sound annoyed with me, babe."

I explain that I've just created a timeline of all our false starts and periods of silence. "I'm scared the pattern is never going to change."

T manages to laugh. "I think you'd like me more if you spent less time with a version of me and our relationship that no longer exists."

I concede that it's not great to have someone dredging up old hurts.

"And," he says, "isn't this 'The *Ex-Boyfriend* Yard Sale'? Why am I in the show if we're still together?"

I don't really know how to justify it, but I feel it's right. I say things like, "We were broken up when I started it," and, "I only talk about our relationship up till the point where we broke up at the airport."

He sighs and says everyone will know it's about him.

I assure him I've changed identifiable details and I'm referring to my exes by using the names of the objects they gave me.

"Reducing us all to objects? Cute."

This mollifies me. "You're cute." We indulge a moment of "no, you're cute" repartee.

"I love you, Haley," he says softly.

"I know, T. And I know me getting whipped up about the past is annoying, but I don't know how not to when we don't have a plan for the future."

A harried edge appears in his tone. He says there are too many unknowns with his work at the moment. "But all I know is that I can't do long distance forever."

I press him on when he'll have more information about work.

He's not sure.

I ask how therapy is going.

It turns out he hasn't been able to afford a session in months. He asks if I'd consider removing him from the show.

"No."

"But you have to cut four and half hours of material, Haley. Surely some of the exes are on the chopping block?"

"No. They're not and you're definitely not. You're my — you're the—"

"I don't want to be the villain of this piece."

"You're not! You're the heart of the show."

Suddenly he's crying.

And I'm consoling him from 3,459 miles away, affirming his benefit in my life. I tell him he taught me to fight and recover. I tell him I love it when he calls me out for being sanctimonious. I tell him the sex is better than anything else I've known. I tell him that I've never dated someone who I hope to know forever, no matter the outcome, whose opinion I prize above all others. And I say, "If it doesn't work out, I really hope that in our sixties, we're great friends who laugh about the years we spent trying to date."

He says he doesn't want to be my friend; he wants to be with me. He says he's sorry; he's just afraid that people will hate him and tell me to leave him. He says he'll think about how we might plan. He doesn't say he'll come here for ten days but I hang up feeling closer to him.

£ + ♥

This morning I woke up to my monthly email from the astrologer at the health shop in Crouch End all about Saturn Return. Saturn Return is an astrological phenomenon that occurs when the planet Saturn returns to the same position it was in when you were born, for the first time in your life. *This happens between the ages of 27–31, which is how long it takes Saturn to make a trip around the sun.* Astrologers consider it a powerful period in one's life: *a bat mitzvah for the soul. It's a time of returning to the true self and making big changes.*

I entered my Saturn Return as I was dating Backpack, only I didn't know it then. After Typewriter, I wanted someone adoring and besotted. I got it with Backpack, but I couldn't give it back. When we met, he'd been retired from his career as a professional lacrosse player for a couple years and was working as a sous chef in a swanky restaurant. His roommate, an actor I'd gone to theatre school with, served tables there. They came to see me perform an excerpt of my show about romantic gestures, *I'm Doing This for You*. Backpack fell in love with my onstage persona. I fell for his good looks and admiration of my talent. Stay in the game long enough and you'll play both sides of every dynamic that's ever rubbed you the wrong way.

Backpack enjoyed a blemish-free life. Literally, I don't think he ever had a zit or went through an awkward physical phase. His skin was creamy and his thick hair never cowlicked sideways or fluffed up like a baby bird; he kept it tightly shorn. I'd lie in bed, tracing the crisp line from his temple, over his ear and across the nape of his neck. His Grecian-sculpture body perpetually smelled like soap. Hands down he is the most objectively beautiful person I've been with. He also spent more time gazing at his reflection in the mirror than anyone else I've known.

Backpack provided the lustiest beginning to a romance I've ever experienced. The first time we kissed was at a house party. We flung our bodies around a storage room, breathlessly tussling on its industrial green carpet. I lost a pearl earring, a sixteenth-birthday gift from my father — mark that down as Collateral Damage — and in our reckless frenzy I whacked my shin against some large piece of metal, acquiring a bruise that outlasted the eleven months of our relationship. Back at my place, we stripped down to our underwear, gorged on dark chocolate and mauled each other, laughing the whole time. The sex itself transpired as a silly after thought. He left for work before I woke up. On my desk was a note that read *I like you* with his number below.

That evening, sitting with Backpack in the basement of an Ethiopian restaurant about to watch an experimental theatre performance, a woman about my age tapped me on the shoulder and asked if I was Haley McGee. I was flattered at being recognised and doubly chuffed that Backpack's narrative about me being a fantastic artist was being stoked. But she wasn't asking for the reason I expected.

"Did you date Typewriter?" She seemed to be imploring me.

Queasiness sloshed in my guts as I tentatively told her I had.

Typewriter had just dumped her. She was the person he'd moved on to by Christmas. Five months had now passed.

I told her I was sorry and offered to go for a coffee and talk about him sometime.

She said she'd love that. "What happened has messed me up so much."

Out of the corner of my eye, I recognised Backpack's jaw twitch as faltering stoicism and rescinded my offer. I apologised and told her I should have thought before I suggested that. "Don't worry about it," she said and returned to her seat. The lights dimmed and I turned back to Backpack, reaching out for his chiselled thigh. He put his hand on mine and squeezed.

We swam through our first three weeks together in a perpetually turned-on, full-blown lust attack. I was too jittery to eat, too horny to sleep. I was in a production of *Uncle Vanya* at the time, funnelling all my lust for Backpack into Sonya's feelings for Astrov.

The stage manager had to take my skirt in, I shrank in size so quickly. I counted the hours till our sleepless nights. So this is what it is to be lovesick, I thought.

One Sunday evening, after he'd worked the brunch shift and I'd had a matinee, he came into my kitchen, pushed me up against the refrigerator, pulled off my shorts and went down on me. I watched the magnetic poetry fly to the floor as I writhed.

He said, "There's a wildness to you. I love it and it scares me."

Whatever web of a persona I was spinning had trapped him entirely. I started to feel guilty, ashamed even, that I was earning more money than he was. I had toiled away slow and steady since theatre school and it was finally paying off, whereas he barely scraped by on his chef's wage, but was resolved to pay his restaurant-industry dues without complaint. His lacrosse career came to an abrupt end when he tore his ACL. He explained to me that because lacrosse is a "non-core" sport, the money is terrible. Though he was lucky to land a couple sponsorships, which he feared were less thanks to his abilities and more about his good looks, all the money he'd earned from them was long gone. An only child, he never knew his father, but his mother had been with her girlfriend since Backpack was twelve. Sometimes he lent his mum money. She liked to play the slots. I thought the fact that he had moved to another volatile industry without a safety net was incredibly sexy.

After three weeks together, I lent him money to cover his rent and then I was off on out of town gigs. Thirty-one of the forty-nine weeks we were together, I was away working, which means 63 per cent of our relationship was an LDR.

He'd insist that I call him when I had insomnia. "Wake me up and I'll be there with you."

I did. I said to him, "I wanna talk to you on the phone every day. I need to."

And he said, "I need to talk to *you* every day. I was worried about coming on too strong."

The weeks apart increased our libidinal desires but because I was working six days a week and he didn't have a driver's licence, it was difficult for him to get to rural Ontario to see me. The first time he managed to, when he saw me waiting for him at the station, he told me he "got off that bus the way people in movies get off buses".

Our sex was acrobatic and rowdy and uninhibited, neither of us looking the other in the eye, but totally immersed in our own physical sensations. That night, as we lay on the floor, his asthma reacting to the spores in my poorly ventilated accommodation, we professed our love for the first time, fervently, desperately, our arms clapped around the other's naked form, unable to hold each other with more urgency. We remained clung through the night, preferring to be sealed together than drift apart in sleep. A song called "Under Your Spell" became our anthem.

The next time he was supposed to visit, he went out with the staff the night before and missed his train in the morning, then refused to apologise. But he found a rideshare and had a three-course meal waiting for me after my evening performance. It was the moistness of his lips when he bowed his head to me that made me instantly forgive him, though.

Then his apartment got bedbugs and his roommate booked a TV series that was shooting in South Africa for six months. He looked at upwards of twenty apartments within his budget, all of which were dumps.

"You should just move in with me." I said it as a joke but then we both got serious. "Actually. Move in with me."

"Really?" he asked, holding his hand over his mouth.

My crotch was hot at the thought of him in my space every day. "Yes. Would we be okay? I think we'd be okay."

"I think we'd be okay too. I want to." It was fast, he said, but "when it's right, you know".

We agreed that the worst that could happen was that he'd move out. The day I got back from out of town, he showed up with his TV, two boxes filled with his various protein shake paraphernalia, a few posters of athletes that I vetoed going up on the walls, four extra-large suitcases and three small ones. My aunt Harlow had given me a bird's eye maple dresser for him, one of her yard sale finds, but even that wasn't big enough for all his clothes and we had to buy two shoe racks for all his footwear.

Technically Backpack and I lived "together" in my apartment for thirty-six weeks, but in actuality, I was only in town for fifteen of them cumulatively. The rest of the time I was living the life of a gigging Canadian theatre actor and out of town working on a variety of projects. The twenty-one remaining weeks, he had the run of the place with his weights and tubs of peanut butter and recipe books.

Financially I took a hit to cohabitate, splitting the rent with him rather than have it covered while I was out of town by a sub-letter. The monetary loss ($103.85 pw x 21 wks = $2,180.85) seemed like an appropriate sacrifice for our new life together. I was less keen, however, to accept our fizzling sexual connection. I still wanted it, but echoing what previously happened with Typewriter and Bicycle, he'd grown increasingly disinterested and resistant. Though unlike Typewriter and Bicycle, he remained otherwise romantic and affectionate; he just didn't want to get naked. What was so off-putting about me, I wondered — was it my labia, or my small boobs, or my face? My tactics — wailing about my physical insecurities or demanding sex — proved ineffective in negotiation. He got stand-offish and quiet. We lived together like this in the apartment for a few weeks before I was off again, this time to Europe.

Our correspondence was sweet but not nearly as erotic as our previous time apart. When I returned from overseas, I hoped my absence would have stoked his desire, but our sex life was entirely laboured and fraught. He'd hold me on the sofa but didn't want to make out and if I reached for his groin, he'd bat my hand away. Around this time, I was in the running for a role in a show that would have taken me out of Toronto for six consecutive months. Backpack heard me tell the artistic director of the company that I'd give my fingernails to be cast and didn't speak to me for the rest of the evening. That night in bed he admitted he'd been hoping I wouldn't get the job. I couldn't discern whether he was jealous of the work or didn't want me to go. But after several call-backs, I did get the job. And after a few more weeks, I was off again.

On tour in France, a dancer made an advance on me. He was Yemeni and was risking imprisonment by taking part in this festival that included Israeli artists. I liked the attention from someone who was risking so much for his art. I let him kiss me on our final night. Pressing his hard-on into my pantyhose, he told me that he would come to Canada and catch me. I had just turned twenty-seven.

Over breakfast at the festival, I chatted to a Spanish translator in her late fifties who had had various long-term relationships. She told me that she'd only get married if she knew she was dying, so she could leave all her money to her partner.

A vivacious sixty-year-old Israeli actress chimed in. "A romance is the cherry on top but not the cake. I have the cake already — my life is entirely mine and I never make false compromises."

I admitted I was miserable with my current boyfriend, but I was also so tired of going through break-ups. I wanted to know when it would just work.

But this is why we travel, to find ourselves in unexpected conversations over a breakfast of fresh baguettes and jam, and then return home with a gigantic paradigm shift about what a good life might look like. In this instance, when I came home my whole place reeked of dirty gym bag and peanut butter. And there was no dish soap.

I flipped at this. "I subsidise your life and you can't replace the dish soap."

He said, "It's nice to see you too."

I half-heartedly took it back and fobbed off my crankiness on PMS. But he'd turned stony and silent, refusing to admit fault.

Because we'd told each other we loved each other early on, I felt I had to stay and fight for the relationship. But I wanted to bolt. Actually, I wanted him out of my house. As my respect for him abated, his face morphed from a specimen of idolised beauty to a heavy-browed asymmetrical puddle, cloudy and remote. He'd cuddle and kiss me when we'd watch TV together, but we had no sensual or sexual intimacy. At best, it was like being a middle-aged couple, too tired to screw but pleased in each other's company, and at worst, awful sexual rejection. With our sex life shrivelling down to nothing, our arguing ramped up to near constant.

He always had an excuse: too tired, not in the mood, distracted by something at the restaurant. If I pushed it, he'd pick a fight. When I'd barter with him, suggesting that if he wasn't in the mood, why didn't he just get me off, he'd refuse, saying that that wasn't balanced or "right". Then I'd go silent, exposed as a lusty, insatiable horny pervert. My sexual frustration compounded as I spent more evenings lying awake beside him, not confident enough to just make myself come.

So after my encounter with the Yemeni dancer in France, I had no moral qualms with lying by omission about it. If Backpack didn't want me, I figured, then I'd go where I was wanted.

Reflecting on this now, I wonder, why did I withhold that information? What dignity was I trying to maintain? Was I trying to preserve my no-fault, no-offences, no-fouls record? I wanted the break-up to be all his fault. I wanted him to carry all the blame for our relationship's demise. I didn't feel guilty about what I'd done. The misgivings I still have with my behaviour back then are around my staying and pretending I was committed to making it work. In truth, I didn't want to stay in one place. My career was my love. I knew that I didn't want a boyfriend anymore. Averse to owning these truths, I avoided the difficult conversation and implicated his failings as the only reason we ended.

After a month without sex, I attempted to initiate it one morning, and he rolled away. A thin line formed in me and my body moved efficiently, without thought. I slipped out of bed, gathered his protein shake accoutrements, cookbooks, specialised oils and professional knives, and lined them up like soldiers on the kitchen counter. I took the low-cost peanut butter out of the fridge and sriracha from the table and added them to the army. I washed his reusable coffee cup in the sink and surveyed the kitchen for stray signs of him while it dried. Out of the freezer I removed his frozen ribs, peas and his icepacks for muscle aches. I stood very still, holding my breath, but I couldn't hear him moving at all. I took the reusable grocery bag I least cared about and, without rustling it, moved the army of his goods into it one by one. My territory once again, I cleaned the kitchen. I used my fingernails to pick hardened bits of avocado and red cabbage off plates, wiped down the table, the counters, the sides of the fridge, the stovetop. I opened the window to let some fresh air in. He hadn't stirred. Unsure how much time had passed, I calmly returned to the bedroom. He was awake now, lying in bed, staring at the ceiling. I changed out of my pajamas into clothes. I even put a pair of running shoes on.

Armed and prepared, I addressed him. "I've packed up your stuff. You can't stay here anymore."

He nodded and said he understood.

In silence, he got dressed and I helped him fill his suitcases with his clothes and shoes.

At one point he asked, "Is this the right thing to do?"

I said, "Yes."

He cracked his knuckles one by one and then told me I was half his life.

He was gone within the hour.

I think a person can only be sexually rejected so many times before their desire is extinguished. Maybe in a more established, mature or compatible partnership it could be rekindled, but despite Backpack telling me he was still in love with me for over a year after it ended, I had no interest in reviving it.

I liked that he still idolised me while I was rejecting him. It gave me a sense of settling the score.

Still intimidated by his aesthetic sense and unparalleled good looks, I sweat when putting myself together for the interview with Backpack. The first thing he tells me when we Skype is that several years after we broke up he had a dream in which he got dropped off at an institute that I happened to be the director of, and where many of the other women he'd dated over the years also worked. In the dream, I called him into my office and told him that we needed to amputate his legs. When Backpack shared the dream with his therapist, he wanted to know what part of his body Backpack most valued. Naturally, Backpack answered, "My legs."

"So," Backpack laughed, "that's my interpretation of the cost of love."

We talk about the backpack itself. He reminds me of the dirty yellow bag I'd been using since high school when we met, how it was ripped and falling apart. I tell him I've worn the bag he got me into the ground as well.

"You're hard on things," he says.

"I get my money's worth," I reply, and we laugh a little.

When we talk about the day he moved out, he chokes up.

"You know when I watched um, *Nocturnal Animals* actually—"

"Yeah, I saw that film," I say.

"Do you remember that line Jake Gyllenhaal says about love in it?"

"What does he say?"

"He says, 'Love is precious'—". His voice breaks and he swallows. "And you have to be careful with it, 'cause you never know when you're going to get it again'. And I dunno. I dunno

I just — I — when I think back to that day, and like, I remember being — afterwards, being like, 'Why didn't I speak up? Why did I just go along with it? Why didn't I fight for it?' And I just wished that at that time, I had said what was on my mind, and at least we could have talked about what had been going on between us, whether we were going to stay together or not."

"I think I . . . started to shut down, or put up the Berlin Wall of Haley, when I felt like you didn't want to have sex with me anymore. It killed something in me and once it was dead . . ." I shrug apologetically.

"You know when we would fight about sex and I — I'm still bad at talking about my emotions, but then I was a thousand per cent worse. So, for me, a big way to express love is physically. And I was not happy about you being gone all the time . . . and I think I felt like you were going to leave me, and so, to protect myself, I pulled away physically. But, uh—"

"It's so wild that we do these things to protect ourselves and yet—" I begin to say.

"Just — sorry — hold on. When you'd ask if I wanted you, or if I was attracted to you, the crazy thing was I was so attracted to you. I'd fantasise about you, and I wanted to say, 'No, no that's not it, I — I love you so much.' But I — I couldn't explain it then and, yeah . . ." He closes his eyes and grimaces.

I want to say something by way of taking responsibility, but all I manage is, "And I interpreted your actions and silence to mean a totally different thing — I made it about my attractiveness. Ugh that's awful."

He raises his chin. "Yeah."

When we hang up, I listen to the recording of this exchange over and over and contemplate the imbalance of our reactions to our split. I shudder, thinking, how can a shared event elicit such divergent responses?

After we broke up, I decided it hadn't been love between us after all, merely blinding lust. But I see now that for him, it was love. I hate that this kind of unequal love exists. Because if it's true in this configuration, it's probable that the people who I thought I loved just a little bit more than they loved me, maybe I loved a lot more. Or maybe I loved them, and they didn't love me at all? In the early days with T, I once declared to Thea that unrequited love isn't real. I said, "Love is a reciprocated feeling that exists between two people. Yearning after someone who doesn't feel it back isn't actually love."

Her response was: "Well, Haley, that point of view discredits some of the best poetry, music, literature and art that has ever existed."

"Right," I said, before we both broke into laughter. And it hit me. I didn't want to admit I might love someone who didn't love me back. I didn't want that to be a possibility.

£ + ♥

"The number seven has no balls," I say.

"What?"

I'm treating Gemma to breakfast in a café in Finsbury Park. We were supposed to meet at my place, but it turns out that Navid is working from home several days this week; my room is too cramped for a work session and the TV is too distracting.

I tell Gemma I heard it on a podcast. "Seven is a lukewarm, cop-out number. Some business tycoon said it. Eight, nine, ten are clearly positive. Six and down — obviously bad. But seven hovers in the no man's land of indecision or politeness. If we eliminate seven, we get strong choices."

Gem agrees, "We definitely want to do strong math."

We decide the number seven must be stricken from our qualitative data. Which means anything rated on a scale from one to ten cannot receive a seven. Anywhere in the spreadsheet

277

there had been a seven, I have to choose either six or eight. But Gemma also wants to discuss something else. She's written a very short but essential phrase for the formula to counteract how my nostalgia was affecting the numbers. It assesses how much time has passed between the break-up and my filling in the spreadsheet, and then, if applicable, how much time has passed between speaking to my ex and filling in the spreadsheet, and if there have been changes or discrepancies between the two.

She was right to do this. After interviewing my exes, I'd snuck into the spreadsheet and increased their scores. Especially after talking with Backpack and understanding the break-up from his point of view.

We title the new phrase the Rose Tint Corrector.

But I'm stuck on Gemma's point that because I am not interviewing all of my exes, the conversations I do have unfairly colour some of my assessments. When I toss out the controversial idea that perhaps we should ask my exes to fill out their own spreadsheets, we debate whether the exes' feelings should be factored into the formula. After a while we decide, no. In the spirit of the history of yard sales, which originated as a way for a ship owner to get rid of unclaimed goods after long journeys, the system should be kept as is.

"I'm the ship's owner. My exes are my former passengers. The objects I have are the goods they left behind after their journeys with me."

"Exactly," says Gemma. "Which means the price of the objects should be determined between you, the ship's owner, and the public. The price has nothing to do with your 'former passengers' anymore."

However, when I ask about those instances when being reminded of an ex's point of view overtakes me with guilt, shame or regret, Gemma and I come up with a new Wild Card that addresses the phenomenon of pain I've inflicted continuing to haunt me. We produce the "I Did Bad Shit" Wild Card, which accounts for the feelings of guilt, shame or regret one may still carry long after a relationship ends. For example, if you still feel bad about hooking up with a Yemeni dancer and never coming clean about it.

'I DID BAD SHIT' WILD CARD

The inverse of the "Bad Shit Happened To Me" Wild Card, this captures how much fun I had while I was doing the bad shit (6/10), how well I got away with it (10/10), how well I apologised (1/10) minus the red flags he ignored (8/10); the law of diminishing returns is also here, where x equals the number of times I did the bad shit (1) multiplied by the percentage of the relationship I was engaging in the shitty behaviour (21 per cent).

On my jaunt home via the Parkland Walk, I call Ollie. He's railroaded himself onto the dating apps, but with each new person he meets, he thinks, "This isn't how it felt with my ex, so what's the point?"

"You need a Rose Tint Corrector, Ollie! You're viewing the past through rosy glasses."

He says the lens his ex sees him through is now a shit cloud. After twenty minutes on that chestnut, Ollie tells me he was offered a job teaching at a university in Singapore.

"That's fantastic!" I exclaim as I manoeuvre around a family of cyclists.

Ollie's worried taking it will fuck up his chances with his ex.

I hold the microphone on my earbuds close to my mouth and say, "Oh my god, Ollie — GO!"

He says he wants to keep the door open, just in case.

"Nothing is more attractive than someone who has moved on."

"The relationship coaching bot said as much." In lieu of hiring a therapist as the lawyer advised, he's been writing in to advice podcasts and doing Internet quizzes. When I challenge him on why he's resisted therapy, he tells me therapy is a racket. "They have you in the basement, looking for cracks in the foundation, hunting for mould and water damage, and next thing you know, the house is down to its skeletal form and it'll be years before it's rebuilt."

"But it's so worth it to redesign the whole thing from the ground up."

He says he really just wants a fresh coat of paint, a deep clean and some new curtains. He tells me he's not like me. He wants to live and *do* things. Not everyone wants to exist in a meta space, constantly dissecting their experiences.

"Well if you want to be a doer," I say defensively, now pacing outside Navid's flat, "then you should take the Singapore job."

Later that night I receive an email from Gemma with an updated draft of the broad formula. She says she'll explain in more depth why she's divided the RI by 1,000, but generally speaking, it has to do with tempering the prices.

DRAFT 2

$$\text{COST OF } \heartsuit = MV \times \left[1 + \frac{NI-t}{t}\right] \times \left[1 + \frac{RI}{1000}\right] \times RTC \times WC$$

280

Legend:

MV — Market Value

NI — Narrative Impact

t — Time Invested

RI — Relationship Index

RTC — Rose Tint Corrector

WC — Wild Cards

£ + ♥

I luxuriate during my ten days in Fi's house. I take over her dining table with my draft of the show, record fundraising update videos from the back garden, and host Milo for brunch. He's all business with tips for donor engagement and thoughts on the lighting design for the show until, on his way out the door, a mishmash of one-night-stand anecdotes tumble from his mouth.

That evening, John Lewis lies on my stomach as I talk to my brother. Kian never demands a call but today he was adamant that we speak. Like Backpack, he too has been perturbed by a dream.

After graduating from a prestigious business school, Kian moved from one "golden handcuff" job to another, earning heartily but with negligible autonomy over his time. The move to Vancouver was meant to get him closer to the mountains so he could partake in his favourite hobby, snowboarding, but he's still miserable.

In the dream, he was walking along a footpath in the woods, somewhere in Frontenac County, where we went canoe camping as children — jagged rocks, coniferous trees and freshwater lakes, untameable and empty. He came across a sign saying that he could fish at this particular spot for free. So he parked it and started pulling up fish. But the fish were rotten and deformed. Nonetheless, he collected his rotten fish in a bucket.

As he fished, his various friends and family members would pass by, pausing to ask him what he was doing. They'd remark that he'd never be able to eat these fish. To which my brother always replied, "Yeah, but I can fish here for free."

When he woke up, he realised that every day he was dying instead of living.

I'm biting my tongue. I want to shriek, "Hallelujah!" but instead I say, "Wow."

He tells me he'd been feeling off for a while but assumed that's just what being an adult felt like — a lot of dissatisfaction.

"So what do you want to do?" I ask.

He says he wants to blow it all up. He has an "Oh Shit" fund with six months' living expenses saved up. His plan is to sell his car, quit his job and spend one month in a different place around the world, beginning with the Galápagos Islands, where he wants to volunteer to help save endangered marine iguanas. "I guess I just needed to talk to someone who'd tell me to pull the trigger."

"You have to. You have to. Pull the trigger. Liberate yourself." I speak so forcefully that John Lewis topples off my stomach. "Delay no more," I say, picking the dog back up.

I listen as he pens his resignation letter and books his flight. It's thrilling to witness.

In the excitement I forget to mention to Kian that there seems to be a market where my artifacts feed other creative work. I got a message through Gumtree from an art director designing a film set in 2013 who is willing to pay two hundred and fifty pounds for my tattered denim Hershel backpack.

Inspired by Kian's boldness, within a week I've crossed the ocean to hole up in a cabin with T, a few hours north of his hometown. It's only three nights and has cost me hundreds, but life is precious, and I don't want to waste it. T's not perfect, what we have is not perfect, but there are no illusions about what it is, and it's mine. That's a strong foundation to build from, surely.

We spend the first two days canoeing and having sex. He's cheerful in this setting and an ease flows between us. On our final evening, sitting at the kitchen table, when the conversation inevitably turns to our relationship, I seize on the opening, pulling out my notebook so I don't sell myself short while I lay my cards on the table.

I hug my knees to my chest and close my eyes before speaking. "I want a partner who is *in* my life. I want us to be in a plan together, to hold a vision that we're both working towards. I want to plan and implement the plan to make it happen, together. And I want you to want that too.

"I want open, easeful communication. When problems arise, I want a relationship where we don't stuff them down or tiptoe around or wallpaper over, but deal with them in real time and with the expertise of two people who really know themselves and each other's inner lives — taking care of each other's soft spots and scars, and wounds.

"I want our relationship to be warm and playful and fun in a deep soulful way, not a frenetic or manic way. Though of course I want to joke around and delight in each other's ideas and silliness and company.

"I want us to laugh together. A lot. A sense of, 'I can't wait to tell T about this, because *he* will get it'. And I want to think of how you'd react to something and for the very thought of your reaction to make me laugh. I want to remember the jokes we've created together and to laugh out loud at them when we're apart.

"I want us to be able to have animated discussions about art but for them to never turn personal. And I want us to be experts at fighting well and recovering quickly.

"I want there to be a sensual quality to our interactions. To run our hands over each other as we cross paths in our home.

And I want sexy moments in the kitchen with you grabbing my bum and pulling me in to kiss before we both move on to do something else. I want us to keep making out, not just as a precursor to sex, but because it preserves romance. And it's scientifically proven to keep couples happier and bonded. And when the sexual desire between us fades, I want us to be able to laugh and talk about it, and enjoy the process of rekindling.

"I love that we value each other's opinions and respect each other's minds — of course, I want to keep that. But I want to add snuggling on the sofa, dancing in the living room, dancing at parties, dancing at weddings, to our repertoire. I want to be with someone who loves to dance as much as I do. And I want sex regularly — in our king-sized bed, in our walk-in shower, on the sofa, on the floor of my home office, in my recording studio.

"I want us to live in a three-bedroom house near Hampstead Heath and to spend Christmases together — for it to be a time that's ours and not something that we hand over to our families. I want us to be able to go on *restful* holidays together — spending time in the sun, reading, eating great food, making love and going on walks and exploring places like Greece and Italy and Croatia ... France ... the hits. Spain, Portugal. Morocco. Brazil. Tibet.

"I want us to want to spend the same amount of time together as we do apart, so there's no conflict around that.

"I want a relationship where we both grow and evolve and support each other's growth and evolution, while we maintain individual lives and friends and pursuits. Where we admire what the other one does. And where, when tragedy strikes, we hold each other. We seek balance over tit-for-tat. We consider our love languages. We're generous with each other, through actions. Where we are committed to our life together.

"People feel welcome in our home and at ease when they're with us. We're one of those couples it's a pleasure to be around because we don't work out our issues in front of friends, because we don't need to, because we did it in real time with our system when the issue arose, and so it hasn't festered or grown. And if conflict does arise in front of pals, we'll feel safe filing it away, trusting we'll address it later.

"We have a sectional sofa in our living room. There's a record player and a sound system that you're in charge of.

"Dog? Cat? Baby? All strong maybes for me — I'm not convinced about any, but you could convince me. Convince me.

"The sex will deepen, and we'll explore new territory together. We'll do things that are vulnerable and scary — all my experience so far has been very vanilla — I want our sex and sexual exploits to be something we really enjoy together.

"Oh — Money. We will have our money under control. We will live in abundance and within our means. We'll have enviable communication around money. We'll discuss our value systems, ingrained and unhelpful beliefs around money, and our financial goals. We'll each have our *own* money and we'll be aligned on the kind of life we desire.

"Mostly we'll have great communication around all things. We won't repress and we'll be adept at resolving our scuffles.

"What else? We'll have nice silences. We'll enjoy cooking and sharing meals just the two of us. We'll love each other well but we'll love ourselves best — we won't be co-dependent. We'll be connected and deeply content.

"That's what I want. That's what I'm interested in building with you."

I look up from my knees. T is running his finger over the rim of his empty wine glass.

"Wow. That sounds like a good life, Haley."

I wait for him to say more, but instead he sits in silence, picking at his nails. "Wow . . . I — wow. You have it all mapped out."

"That's what I want." I suddenly feel very tired. Deflated by his lack of enthusiasm after pouring all that out, I go and lie on the sofa. "Now you go."

He refills his glass. "I . . . I don't know as much I . . . It all sounds good, but I — I can't see myself in it. I want — I want to want it, but I don't see it."

Hand over my forehead, I ask him what he sees.

He says he doesn't know.

"But, what do you want?" I prompt him with, "You can say anything."

"I . . . I don't know." He talks about the things I mentioned that he doesn't want or like, such as, he likes eating in restaurants, and he doesn't like hosting or vacations where you just lie around doing nothing, and he says sex as-is dazzles him enough.

I ask him what kind of configuration he'd like our relationship to have.

He doesn't know.

"What happened to the British passport you were going to get?" I ask. "And the month you promised me in London? If you don't want to live in the UK anymore then I need to know that." At this, T pinches the space between his eyes. I want to tell him about Navid's move and proposition that we take over the flat. But instead I ask if he wished I would relocate to one of his four cities.

He says no.

I ask if he wished I'd follow him around as he trots the globe.

He says no.

I propose a life in two cities, one London and the other one his choice.

He can't see it.

Searching for some compromise point, I propose three months together in London each year, three months together in a city of his choice each year, and for the remaining six months I'll live in London and he can be wherever he wants to be. That gives us half the year together, but only ever out of our routine for three months. "I'm up for unconventional; I'm not up for limbo."

He says it sounds unsustainable.

I grow impatient. "Forget where you live. I don't know what you *want*. What do you want?" I repeat this several times, bringing the edge of my palm down on the top of the sofa for emphasis.

His shoulders round and his head droops down to his chest. "I don't know? I don't know. I need some time to think. I don't know. I'm sorry."

"I need to know."

"I know you do. I want to give you something concrete. I'm sorry I don't have an essay inside me to counter yours. I have to get back to you."

The energy is sucked out of the room for a while, until the I-love-you-I'm-sorry dance begins and we find ourselves kissing. We quiver together like teenagers, tentatively grazing our fingers over the other's limbs, and my labia shame dissipates under his tongue. I come six times before we melt into each other. The next morning, we eat the most sublime pancakes at a local institution and then I leave, glad not to have lost the love I have. Hopeful for a counter-offer. And keen to get back to my fundraising and preparations for the show. Milo meets me at the airport and drives me back to Navid's.

I went with the express purpose of saying what I wanted but now I'm lost. How long do I wait for his reply?

THE LEDGER

Love	T knows what I want
	Still waiting to learn what T wants
Money	+ £18,860 for a voiceover commercial
	+ £2,870 from insurance commercial going to air
	+ £10,710 from Arts Council
	+ £3,000 from fundraising
	Cleared debt!
	Put £4k from VO money towards show budget
	Show budget = £29,532 (box office will hopefully make up shortfall)
	£8k in bank to live off for next several months
	Paid Thea £2,176.06 ($3,770: @ $65 per session x 58 sessions)
	£516 on last minute trip to visit T
Career	Dedicating all my time & energy to *The Ex-Boyfriend Yard Sale* & available for voiceovers
	Pausing Joe-jobs
Total	*? Better?*

16. DOLLAR TODAY

*"Good economic theory must give the people the
chance to use their talents to build their own lives."*
Muhammad Yunus

Rehearsals begin in three weeks. I surpassed my fundraising goal by a couple hundred quid but after all the fees to the online platform came off the total, I actually just met it. Still, it's a massive relief. Rehearsal space has been booked, an entire team has been officially contracted by my new producer, my bank account is bountiful and I'm debt-free. The flyers that Milo designed are being distributed around the city by my terrific admin assistant. The video trailers, also made by Milo, went live last week and have already had over 2,000 views. Ticket sales aren't great, and I blame myself for not working harder to build my online presence by posting more regularly on social media.

In the midst of winnowing the script down to "ninety minutes max" from its current two-and-a-half-hour form, practising with my bubble wrap every day, attempting to memorise my lines for the parts of the show I'm confident won't be cut, and keeping the peace with T while I await his reply, I'm waking up at 6 a.m. to gather any and all bits of necessary research and relevant information to make the formula work. I want it to be something useful and worthwhile and virtuosic. The design team needs the final script so they can begin building, but I can only send it once the formula is complete.

This morning I'm meeting with Albert Everett Fry again and then Gemma and I are doing a catch-all, tying-up-loose-threads session on the formula this afternoon.

Albert asks me how it's going with T.

I tell him a few details, but when Albert begins to narrow his eyes, I bark, "I don't want to talk about my relationship anymore. I wanna talk about economics."

"Okay." Albert doesn't take much personally. He launches into a theory about radical uncertainty, and I scramble to take notes.

The theory goes along these lines: in order to take action in our lives, and not be completely paralysed by how uncertain everything actually is, we tell ourselves stories about how our actions will affect the world. It's the emotional investment in these narratives, not a rational calculation, that gives us the confidence to act in an environment of persistent radical uncertainty. Things go off the rails, however, when we get so invested emotionally in a narrative that we start ignoring red flags.

Albert draws a graph in my notebook. "You see the signs, but you segregate your emotional dedication to the narrative away from the facts, and continue to take actions that are increasingly wrong, until your narrative becomes a complete fantasy, then you have a collapse, emotionally or financially — often both — since you've been making increasingly insane investments."

"Am I the deluded one making insane investments? Is T the one who is too cautious, paralysed by the fear of all the things that could actually go wrong?"

"I mean, I don't know. It's just a theory. Mostly it has to do with how people spend money or make political decisions, but it can have other applications too." Albert's southern twang amplifies. "And I'm rooting for you guys."

Later on, in the basement of the theatre, both hands wrapped around a flat white, Gemma nods as I pace the room, spewing ideas one after the other.

"We've got to look at: What's the difference between a deep bond and a sick compulsion? We need to account for how much this project is costing me, financially — it's supposed to be getting me out of debt and I've siphoned money from a voice-over payment into the show — but also the emotional toll it takes remembering moments I'd rather have forgotten and also falling a little bit back in love with each of the exes that I speak to."

For the discomfort and anguish I experience mining my past and reopening old wounds, Gem suggests we add a new data point that measures how easy or difficult it was for me to work with each item for the show.

I agree, jot it down and slap another Post-it note to the concrete wall.

I remind Gem that we *still* need to figure out a tipping point for a waste of time. When she shows me the math she's been working on for this, I notice it's a return on investment model, which we're already using in the formula. "I don't want another ROI basic thing," I say frankly. "I want beautiful math."

Gemma laughs, but I can tell that this has irked her. "I'm focused on poetry."

"Great," I say, recovering my good-natured tone. "You're focused on poetry." I sift through my loose pages of notes. "Now I want to focus on pet names. I read an article about a study that found seventy-six per cent of people who claimed to be in 'very happy relationships' have pet names for each other. It's research-proven. Being called baby for the first time is almost as good as being told someone loves me, but it's more titillating." I point at our drawings of the objects, rattling off, "He called me baby, he called me baby, he didn't have a pet name for me, he called me baby, he called me dolly, he said come here baby and it was the best moment of our whole visit."

She takes a sip of her coffee. I notice she isn't taking notes.

"I also want to do something with the stat that says most people find 'the one' after dating seven and kissing fifteen people. Fifteen?" Incredulous, I look up to the low ceiling. "Fifteen?! Who's only kissed fifteen people?"

Matter of factly, Gemma says, "I don't think I've kissed more than fifteen people." She avoids my eyes, inspecting the ends of her ponytail instead.

I move on. "I did some research at the Center for the Study of Long Distance Relationships. And guess what?" I say, flipping through my notebook. *"Research shows that, despite what many people think, LDRs do not have any greater chance of breaking up than any other relationship. LDRs report just as much satisfaction, intimacy, trust, and commitment as traditional relationships. LDRs are NOT a 'bad idea'.* So we've got to get the LDR variable out of the formula." As I say this, I move to the draft of the Time Invested phrase and scribble over the symbol that represents the percentage of a relationship that was long distance.

Gemma says that makes sense and begins to unpack her lunch. The smell of garlic permeates the room.

I tell her that I've been thinking about all the things that aren't captured in the formula simply because they're outside my lived experience, wondering if that's exclusionary or irresponsible. "Audiences don't want to know about my life, they want to project theirs onto *The Ex-Boyfriend Yard Sale* and we have to give them the space to do that." Gemma tries to interject at this, but I interrupt her. "How can we trace all the reasons we fall in love with the people we fall in love with? Are all loves just antidotes? Is that such a bad thing?" I hear my voice rising as I ask, "And what about divorced people being able to use this formula?"

"Haley," Gemma says calmly, "if this formula is going to be used by people who aren't you, we'd have major changes to make. At the moment the whole thing is skewed to reflect your value system. If anyone else was to use it, we'd first have to get them to fill out some kind of survey about their values so that their data points would be weighted appropriately and the relationships between data points were in line with their belief systems. I don't think we have the funds or the time to create something like that." She adds that some of the ideas I'm bringing forward may already be captured under other data points. The aim now is to edit and refine.

"Just a few more!" I frantically dig through my bag till I find the Post-it notes I wrote on last night. "I want to include: Did we break up well? Are we still friends now? Would I sleep with them again? We need to figure out: Is having your heart broken more than once a benefit or a hindrance? Does the current state of my relationship with an ex nullify the pain felt in the past? If every time you go on a date with someone new it just makes you miss your ex more, does that make the T-shirt they gave you more precious or a burden? And what about how often you use the object? And how many compliments you get on it? And what about the people I'm selling these things to? Shouldn't all this be relatively scaled to the buyer's income? Because £10k to a person who makes £500k a year is a lot different than it is to someone who makes £20k? The buyer needs to feel the magnitude of the cost!"

Gemma raises her eyebrows at me.

And I concede, "I know it's too much. But it's also not enough." It's never enough for me. I'm like that. Being with me is being with that. Fair warning.

Brusque, Gemma says to email her this list and she'll see what she can do.

"That would be terrific," I say, sheepishly collecting the Post-it notes from the floor.

She says I have to stop adding more factors so we can begin streamlining soon.

I agree, but I tell myself I can do whatever I want so long as I keep Gemma onside. On the journey home, I wrestle with myself. I wish I'd mentioned that I was expecting a period of testing different models. I was expecting Gemma to be equally intent on excellence. But this disappointment is my own fault. Everything I touch becomes jumbled, despite my best efforts up front to be orderly. Besides, what other mathematician would understand me and stick around when things get emotionally charged?

I get off the Tube at Archway to walk uphill as penance. Huffing and puffing with my heavy backpack, I run through all the times my shadow's been caught by my exes.

Mix Tape said, "You're a jealous person." Necklace said, "You're too sensitive." Ukulele said, "Lower your voice. You're embarrassing me." Bicycle said, "You have emotions I didn't know existed. I want off the rollercoaster." He also called me "emotionally manipulative". Typewriter said, "You're exhausting." Backpack said, "You're extreme." Jewellery Box said, "My father warned me, this is why you never date an actress." T-shirt said, "You're always disappointed with me. Nothing is ever good enough for you." Actually, many of them said, "Nothing is ever good enough for you." And what's the common denominator? Me. I am.

To snap myself out of the seductive call of the wallow, I phone Sam to ask about the lighting grid, but end up revealing that I've locked horns with Gemma.

He refuses to sympathise with me. "If you want the project to be perfect it will never be done."

"Sam," I seethe, "I want it to be good and accurate and useful. I don't want to make a fluffy, futile piece of shit."

"Absolutely." His tone softens, "But do you want to finish the show?"

I pause under the suicide bridge as cars zip past me. There's graffiti on the wall and I'm trying to read it. An elderly woman with a cane marches towards me, shoulder pressed into the wind.

"Yes," I say at last. "Of course I do. I do. I do." I let out a self-deprecating laugh, and sigh. "Okay, I'll let you go."

£ + ♥

With a week to go before rehearsals begin, I'm saying goodbye to Fi after my boozy Sunday afternoon improv show. She's pregnant again, so not imbibing. It's very early on and mornings are hell, but she has about three good hours every day and this show was right in the pocket. One of my teammates unwittingly cast me as a pregnant woman, and I did my best to fight the clichés. I played it eerily even-keeled emotionally, repeatedly relinquishing my seat to others and offering to pay for everything that came up in conversation. I was worried Fi would be offended but she said it was brilliant. Not my funniest work but deft.

I watch her skirt around her dislike for T when she asks after him. The main thing she wants to know is if I really do think I had to pay for everything in my relationships. She says the only fair way to do it is to take each person's salary, or average yearly earnings if they're self-employed, look at what that ratio is and split every expense at that ratio.

I guffaw.

"I'm serious," she says. That's what she and her husband do. It was his idea since he was earning so much more than she was when they got together, and they've carried it forward. He tallies up all the expenditures at the end of each quarter and he usually gives her a refund. The ratio is now 1 to .74. She says it's bollocks because the national gender pay gap is for every £1 a man earns a woman earns £0.83, but at least within her marriage it's equitable.

On the walk home I want to leave Gemma a voice note saying that the "who paid for more things in the relationship" data point also needs to consider the gender pay gap at that time and the pay gap inside the relationship, but wary of annoying her any more than I already have, I record it in my own voice notes instead.

I'm about to call Ollie to see how he's doing — he accepted the job in Singapore and he's currently on a lonely solo trip in Mexico City, getting to grips with his divorcee status and getting a tan before the big move — when I see I have several notifications on Twitter. This is odd because I don't use my Twitter account. Anticipating some much-needed preview press for the show, instead I discover a series of direct messages from Jewellery Box. Without reading them, I close Twitter and put the phone back in my coat pocket.

Unlike the rest of my exes, I don't like Jewellery Box. He belongs to the camp of partners I hooked up with, committed to and only unearthed their real personality after the commitment was made.

After Backpack, my numerous trysts ranged from a Slovenian TV star to a Welsh arborist — they were all a hoot and learning curves on how to keep a relationship casual. I discovered that the key to preventing a fling from falling in love with you is to clamp down on the impulse to utter effusive compliments or machinations of a hypothetical future together, especially post-coitus. Those words get you into trouble; they create a shared story in which you both play a role. I got good at keeping my mouth shut, but I missed the romance.

Coming out of my Saturn Return, I was ready to find the one, or at least the next one, and I found myself on a writing residency in Helsinki working on my second solo show. Jewellery Box was the handsome artist host, an American who'd been living in Finland for a couple decades. He gave my cohort of playwrights a tour of the city and at the end of the night he and I agreed to meet on our own in a couple days. A flash freeze had left the city covered in ice and we tottered around Töölönlahti park together. I wore my grandfather's parka, wool socks layered over two pairs of pantyhose and hiking boots. Each time I slipped he caught me.

As a professional ceramicist, he mostly made functional tableware for high-end restaurants and hotels. The purpose of art, he said that day, was to contribute something meaningful to the larger human conversation. Or try to. I didn't know it then, but it would be the most valuable thing he would say to me. It reframed the purpose of artistic output for me. I wagered on more nuggets like that coming my way, but mostly he just denounced capitalism. His nose was constantly stuffed due to the dust in his studio. But, he said, it was pointless to try to keep it clean: "all ecosystems revert to chaos."

After the two-week residency, I was off on another six-month leg of the contract I'd been willing to give up my fingernails for — the same one that Backpack did not want me to get. It turned out to be a lucrative gig that just kept giving. Splitting the price of the trips between us, I returned to Helsinki on my week off and Jewellery Box visited me in one of the remote towns where we were rehearsing, and then in two tour destinations. Yet the more I knew Jewellery Box, the less I liked him. He insulted the work of Joni Mitchell, who held icon status in my childhood home. And his sense of humour was truly heinous.

I record another voice note to share with Gemma at a more appropriate juncture: "Can we go into negative numbers if his sense of humour wasn't just not funny, but gob-smackingly poor, while he was convinced of his hilarity? This is doubly offensive when you're dating someone who is literally paid for their comedic timing."

Eighteen years my senior, a few months in he told me part of his reason for dating a cis woman under thirty was because he was still hoping to have children. Not long after that, he revealed that not only had he and his ex-partner been together for twelve years, they had only split up a few months before I met him. I was shocked when he said that break-up had initially required a restraining order to be issued. Apparently, in the subsequent months they'd reached civil terms, but I couldn't help but feel protective of him.

During my visit to Helsinki on my week off, I was excited to sleep late, lounge around and rejuvenate. After this precious break, I'd be heading into another eight-week period of six-day weeks. But every morning at 8 a.m., he'd wake me by bringing me a coffee in bed. I asked repeatedly that he let me sleep in, which he'd agree to, until the next day when he'd be wafting his handcrafted mug of espresso under my nose. A controlling gesture wrapped in a bow.

Early on, I'd been taken by Jewellery Box's intelligence, and fed a kind of professor–pupil dynamic by asking him questions and hanging on his answers. But soon I found myself bored of his lectures, yet I wasn't sure how to create a new role for myself.

When we Skyped, Jewellery Box often complained that while others led lives filled with right-time-right-place good fortunes, he fell through the cracks, destined to be left behind and forgotten.

I wanted to say, "With that attitude, that's precisely the future you're writing." But he'd just arrived home after his recent trip to see me to find his beloved, seventy-year-old pet tortoise, which he'd grown up with and inherited, gravely ill. During the several weeks where Jewellery Box sat vigil for his tortoise, I increasingly found myself rolling my eyes when he called.

On the opening night of the show I was performing in, I'd been texting with Ollie, debating if I should tell Jewellery Box about my crush on one of the theatre technicians, who was younger and funnier and firmer — physically and metaphysically. Jewellery Box had hopped on a plane to catch the show, and I hoped his visit would quash my infatuation and remind me where my allegiance lay without me having to confess anything, but the tension of my secret feelings made me giddy.

Amidst the post-show reception, he handed me flowers and kissed me a little longer than I would have liked, before telling me he couldn't understand why the audience was laughing and repeating punchlines during the show. To him the story was crass and uninspired. I laughed it off and trotted out the only Latin I know, *"De gustibus non disputandum (est)."* There's no accounting for taste. Jewellery Box mimed tipping a hat to me.

Nearing midnight, after dinner in a diner, my eyes were starting to droop. I suggested we take a taxi back to my digs, but he refused, saying that he'd taken a taxi after a large meal with me in Helsinki and it had given him indigestion. He needed to walk it off. I had a matinee and evening show the following day, and I was keen to forgo the forty-minute walk and get to sleep. I suggested that I take a taxi and he walk home.

In a low, controlled tone he said, "You're being very selfish, Haley. I'd never suggest you walk alone at night in Helsinki."

"We just opened the show," I explained, "and you saw how taxing it is."

His enunciation sharpened. "This is the problem with actresses, they keep themselves at the centre of everything."

Giving up, I nodded.

He asked what was the point of spending all this time and money to come and see me if I wasn't committed to his well-being? He said he was in danger of bankrupting himself with all these expenses and he could lose his house.

I told him I thought he'd inherited his house from his grandmother and owned it outright.

He sneered that he'd remortgaged it six years ago.

We walked back to my accommodation.

I admitted I'd been struggling with a crush.

"Is it the obvious person?" he asked with disgust.

"The person I was talking to, all in black? Yes." I told him my feelings had diminished just by admitting it to him. And that was partially true.

That night I couldn't sleep. I was tossing and turning, then suddenly I sat up in bed, and questions I hadn't consciously thought of cascaded from my mouth.

"Was your ex with you when you put down your tortoise?"

Pause. Then, "Yes," he replied from the pillow.

"And the two of you spent the night together after that, didn't you?"

Pause. "Yes."

"Did you have sex?"

"I don't have to answer that." His voice got louder and he turned away.

I took a pillow and moved to the living room. As I was dozing off on the sofa, the bedroom door banged open. Startled, I inhaled sharply.

My eyes found his silhouette in the door frame, hair puffed up, gut loose.

"What's the matter?"

"You scared me," I said.

"Oh, I scared you?" he snarled as his flat feet flumped through the living room into the kitchen.

I sat up, hugged the pillow to my chest and listened carefully. I could hear Jewellery Box grunting, opening and closing drawers, rummaging in the cupboards. I wondered if he was getting a knife, but he came back into the living room empty handed. I sat very still. He was pacing and raving.

"Maybe I should have killed myself, along with my tortoise, because nobody wants me!"

I did a quick calculation. Calm him down, make nice, after he leaves tomorrow end it and never see him again. I apologised and babied him. I held his face in my hands and kissed his chapped lips. I rubbed his beefy chest and said let's go back to bed. In the morning I sat on his lap while he rolled his cigarettes for the day.

A couple days after he left, I called him and told him that I didn't want to be in a relationship anymore.

He yelled, "Good luck." And hung up on me.

A couple days later he wrote to me as though the fights had never happened, telling me about his day-to-day goings on. That's when it hit me that the restraining order that he alluded to might have been against him, rather than his "crazy ex".

The last time we spoke, the day after he'd sent his denial-ridden email, I reiterated that I wanted to be alone. He accused me of never really liking him but simply keeping him around for support while I worked on a challenging project away from home. He wasn't entirely wrong. I didn't dispute his claims or defend myself and he didn't go berserk. I hung up and thought, Jackpot. I'm free. He deleted and blocked me on social media, and we have not had any contact since.

I sit on a bench around the corner from Navid's and open Jewellery Box's messages on Twitter. My bowels surge as I read:

Dear Haley,

Johannes sent me a link to the festival he programs in the Netherlands. I noticed your picture was on the main page and in the background of your photo was the jewellery box I made. This, coupled with your rather twee title, has given me pause. I sincerely hope you are not using my name, any of my identifying features or any of our correspondence in this show.

As a person who has experience using one's life as fodder for works of art, I advise you to think carefully about your intentions. Your title alone suggests that you are striving to satiate a mainstream hunger for tell-all voyeurism perpetuated by the millennial self-branding obsession and relentless objectification of experience in the social-media age.

You're a wonderfully gifted actress, Haley. You excel at playing characters created by other people. Why are you succumbing to this trend when your talent lies in a staid tradition? I digress.

Though I regret getting involved with you so quickly and all the money I lost visiting you, which as you know nearly caused

*me to default on my mortgage and lose my home, I am grateful
for the idea you helped me come up with about the lighthouse
and the lizard, which has been instrumental in my new sculp-
tural work about my life, set to be exhibited in the new year.*

*I hope you are well, and I wish you good luck, but I wanted to
make very clear, I do not consent to being in your show.*

Kind regards,

Jewellery Box

Trembling, I call T, but he doesn't answer. Milo tells me he's on
his way; he's taking me to Franco Manca's. And now I urgently
need the bathroom.

I dash past Navid, who is watching a reality TV show, and
barely manage to shut the bathroom door before exploding
stress-diarrhoea into the toilet bowl. Jewellery Box literally
scared the shit out of me. But it's not funny yet. I take off all my
clothes and look in the mirror. I'm thinner than I expected. I
shake in the shower and forget whether I've shampooed my
hair before slathering it with conditioner.

By the time I'm dressed, I tell Navid that I've received a cease
and desist letter and ask if he has a lawyer friend who could
help me.

He looks at the Twitter messages and tells me to relax. "You're
giving this guy too much credit — he's all talk. I know his type."
Navid invites me to join him and his mates out in Shoreditch
later, to blow off some steam. I tell him Milo and I will take him
up on that after our meal.

I want to whip out the hot iron and straighten my hair, but I
don't have time to dry it thoroughly. I drag liquid eyeliner over
my eyelids, rub blush into my cheekbones and smooth bright
red lipstick across my lips.

Waiting for Milo to arrive, I sneak a quick swig from Navid's
tequila collection. Its heat mellows my insides. Fucking
Jewellery Box.

I yank open the car door. "I've changed his name and so many distinguishing details!"

Milo says, "Let's take your mind off this." We drop the car at his flat and walk to the high street in his neighbourhood. He's still living with Julie, but as flatmates who occasionally sleep together. We order a carafe of red wine and two pizzas. Milo reads the messages, and then says, "To be fair, he has a point."

"Seriously?"

"He's saying he doesn't want to be in your show."

"Nobody knows it's him!"

"But that's really the jewellery box he gave you?"

"Yes."

"Well."

"His name isn't even signed on the bottom of the box!"

Milo is in one of his contrarian moods. Fighting tears, I threaten to leave if he refuses to take my side.

"What? No. Come on. Just take him out of the show. It's just a show."

I look at Milo's broad golden retriever face, gobbling the crusts he's saved to douse with oil. T would take my side. T would be incensed on my behalf. T would have litigious-sounding suggestions for rebuttals. T would never diminish what I'm working on.

"You're bugging me," I say, dropping my greasy napkin to my plate.

"Whoa."

I can see I've hurt him. The server asks if we want more wine or dessert.

Milo says, "Dessert yes. And maybe a whiskey?"

"Oh, hell," I capitulate.

Somehow Milo and I recover our rapport, and when I announce that I'm going to meet Navid, he agrees to come along.

In the Uber he asks about T. A topic we'd both pretended to forget till now. I should lie and say it's great. But I sigh. "I love him, but . . ." I press my forehead into the cool window of the car. "It's not what I want, ultimately." T's been in touch a lot, but he still hasn't made me a counter-offer.

"Mate." Milo puts a hand on my shoulder.

"Don't be happy," I caution.

He swears he's not. But he's smiling.

The moment we enter the club in Shoreditch I remember that I hate clubs. We find Navid and his pals, who are happy to see me. Milo buys rounds and I dance for a spell, till I'm drunk and time slips and I'm in the basement, outside the ladies' toilet, with Milo holding my arm saying, "McGee."

When he kisses me, I allow it, but I let myself go slack in the knees. "Steady now." He pulls me back up. I'm a rag doll. I'm drunk. I am too drunk. Moments collide. Navid's friend holding my hand. Hopping into the men's toilet behind him. Screaking at the coat-check girl that my wallet and phone are missing. Milo telling me to calm down. I snap at him to quit patronising me, then open my eyes wide and race up the stairs. Suddenly sober. He follows.

"They're in your pockets!" I hiss.

"What?"

"My wallet and phone."

He laughs, taking them out. "Wow. I've never seen the hysterical side of you."

Outside now, I fumble with my phone.

"What are you doing?" he asks, wrapping an arm around my waist.

"Getting an Uber." I stumble even though I'm standing still.

"I'll get one." He takes out his phone.

"No, I—" I manage to get one ordered.

He breathes on my neck. "McGee, I'm crazy about you."

I shake my head. "I want to go home. I want to go home alone."

"McGee." He pulls me close and shushes me.

"I WANT TO GO HOME ALONE!" I shout, prying myself out of his embrace.

When my Uber arrives, Milo opens the door for me. The driver yells at him to get in or get out. He shuts the door and I slump in the seat, apologising.

£ + ♥

I wake up the next morning naked, too hot, a static feeling on my skin. My head thumps as though a crew of workmen are climbing a ladder running from between my eyes to the crown of my skull. Any self-flagellation is superseded by the urgency to get to rehearsal.

I brush my teeth, smear coconut oil all over my face to remove the imprint of last night, knock back some paracetamol and latch myself into a pair of overalls. This morning, the entire production team will meet for the first time.

When I slink into the theatre's lobby, Elson is chipper, and the stage manager has an agenda she wants to run by me. My admin assistant holds up a steaming cafetière in my eyeline as I listen to the scenic designer's concerns about the plinths I sourced for free. I give her a thumbs up and nod vigorously when she holds up the milk. Determined to begin well and be a strong leader, I compliment Gemma's outfit and thank her for the math she sent through. My contrition in recent days seems to have repaired the damage I inflicted in our last meet-up. I force a smile as I greet my producer. All the designers are here today too, including a sullen Milo, along with Sam and a couple of the theatre's staff. This should be an auspicious day.

The ghost light is still on when we congregate inside the theatre. After the introductions, we talk budget and production schedule — the designers share where they're at. I apologise for not having cut the script down enough yet. Elson says we'll get there by the end of the first week and Gemma adds that we're really close with the formula. Elson talks about how we're going to work in rehearsal, and I talk about the themes in the show and how I see them manifesting in the space. The tissue of my lungs seems to be dissolving as I speak. I pop up to demonstrate how I think we should rig a zipline from behind the audience to meet me on stage.

Standing on stage with my back to my collaborators, I'm overcome with panic. I can't keep pretending everything's fine. Suddenly I say, "We have to cancel the show," then proceed, tearfully, to read them Jewellery Box's direct messages, letting out a few whelps as I reach his sign off.

My producer gently removes my phone from my hand and scrolls through the messages. My assistant passes me some toilet paper. She really is a keeper. Milo looks at the lighting gels.

I honk my nose and say, "It was an impossible task. There's no way to actually know what it's all worth. The show is costing me, and I can't afford a lawsuit." And I apologise. I apologise so much it's aggressive.

Elson says, "Let's finish the meeting and then we can go for breakfast."

Gemma hugs me.

My stage manager says, "Please don't cancel the show, my flatmates are all looking forward to it."

Sam assures me it'll be fine and my producer seconds that claim.

I'm humiliated by their kindness. I do my best to stay composed, puffy face and all, while the others echo Sam. There's an update on ticket sales. The producer is pleased with them, but I don't clock the numbers. Milo ducks out before we wrap up.

When I charge my phone, there are several missed calls and texts from T. At breakfast with Elson, I excuse myself midway through my poached eggs and hash browns to throw up in the bathroom. I return feeling marginally better. The best theatre directors are highly sensitive, understanding how to draw out specific qualities from skittish and highly strung actors through nimble communication. Elson is a master. By the time I've had my third coffee he's convinced me this isn't worth considering cancelling the show over.

I take a forty-five-minute shower when I get home. The kind where you sit on the floor of the bathtub and hug your knees till the hot water tank runs out.

Thea is firm in her belief that Jewellery Box won't be able to touch me. Her sister is a lawyer. She recommends I meet with one for peace of mind. We discuss my masochistic behaviour with Milo, how I might be complicit in creating a dynamic I don't like or want.

I tell her I just want T full-time.

She says that might mean letting go of the crutch I've been using.

"Milo's the crutch?" I consider this. "Yeah, he is."

As soon as I know he'll be caffeinated I call T and tell him about the cease and desist letter. He demands I send him screenshots of the messages and then spontaneously assassinates Jewellery Box's character, penning a scathing, intimidating reply. It's the most romantic piece of writing I've received. I don't send it, but I print it out and carry it in a hidden compartment of my purse, a document of T's fierce loyalty. Only after we get off the call do I realise I neglected to tell him about Milo.

I put a moratorium on booze until I'm done with the show. This conversation with T turns out to be the first in a trinity of good things coming at me.

Agnes calls. The gambling advert that fell apart over a year ago is now going ahead after all. Its usage is significantly reduced, which means the buyout is only a sixth of the thirteen thousand pounds they were initially going to pay me, but it means I have some breathing room.

Knowing this money is coming, I arrange a quick meeting with a lawyer tomorrow morning. The lawyer is my improv coach's stepmother. Her office is in Bloomsbury and her assistant brings me a complimentary cappuccino while I wait.

After reading the messages, the lawyer tells me not to worry about Jewellery Box's reproach. Because I'm not using his name or any distinguishing features, and I've changed around loads of details, he has no grounds. "Hell, edit the shit out of the messages and read them in the play!"

I take my first deep breath since Jewellery Box's re-emergence.

"But for fun," she says, a mischievous glint in her eyes, "let's calculate how much hush money he'd have to pay you, if he wanted you to remove him from the show." She says to do this we look at the greatest potential outcome — the greatest potential revenue I could accrue as a result of the show, and therefore the greatest potential economic loss I'd incur by removing him.

The lawyer's been divorced twice, and she thinks my show is going to be a hit. She talks fast and smooth. She says she wouldn't be surprised if *The Ex-Boyfriend Yard Sale* gets a West End transfer before heading to "a little street called Broadway". When I raise my eyebrows, she assures me that the Cost of Love formula will end up on BuzzFeed and Freakonomics. "Without a doubt, you'll get a book deal and write a bestseller, garnering international press and accolades along with celebrity endorsements."

"Really?" I ask, catching her excitement.

"Oh, I expect you'll end up with your own BBC Radio show talking to people about love and money and whether it was worth it. But it won't be long till the BBC realises that the show belongs on television. And the ground-breaking series will be hilarious and accessible with a sneaky feminist message and political tilt. The TV show will have mass appeal, be a critical darling, and launch you into stardom. And as a result of all of that—" she takes her glasses off and uses them to punctuate her speech — "I believe you will be able to enter the London real estate market.

"So!" she says, pulling the lid off her pen with a flourish. "Given that a house in London is about what? Two million?"

"Sounds about right," I say.

"And given that the jewellery box is one of eight objects you've chosen to feature in your show, Jewellery Box himself would have to pay you one eighth of two million to *legally force* you to remove him from the show. He'd have to fork over a quarter million pounds to hush you up."

"He'd have to sell his house."

She spins the page of figures she's scrawled towards me. And then draws a big smiley face.

Floored, I lean back in her plush chair. "So, what do I do?" I ask.

"Carry on," she says triumphantly.

"Do I write him back?"

"God no."

When Gem and I next convene Elson joins us. He purports it's because he wants to gain a better understanding of the math before we begin rehearsals in two days, but I suspect he's here to stop me adding anything to the formula that would slow Gemma down.

His position notwithstanding, I've been back through my notes with vim and vigour, and I am in full-steam-ahead-take-no-prisoners-bloodhound-at-the-gates-ready-to-roll-up-my-sleeves-and-not-look-down mode.

I stand erect before my collaborators and calmly say, "Dollar Today."

"I was thinking that too!" shrieks Gemma. She and I pull math notes out of our backpacks as Elson looks on, puzzled.

Breathlessly I relay another economic theory that Albert shared with me the last time we met. It says that a dollar today is always worth more than a dollar tomorrow. For instance, if you get a dollar today and use it to buy a piece of wood, you can spend the rest of the day — i.e. your time — applying your skills as a wood carver to turn the piece of wood into something that can be sold at market tomorrow for a higher price. Whereas if you'd been given the dollar even a day later, all you'd have is a dollar.

Gemma chimes in, "But we didn't have a practical application for it until this Jewellery Box hitch."

"So for us," I almost shout, "my objects from my exes are my wood. And I've used my time to apply my storytelling and performance skills to them to enhance their price."

Elson says it's fantastic.

With this theory in mind, along with the costs of creating the show (in money, time and emotion), and the potential earnings at stake as estimated by the lawyer, we add a special phrase to the formula, which looks at how the show itself is adding value to my objects. We call it "Dollar Today" (DT).

It takes into account who paid for more things in the relationship because this colours immediately how much value the object already holds for me. If I paid for more things, the object is automatically worth more because I need to be compensated for that. Of course this is difficult to measure, and so we decide to call this data point *my perception of the ratio of who paid for more things in the relationship,* factoring in who earned more, and the gender pay gap at that time.

Dollar Today is the best kind of gift, the kind you didn't realise you'd always needed until it was in your lap.

$$ \frac{?}{£} \left[\frac{\Delta\#}{\odot} \times \left(1 + \frac{\log(\square) + \log(p \cdot £) + \log(\ast) - \log(£+t)}{\log(avg \, £ \, in \, \heartsuit)} \right) \times \left(\frac{RANK}{1-8} \times \frac{\%\,AIR}{\%\,TIME} \right) \right] $$

DOLLAR TODAY

The phrase also includes the number of tickets sold on a given night, and that number is divided by the emotional cost of writing about the object in question — which in the case of the jewellery box is quite high (8/10). This is to measure how much I suffered for each audience member present.

Gemma says this is a perfect place to use logarithms.

In unison Elson and I ask, "What's a logarithm?" and chortle.

She doesn't want to get lost in the esoteric, but tells us that she likes to think of logarithms as being able to undo an exponent. They scale down big numbers. This is useful for us because these dollar amounts could quickly overrun the other phrases in the formula *and* logarithms inherently allow for ever-changing data.

We're using logarithms as they pertain to ticket sales, potential earnings (as calculated by the lawyer), my celebrity status, the hard costs of producing and running the show (in time and money) and my average income during the relationship in question.

My "celebrity status" is calculated by tracking how many followers I have on social media, how that grows over the course of the show's run, and the amount of, *and quality* of, the press the show receives. A five-star review in a national paper has more cachet than a positive Tweet from an audience member, though those Tweets matter too. As our trip to the auction house taught us, celebrity is the number one thing that can spike the value of an innocuous item. Gemma puts Google Alerts on my name to keep tabs on this.

Elson and I add an interactive element to the opening of the show. The audience will appraise my goods upon entering the theatre, before they have any context, and then we'll get them to do a reassessment midway through the show, once they have more context, by revealing their initial bids and getting them to cheer or boo if they now think the price should go up or down. And the assistant stage manager will record the audience response. Gemma says we'll use the initial bids in the Market Value phrase, but also how the audience appraises the items without and then with context will determine their rank from least to most valuable, from first to eighth. This works with the idea of the dilution effect because it looks at each object in the context of a collection.

We decide to multiply the object's rank by the percentage of airtime it receives in the show. Airtime is a tangible measurement of how valuable I have deemed each of these relationships in terms of how entertaining or impactful the stories associated with them are.

Gemma and I are sky-punching giddy when we figure this out. She leaves to work this into a spreadsheet, complete this draft of the formula and get the figures.

17. THE FORMULA

"A work of art is never finished. It is merely abandoned."
E. M. Forster

Admittedly my in-for-a-penny, in-for-a-pound-of-flesh approach to this project has me at the end of my tether on the night before we begin rehearsal. I've committed to making all my own lunches to save money, creating the copious paper props used in the show, organising three ancillary events that will happen during the three-week run and building an interactive Cost of Love installation for the theatre lobby and a window display for the theatre's street-facing windows. It's all proving too much.

I want T to talk me down from the ledge, put it in perspective, give me permission to buy lunch, offer platitudes and tell me I'm competent and capable. But he's writing to a deadline and can't chat. And I don't feel like speaking to Navid because every conversion wends back to how sensational Ísleif is. "You need to have sex," Ollie tells me. "But if that's impossible put your head down and work." So I do. The evening passes swiftly inside my cell, lying on my bed, muttering through my script and making yet more changes. I pause to email my brother about the few Gumtree offers I got for the jewellery box, all below thirty pounds. No bites for the T-shirt so far.

It's late when T returns my call. I'm now under the covers with the lights out. I should just let it ring and talk to him later, but I answer. He's been working on an assignment about influencer culture, which he detests, and plummets into a complaint about people who shove their self-improvement in your face. I listen, but his words cause me ever-greater offence — he knows I read self-help books. I tell him I don't want a boring call like this in the middle of the night. I want more intimacy, more sex, more affection.

He balks at this.

A speech I've had simmering on the back burner boils up. "If we don't have a plan to be together soon, and you won't make plans, then I need sensuality in our communication."

"I don't like phone sex; it doesn't turn me on."

"Then what do you propose?" I whisper with venom. I listen to the wheels of his bike spinning. "T. You're asking me to be in a neutered relationship."

He's exasperated. "If this is a deal breaker for you Haley—"

"It is." I say it without thinking, and definitively. "It is a deal breaker."

And now we're in break-up-conversation territory again. Rancour fills me. I tell him I can't do this now, remind him it's the middle of the night here. He says he'll speak to me once he submits his piece at the end of the week. Furious and exhausted, I sleep.

At 9 a.m. I fill an Uber with all the props I've been housing at Navid's, promising the driver I'll give him a good tip for the accommodation. London traffic moves at a sputtering creep. I'm late to our first day.

I sob through my first reading of the *The Ex-Boyfriend Yard Sale* script. I apologise to the team, guaranteeing that I'm not unhinged, just struggling with insomnia. But eventually I bounce back and I throw myself into rehearsal, joyously arguing with Elson as we ferret out material to cut from the script and establish the "physical language of the show" — what does it mean for me to be on the Astroturf versus off? When is it important for me to be close to the audience? And where will we situate our various paper props around the space?

Over lunch Ollie sends a text that reads, *Fuck packing your own lunches. Sleep and do not do anything dramatic with T. Do like me: don't worry — work.* The Singapore job is a mammoth task that Ollie has added to by joining every available committee. He moans, but the panic in his voice has settled. He sounds like himself again.

When we reconvene, Elson asks me to talk him through the T-shirt timeline string that I made. Though I only refer to a few points on it during the show text, it's a key prop and he wants to understand its scope.

Looking at it, I suddenly don't want to do it. I can't stand to see all the ways I ignored the signs and repeated and repeated and repeated variations of a pattern, hoping each time for a different end. But I can't say no, not on the first day. So the stage manager fixes a hook at either end of the studio wall and I take my time unspooling it. Once it's suspended, I stand at the beginning of the timeline and start.

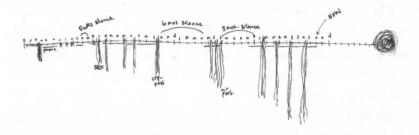

"You smell good" was the first thing T ever said to me. I was unpacking my backpack at The Common, the coffee shop across the road from my Toronto apartment.

I had seen T around my neighbourhood before, often at this café. We ran in overlapping circles and had a few friends in common but hadn't met until now. I'd just been cast as a journalist in a play and when I mentioned I was looking to do some research, a mutual friend suggested I have a coffee with him. The mutual friend also told me, out of sheer malaise, that she'd recently considered asking T out. When she said it, I was silent, but inside, a possessive, territorial urge reared in me. No, I thought sternly, if anyone is going out with T, it's *me*. Later he'd admit he had a similar premonition about me.

His comment about my scent, which happened to be my deodorant, disarmed me and we tumbled into a funny and frank conversation about body odour. I was intimidated by his intelligence but delighted at our playful repartee.

During a dip in our conversation he asked what kind of music I listened to. My answer remains one of my biggest regrets.

On the tip of my tongue lay a vivifying response. I could have, should have, said, "Nope," and paused for effect.

He would have laughed and repeated it back with a question mark.

Then I would have grinned and given him the gears. "I don't want to play some game where your image of me is defined by the music I listen to. Besides, that sounds like a bit you do."

To this, he would have nodded once, impressed, and said, "Fair."

The entire tone of our relationship could have been established as forthright, bold and lively in that moment. Alas I got bashful, added a caveat that I didn't really listen to music, before revealing I'd been listening to Tracy Chapman's "Fast Car" on repeat.

He replied with a "Hunh." And the following day he emailed me an old rap song that used a sample from "Fast Car".

From this, an epistolary exchange took hold, and we'd often "run into each other" at The Common, both of us frequenting it more regularly in the hopes of a chance encounter. He'd usually be there when I popped in to pick up a coffee before heading to rehearsal. I started going earlier so I could sit with him and take time to chat instead of dashing off after a quick hello.

I had a lot of questions about his work — how he sniffed out stories, how he knew what kinds of questions to ask. He loved to talk about process and he was deeply curious about the theatre. His grandmother had been an actress and he admired the fact that I was one too.

I had a crush on him, but it also seemed we were developing an incredible rapport as friends. I was navigating a difficult relationship with the director, being the only woman in the show and twenty years junior to the other actors, but T counselled me on how to adroitly put the director in his place and reclaim my voice in the rehearsal room. And when he was struggling with a source who'd clamped up, I was able to give him the tools to charm them into divulging more: self-deprecating humour and flattery. He told me I was a better manipulator than he was, which I took as a supreme compliment.

On one of my days off, after our chat over coffee, he invited me to visit a sound installation in Kensington Market. We shuffled there through the snow. It was January in Toronto, minus-twenty degrees. We had both joined the YMCA and stopped drinking for the month. He walked me home from the gym one evening, and when we got to my door he high-fived me mitt to mitt.

Everyone in my life knew about my towering crush on T, and though I was dying to broach the topic, I also wanted him to do it. Besides, there was something delicious in this prolonged pining time. I felt like I was sixteen again. Outside a concert venue I grabbed the lapels of his coat and hungrily whispered his name. I wanted to assure him his new jacket was indeed flattering. He put his hands on my hips, looked me in the eyes and told me I was his favourite person. Once our sober month was complete, we shared a bottle of wine, then polished off an old bottle of rum, and professed our feelings for each other.

He came to the closing matinee performance of the show where I was playing the journalist. He said I was extraordinarily good, that I surpassed his expectations. He was leaving for a project in another city in a couple days. Emboldened, I stood before him in his kitchen, stone cold sober, and said, "I think there's something between us that's rare and shouldn't be ignored."

He said, "But I'm going away and you're working in Toronto."

"So?" I replied.

I interpreted the nerves in his voice as fear and anxiety, not a symptom of an inability to commit. He had to finish a piece and submit it, so I went home and ate a grilled cheese sandwich. When he rejoined me there several hours later for our first 'date', he was more dizzy with neurosis, compounding what-ifs spinning in his head. Eventually I proposed taking hooking up off the table and just enjoying each other's company, but when it was a reasonable time for him to go home, he didn't want to leave. He laughed with delight slipping into the cosiness of my flannel sheets. I placed a pillow between our torsos as a barrier. My nod to respecting boundaries.

But before long his feet grazed mine. We tangled our legs and hovered our faces millimetres apart in the dark, breathing into each other's mouths, until we finally, finally, kissed. The kiss lasted for ages in the deep winter night, a bit drunk and exhausted. It was followed by a blur of weight shifting, skin brushing on skin and then his fingers sliding down my under-wear. My breath short, light moans from the back of my throat in response to the right pressure from his fingers. He whispered that he thought about doing this a lot.

"Like when?" I wanted to know.

"Every time we talk," he said distractedly. "And sometimes when you're not there." He kissed me as I came but then hesi-tated at the threshold of sex. "Now hold on," he said. "So far, we haven't done anything we'll regret."

Sufficiently satisfied, I pressed my cheek into his chest. Now I've got you, I thought as I hugged him tight. You're mine.

He left town in the morning and I went on vacation with my mum and aunt Harlow to Bali. An otherwise terrific week was tainted with the angst of not hearing from T on Valentine's Day, nor the days before and after.

Harlow said, "Mark him with an X and move on."

Ollie texted, *Ugh these men! These predictably unreliable men.*
Thea told me, "All the information we need about a person reveals itself in our early interactions."

Predictably enough, T resurfaced not long after my week in the sun. We spoke regularly, until I started asking for a plan to see each other, more contact and a label of dating. A sobering conversation about expectations caused him to write me this email:

> . . . *I need this to slow down. I do think there's something special between us, but I don't know you well enough yet to dive in, especially not long distance which has been the demise of all my previous relationships. I'm sorry this reads like a break-up letter. Preposterous, I know, because we're not together. Before I'm able to make any kind of commitment — which you most definitely deserve — I need more certainty, which can only be gained through more experiences together in the same time and place. And given my work and what I understand about your upcoming year, I don't see how that's possible. I'm sorry my pace is slower. It might be best if we don't speak for a while. You're clearly ready for something significant and I couldn't forgive myself for wasting your time.*

Humiliated by the grain of condescension I detected, livid at his cowardice and devastated by the rejection, not just of me but of the connection between us, I didn't respond for a week. It seemed I was being pulled into a betrayal of the cosmos. And I was mystified by his pedantic attitude. Logistics are solvable, I wanted to tell him, if both parties are game — people make all kinds of scenarios work.

A week later I phoned him to say that I understood where he was coming from and goodbye. It was a kind conversation. He asked if he could call me sometimes, just to talk. I said sure. Ollie predicted I'd hear from him in a month or two but in fact, I heard from him the next day and every day after that. I only ever returned his calls, never initiated contact myself. With the pressure off he came towards me. But we were not together. He'd made sure not to mince words in his email: He didn't want to begin a relationship with me.

When he visited Toronto in the summer, we made an ice-cream cake together and I hugged his neck after he bought me a coffee, but that was the extent of our physical contact. I had started dating someone new but kept this a secret from T. The new person I was dating was funny and well-liked, or "excellent second husband material" as I liked to think of it. He was also on the rebound, never got enough sleep and more than once told me to "calm down". Most importantly though, we generated no heat as a duo — there was no potential for great healing, no recognition between our lizard brains — all of which amplified why T was right for me.

In the autumn, T eventually asked if I was seeing someone. He could hear a change in my voice and was crestfallen to have his hunch confirmed. "I never feel this way about people," he lamented. "I was just feeling ready for a relationship." I told him I felt like I'd been in love with a ghost. He said he wanted to fight, but knew if he really cared for me, he had to let me go peaceably. Later that day he wrote, *I truly wish you the best for this new relationship, Haley. I care about you deeply and want you to be happy. If, down the road, it doesn't work out, please tell me. I will come to you.*

Not long after that, the relationship with the other guy ended. We were both using the other to distract from stubborn heartaches. I made myself wait a month before contacting T again. I didn't want to seem desperate or fickle. While on tour in the UK, I reached out to let him know that things hadn't worked out, and I was available to try with him. I made it clear that the reason I ended it with the other guy was because I couldn't get T out of my head. I didn't get the reaction I anticipated. T replied saying that five weeks was a long time and he wasn't sure of his feelings anymore.

Irate and confused, I blamed his fear and persevered. We made plans to meet in Toronto over the Christmas holidays.

Over burgers, one of the things he mentioned was that he wasn't attracted to skinny girls, which I interpreted to mean, "I don't find you attractive." I was immediately mortified by the oversized grey sweater I was wearing, even though it was a new purchase from Europe. I tried to form an inquisitive smile on my face.

"And besides," he continued, "you'll be in London and I'm in New York."

Determined to save face, I took a breath and put on an upbeat tone. "Okay, forget it. Let's just be friends."

After the meal he walked me home and gripped my jacket when I slipped on a bit of ice and started to topple into a snowbank.

At my door he said, "Well now I don't feel like saying goodbye."

I shrugged, went inside and lay on the sofa. It was as though my guts had been scraped out with a melon baller. I stayed on the sofa through the night, unable to move, stunned numb, flattened by his retraction. Because I didn't believe I was entitled to be heartbroken over something that never was, I couldn't make sense of my reaction.

I hosted my family for Christmas and while they went skating, I cried on the toilet, clutching at the padded bra I wore to mask how much weight I'd lost. I didn't eat the meal. Couldn't.

I was moving to the UK in six weeks. T kept calling and I always answered, my pulse galloping at the sight of his name on my phone. His words didn't add up with his actions.

So, eventually, with Thea's help, I spoke my mind. "I think we're two people in the world who should have slept together." After this call I flew to Arizona, where he was on assignment, to consummate our connection for a sense of closure. He said my body possessed witchy properties — it was a compliment — there was an electric heat radiating from my vulva. My ordinary heartache was thrown into perspective by the splendour of the Grand Canyon. I wept the whole journey home.

I wasn't back in Toronto for more than a week before T texted, offering to fly me to New York. He wrote that he knew he was breaking our agreement, but he'd like to see me again. *Life is short. I'd be an idiot to let this go.* I darted off to NYC shortly before I moved to London, where he introduced me to all his favourite diners and I had an orgasm that lasted for three minutes. I was grateful for my small breasts because they made it nearly possible to press my heart against his.

Once I was in London we were in touch regularly. He promised to visit as soon as possible. By the time he did, several months later, I wanted the boyfriend label and to be told he loved me, though didn't explicitly ask for either, while his feelings had diffused, and he insisted that we were not yet a couple.

That summer we met in Canada and camped for a night. On the car ride to the sticks, he emphasised that in order for us to progress in our relationship he needed an equal. My feelings had been hurt because when I'd arrived at his house, he yelled, "Come in," and stayed seated at his kitchen table, looking at something on his computer, rather than standing to greet me and help me with my bags, not to mention embrace me. He was frustrated that I got weepy about that rather than angry. Later I'd think, I need you to be equally invested, but at the time I stoically nursed my doubly hurt feelings. Keeping his eyes glued to the road, he reached down my denim cut-offs and made me come.

Completely secluded on an island, we pitched our tent and fooled around before cooking over a fire. We headed into the tent to escape the mosquitos. But the night was warm and clear and I wanted to go skinny dipping in the moonlight. He refused to join me. Illuminated by our battery-operated lantern, I pulled off my clothes while he described the ferocity of a beaver's bite. "They clamp their teeth and don't let go."

"Who do you know who's ever been bitten by a beaver?" I said.
He didn't know anyone.

I unzipped the door flap, tiptoed over soft pine needles and slipped into the lake. In the water, I floated on my back, calmed and awestruck by the thick web of stars, dunked my head under and got out, glad I hadn't listened to him.

Back in the tent, T decided he also would go swimming alone. After what seemed like too long, I crawled out to look for him. He was standing knee deep in the lake. When I called out to him, he ordered me to leave him alone. As I fastened the Velcro on my sleeping bag, I resigned myself to get through the night and once we were back to Toronto, I'd be done.

After his swim, his mood had shifted and he tried to kiss me. Infuriated by his inconsistency, I dodged him and erupted, "You push me and push me and push me away and it's working."

He backed up.

"You don't owe me anything. You're released," I hissed, slapping the sleeping bag.

"I don't want to be released," he said mournfully.

"Stop changing your mind."

But I was the one who had to make a choice. A few months later, performing at the Edinburgh Festival, I met Milo and had a fling with a Kiwi circus performer to distract myself from T's distance and my career woes. The circus performer, however, refused to fulfil his function and lost all interest in me once we slept together. After Edinburgh, both of us in Toronto, T said, "I don't want to know about you, but I haven't been with anyone else." I stilled all the muscles in my face, attempting to reveal neither confirmation nor denial. My dalliance with the circus performer was a product of T's design, but admitting it seemed risky.

The day after my thirty-first birthday, we met with the express purpose of discussing our future — were we going to quit or commit?

He said, "I don't want to say goodbye to you," then started to cry. Then I started to cry. And we cried from 8 p.m. that evening until 11 a.m. the next day. We cried for fifteen hours at the thought of saying goodbye. But when we were finished crying, he said, "I just don't know that I'm totally in love with you. Because so much of what we've had has been long distance, it's imaginary. It's not real." That's when I laid down the ultimatum: Boyfriend or bust.

Paradoxically, the frankness he demanded from me ultimately gave me the strength to walk away.

The ultimatum was followed by six months of silence, which he eventually broke by telling me that he wanted to try to commit. Then we met in Canada and tried, but he changed his mind, and told me so before doubling me to the airport on his bike.

Then we had another five months of silence, during which I started *The Ex-Boyfriend Yard Sale*, that ended with T's declaration of love.

"And now here we are." I hold a point on the string that approximately represents the present. "It's better than ever before, but it's still not satisfying in all respects and to be honest . . ." I avoid the fine-grained details of our disagreement last night and simply say, "I'm not sure where we stand." I now pick up the tightly wound spool of string.

"So I guess this," I say, nodding to it, "is my future."

Elson says this is a very useful prop. He suggests having it strung up across the stage for a portion of the show. When I say that it'll get in my way, he's excited. It's a metaphor of how a relationship can interfere with everything else we try to do.

In the bathroom I tell T off in my mind. How could he have the gall to threaten me with a break-up last night? If anyone is going to end this relationship, I am. He's lost all rights and privileges to call it off.

Gemma shows up at the end of the day with a draft of the formula and according to her first run, the mix tape is worth £4.39.

"Did you say the mix tape is four pounds?" I ask, positive I have misheard.

"Yep." She nods.

"No. No, no." I'm shaking my head. "That can't be right."

Elson agrees it seems a little low.

I explain that there were so many firsts in that relationship; I came away with baggage that changed the way I love; it's one of my most monumental heartbreaks; I've never loved as fearlessly since.

"Okay," she says, scrolling through the spreadsheet and glancing at her notes. "We can manipulate how things are weighted. We can make the formula do what you want it to do."

Elson begins asking Gemma some questions, and I stare out the window at the sombre buildings of Moorgate. It hits me: the math I was relying on to be cold and objective is malleable. And the person I've been bending towards me, hammering into the relationship I desire, is immovable.

On the Northern line home, I think about how I have blamed, chased, berated and shamed T for not being a different person. I have kept secrets and withheld the truth so I could feel superior without having to step down from a pedestal or withstand the heat of a confrontation. I have bitten my tongue and rolled my eyes when he wasn't looking. I accepted less than I wanted, and silently harboured resentment. I used our relationship as a means to be with someone while maintaining my autonomy, and it suited me. And all the ways I've tried to control the outcome have left me more alone.

When I have my session with Thea, she commends me for recognising my complicity in my dissatisfying dynamic with T. And when I say I can't handle going through a break-up right now, she tells me it's sensible not to make any big changes while I'm immersed in this project.

Once I know T's deadline has passed, I call him and say, "Please, let's not break up until I'm done with this show."

He says he doesn't want to break up with me, but we do need to have a serious conversation.

I agree. "But I need you in my corner right now."

He tells me he'd love nothing more than to support me.

£ + ♥

Gemma and I are in a trendy, poorly insulated café in London Bridge. Within moments of spreading our papers across a wobbly table I spot a mouse scurry over a woman's boot. I long for Canada's stringent health and safety regulations, but it's good motivation for me not to dilly-dally.

We're taking weekends off rehearsal, rather than working six days a week, so I have time to make changes to the script, learn my lines and finish the formula with Gemma.

"This is my last one, I promise." I have snuck in a small list of possible additions and I'm humbly putting them forth. None of them will change the broad formula but they may have ripple effects on the nuanced work within each phrase. "Unspeakable bliss. Did it exist?"

"It's a yes or no binary?" she asks hopefully.

"Yes. There was either a moment of it, or not."

She says then that's simple enough.

This will be our final Wild Card. After some time on the Internet, we create a symbol for it, based on the Japanese character for cloud nine: 吉. And cheekily, if the unspeakable bliss distinction is given to an object, the buyer must include some form of non-monetary payment, in addition to the cash price, as the physicist Luis Bay suggested.

"Let's say I wanted to buy it," Gem says. "Could I wash dishes, the way they make you do if you can't pay your tab at the pub?"

I close my eyes and cock my head to the left. "I think more important than time or labour is sharing a tale of equal emotional impact. It can be a similar story or one that offers ballast."

We agree that for anything marked with 吉, an "Unspeakable Bliss" Wild Card, the buyer must impart a story that empathises (either commiserating or co-celebrating) or contrasts with my stories associated with the object. In short, 吉 demands a meaningful emotional exchange.

Poetic justice would have Gemma divulging a story from her life now, but she's spotted a mouse too and so she quickly draws the symbol on the formula with her perfect penmanship, and replaces her pencil in her ponytail.

The final version of the broad formula looks like this:

FINAL DRAFT

$$\text{COST OF } \heartsuit = MV \times \left[1 + \frac{NI + DT - t}{t}\right] \times \left[1 + \frac{RI^{\heartsuit}}{1000}\right] \times RTC \times WC$$

And it works like this: the Cost of Love equals Market Value (MV) multiplied by one plus Narrative Impact (NI) plus Dollar Today (DT) minus Time Invested (t) divided by Time Invested (t). This is multiplied by one plus the Relationship Index (RI) to the power of love divided by one thousand. And then that is multiplied by the Rose Tint Corrector (RTC) and any applicable Wild Cards.

Remember, each phrase (MV, NI, DT, t, RI, RTC & WC) represents a series of mathematical functions working with all our variables.

We decide to do a test run with some dummy numbers standing in for audience bids. Gemma's made adjustments over the last few days, primarily increasing the weight of rites of passage and stories that had large emotional impact. She pops a few invented audience bids and reassessments into the spreadsheet and reads out the prices to me. The T-shirt is worth £245,698. And the sum total of my assets is: £389,098. When she asks if they feel right, I say they do. They do.

I give a muted, coffee-shop-appropriate whoop and, smiling, pat her on the back. "Well done, Gemma. Well done." But my heart's not in it. I watch myself putting on a show — an approximation of my imagined reaction, if I felt the satisfaction the moment deserves. "We figured it out. We solved it." After this year with Gemma, revealing my sordid and banal vulnerabilities, here I am performing for her, playing a more palatable rendition of Haley McGee.

I hear Gemma's cup clink in its saucer. "I don't know who you're going to get to pay those steep prices, though. You need to become a celebrity."

"Or," I say, as my cogs turn, "if the lawyer's prophecy comes true, and I earn £389,098 from work I accrue as a result of this project, does that mean that my eight objects are responsible for it?"

Gemma nods, smiling. "In a sense yes, they are responsible, but in the formula we've created, the prices will continue to increase along with your social cachet. The data is ever-evolving — as more people appraise the objects, and as your profile raises, the prices will rise. So long as the correlation between provenance and value is as the auctioneer describes. Unless, of course, we discover there is a tipping point, where the price plateaus or perhaps begins to diminish."

"Right. So, I have to wait and see if this investment pays off." And though we understand the sum total of my assets is liable to keep increasing, we agree that if I earn close to £400k from any work that can be traced back to the show, that's when all the love and pain, and the project itself, will have truly been worth it. That's when I'll have been compensated for the cost of love.

We gaze down at the final draft of our completed formula.

It dawns on me that without the formula to band us together, I'm not sure whether Gemma and I will be friends. The nature of our work means there's an imbalance in how much we know about each other. Do we have anything in common once the formula is removed from our equation? This must be a modicum of what it's like to find yourself, an empty nester, staring at your spouse, wondering who you are to each other without your shared focus, no longer gazing in the same direction but at each other.

Our cups now drained, we notice other customers hovering with hot drinks balanced on clattering saucers, scanning for seats. Gemma hands over the formula and we close our backpacks and leave. That evening I transfer her the money she's owed.

£ + ♥

Despite my best efforts to set up the strongest team and support system, the rehearsal period is utterly chaotic and wipes me out. I don't manage to pack any lunches and my financial tracking goes by the wayside. I regret not having more of the script memorised before we began. Fi runs lines with me a couple times but her thoughts on the show's themes make it hard for her to keep her eyes on the page to prompt me when I mess up.

The day we move into the theatre, I lash out at the team. I'm disappointed the design isn't complete and that I won't be able to rehearse with the plinths until the day before we have our first preview audience. I'm also miffed that while opening night is sold out, the rest of the opening weekend has only sold at 30 per cent capacity. I spray my bad mood around, stomping my feet and snapping morosely when I'm asked questions, until Elson intervenes. "What's going on Haley?"

Something in the way he asks it makes my self-righteousness fall away, and I confess to the room that I'm terrified the show is going to be bad. And I apologise but my eyes stay dry.

Everything gets easier after that. The long days teching the show become delirious and fun. Milo and I are congenial, stuffing our sloppy night out in Shoreditch under the rug and focusing on getting the show up. He's only in rehearsal for a couple hours each week, yet every tea break without fail, he casually mentions the various women he's seeing.

And just like that, it's mid-November and opening night. I arrive at the theatre early enough to distribute my thank you cards to everyone involved in the production and shower them with praise. I haven't heard from T. I thought he would have sent flowers, but nothing has arrived yet.

Nine critics will be in attendance tonight along with my producer's family, Gemma and her boyfriend, the theatre's staff and my improv teammates. My nerves have made it impossible to eat more than a few rice cakes and I've taken about forty-eight trips to the toilet. I got my period this morning and my costume is a pair of white underpants and a tank top. I've done my warm-up — some stretches, some air punches and some strange vocal noises. I've recited my pre-show mantras: "Do not be afraid to be weak. Do not be afraid to be tired. Keep the channel open." And I dedicate the performance to the enlightenment of all beings, including myself, and give thanks to whoever's up there for the chance to be a messenger.

Sitting at the dressing room table, I regard my flushed face framed by exposed lightbulbs, and coach myself to take slow breaths. I remind myself what I know. I know my lines; I've honed the beats of the show; Elson has instructed me to lean into the "scientist" archetype and resist my tendency to sit in any of the emotional material.

The stage manager pops her head in to let me know we'll start letting the audience in in five minutes. "Break a leg."

I jam my retractable pointer into my ponytail and my receipt roll with the variables written on it in my bra and give the air a couple more jabs.

I check my phone one final time. Still no word from T. Oh my god, I think, he secretly got on an airplane and he's coming to the show. I'm on tenterhooks throughout the pre-show appraisals, distractedly asking audience members to write down what they'd pay for my items if they saw them at a yard sale, while keeping an eye on the door for T's entrance. But he doesn't turn up. And I don't have time to ruminate on it.

The audience leans forward as I command the stage. I ride their waves of laughter, of quiet contemplation, of solidarity and catharsis. After encasing myself in bubble wrap, brown paper and twine, while recounting how I tortured my collaborators in my relentless pursuit of the formula, I call out, "Fair warning!" The audience cheers. And I rip it all off. Then, exhausted but not defeated, I use a thick Sharpie on a piece of brown butcher's paper stretched across the back wall of the theatre, to write out the Formula for the Cost of Love at record speed. The paper is five metres long and it takes me just over five minutes to complete. I explain the symbols and functions as I go.

Partway through, the marker dies. Heroically I pull another one out of my bra. When I get to the end, I have to pause for an applause break. The final prices arrive on the zipline from the stage manager's booth and I read them out, reminding the audience that these numbers take into account all my data and assessments as well as their initial bids and their reassessments via clapping.

Item	Audience Initial Bids	Final Prices via Formula
Mix Tape	£3.54	£20,550.55
T-shirt	£5.45	£57,926.68 + 吉
Jewellery Box	£5.84	£66.01
Backpack	£8.55	£180.49 + 吉
Necklace	£20.03	£321.59
Ukulele	£23.16	£20.82
Typewriter	£38.45	£2077.91
Bicycle	£80.68	£242,215.74 + 吉
Total:		£323,359.79

"And tonight, the sum total of my assets is £323,359.79," I say, writing the number on the back wall.

I bring the show to a close and the sold-out audience leaps to its feet. I bow deep, sweeping the floor with my ponytail. My expression of thanks and relief.

After I've changed into my own clothes, Elson bursts into the dressing room, hugs me and says, "You should be proud of yourself."

"I am." I cry for fifteen seconds and apologise.

When I came off stage, I checked my phone. Lots of love from friends and Tweets of praise, but nothing from T. Sometime during the post-show reception he sends a *How did it go?* text.

I'm ashamed of how disappointed I am that he failed to celebrate this momentous day with me. When I raise it, he'll say, "But flowers and platitudes don't mean anything to me. Do you really want an empty gesture?"

I do.

But for now, my exuberance is high. In the dressing room, I took a moment to crumple all my rage and disappointment with T into a tiny ball the size of a pea and stuff it in my pocket. My improv compatriots, the design team, theatre staff and I all pile into an Indian restaurant on Drummond Street, wolfing down dosas and pickles and chugging booze from the off-licence next door. I have a jubilant night, even forgetting the ball is there, until I turn too quickly and it begins to unfurl, stabbing my thigh. It takes a few minutes to compress it back down to the size of a pea.

The show struggles for audiences in the beginning, but by the end of its three-week run, the reviews have been strong and the buzz hot. To boot, we were granted great fortune by being featured in the *Guardian*. Ticket sales spike, the show sells out, the rest of the run is waiting list only and miraculously, a literary agent approaches me. She believes *The Ex-Boyfriend Yard Sale* could make a commercially viable book. I'm dancing with fancy footwork and picking up my stage manager to spin her around. I email the lawyer, who responds with, *Told ya.*

£ + ♥

By the time the show closes my body is gaunt and I'm running on fumes. Verity, my new literary agent, and I get to work on the book proposal. It's been a year since T and I rekindled things, but we don't celebrate an anniversary. There's nothing to celebrate. I wasn't even able to raise my point about the opening-night flowers. By requesting that we not break up at the beginning of the rehearsal process, I seem to have surrendered my rights to demand anything. All his actions are on credit. I have to maintain civility. I have no idea what's going on with my brother or Ollie, it's been entirely me me me.

After a flurry of meetings with TV producers, arranged by Verity — all of which I managed to tediously botch due to my lack of TV knowledge and propensity for experimental projects — I snuggle into the flat, decorate my Norfolk pine and bake oodles of cookies with Fi. They sit in a giant Tupperware box above the sink. I munch on them as I pat around the carpet in my housecoat, studying book proposals, figuring out how to transform my solo show into a literary object.

No voice work comes. My producer and I settle the financials for the show. I have to dip deeper into my own money because of low box office numbers early in the run and the number of concession tickets sold that we failed to account for. The meetings and Christmas parties run their course. I'm staying in London again this year.

Navid is spending the holidays in Iceland with Ísleif. T is with his family commemorating the loss of his brother. When I catch up with Ollie, he's settling into his new pad in Holland Village, the "Bohemian" neighbourhood best suited to his tastes.

I love London at Christmas. The place empties out. And with

the congestion cleared, its lungs have room to breathe. The quiet of the city centre is precious, akin to my reverence for fresh fallen snow. As I wander through Piccadilly Circus, I think about how my enjoyment of this quiet is similar to the sensation of exploring a neighbour's house when I've been asked to bring in their mail while they're on vacation.

I get rested. On Christmas morning, I sleep in late and make myself a pancake feast while listening to a podcast. It's mostly on to fill the silence, but when the guest, Jim Dethmer, speaks about "integrity breaches" I put the ladle down and pay attention. He says that the definition of integrity he prefers is taken from the word "integer", which means a whole number and comes from the Latin word for "whole". "Am I living in a state of wholeness? Am I living in alignment with myself? Am I energetically whole and alive?" He explains integrity is just energy and alignment — it's not moral or ethical. Integrity breaches are anything that interrupts a person's aliveness or wholeness.

Over pancakes I look up the definition of integrity.

> *Integrity, noun*
> 1. *The quality of being honest and morally upright*
> 2. *State of being whole or unified*

It springs to my mind to look up the definition of dignity once again alongside this.

> *Dignity, noun*
> 1. *The state of being worthy of respect*
> 2. *A calm or serious manner*
> 3. *A sense of pride in yourself*

I drag my index finger through the puddle of leftover maple syrup on my plate, not missing out on a drop while I consider the difference between these two guiding principles.

The difference to me is that "integrity" is internal. It's about being whole, matching your innards, your inner feelings and desires with your outward actions and expression — a sense of being unified as a self. Whereas "dignity" is about garnering respect, from others *and yourself*. It seems to be more about judgement and seeking approval instead of simply being whole.

I've now moved on to pouring a little bit of maple syrup onto my knife and licking it off.

Dignity, even when it's in the self-respect realm, is concerned with optics. Dignity is reliant on an assessment.

Just then, Milo texts:

Happy Christmas, McGee. You're welcome to join for dinner if you decide the solo day is too lonesome. My clan would love to have you. :)

I lie down on the carpet. I've been living wrong. I've got some serious integrity breaches. I have to stop lying in my actions. I have to get back in alignment. I resolve to be a person of integrity. And unequivocally I know what I have to do. I have to lose the pseudo-boyfriend and the not-enough boyfriend too. It's a sobering revelation but leavening as well. I write Milo and say how about coffee in a few days instead.

T and I don't exchange gifts. We speak later but I'm conscious I can't interpose a break-up around the anniversary of his brother's death. We keep it convivial. He's heading back to New York in a few days and we'll "connect properly" then. Knowing that I'm on my way out makes it easier to love him, to be generous about his grief. If I could love a partner without desiring reciprocity all my suffering would vanish. Is that what the Buddhists preach? I wish I could ask Milo. I don't think I'll ever meditate enough to be a selfless lover.

I spot Milo, eternally early, sucking hard on a cigarette, pacing. Just coffee today, no pizza. My dime.

"McGee." He bows to me.

I imitate his affect and bow back. "Milo."

The café is empty except for us. It's hard to drive to the heart of my message. He's become jovial, nervously jokey. As I requested this coffee, I have to lead the charge.

"Okay so listen," I say, lengthening my spine.

He looks into his cup.

"I feel really bad." I practised this with Thea. I even have notes in my purse, but I won't refer to them.

This is what they say (Ollie helped me cross out the stuff that was unnecessary):

I haven't been totally proud of my behaviour with you. ~~I've been duplicitous, I think~~. I really like our friendship but since you told me how you felt about me, I've been giving you mixed messages. ~~Not because I like you but because I'm dissatisfied with T. And I really enjoyed your attention.~~ Don't worry I'm not going to condescend to you by saying something like "you deserve better", though I do think you deserve something one-hundred-percent reciprocated — we both do — we all do. Our relationship is bad for me.

I manage to get a lot of it out, albeit in a somewhat mangled way. He's very still, head bowed. I think he's still listening. I carry on, "I know I've been ambivalent and ambiguous about this thing between us." I take a beat before I come to the thesis: "I don't see a romantic future for us."

He lifts his face. "And you never will?"

Now it's my turn to stare into my cup. "Probably not."

"But you did."

I nod. Then shrug. Then move my head side to side, maybe yes, maybe no. Then say, "I think so?"

"But now it's just, what? Dead?" There's a tenor of puzzlement in his voice. He sounds close to tears.

I tell him I'm sorry. I wish I did. In so many ways my life would be simpler if I could will myself into a romantic place with him, but—

"I get it." He's heard enough but I have to finish my sentence. "I can't."

"I get it, McGee." He eyes me with weary disappointment.

A couple plunks themselves down beside us and we take our cue to leave. We wander through the Heath for a bit. Milo says he can't be friends with me. Maybe forever. At least for a while. I was expecting this. I know that historically he'd been an all or nothing person, but the amicable split he's had with Julie gave me hope that we could salvage our friendship.

A small child in a dinosaur mask and tutu crosses our path on a scooter, singing "That's Amore" at the top of her lungs. Milo and I look at each other and laugh as her parents chase after her.

"We could have a great life McGee," Milo says half wistfully, half admonishing me.

"I know." I offer it to be kind. But it's only 60 per cent true.

"T doesn't live here."

Here we go, I think, reconnaissance. "I know," I say, laying down arms.

"And you're not happy with him." Milo nearly yells this.

I don't argue.

"You're miserable." He stops in the middle of the path.

I turn to look at him, thoughts formulating as I speak: "Just because it's probably not T, doesn't mean it's you."

Rain sprinkles and we quicken our pace. When dark clouds capture the sky, we run. Milo dives into his car and I remain outside. He rolls down the window and offers me a ride, but I decline and begin to walk instead. Milo speeds though a puddle as he passes me, soaking my boots. Fair.

One down, one to go. I will head into the new year with this equation balanced.

THE LEDGER

Love	Barely with T
	Pseudo-boyfriend is gone
Money	Burned through £8k & had to borrow from self to make up from shortfall on box office earnings
	– £890.82 in debt
	£436.40 in bank
Career	No voice work since Sept
	No success at TV meetings
	No Joe-job work available
	Working on book proposal
	Preparing to tour *The Ex-Boyfriend Yard Sale* in Toronto and Rotterdam

---

Total ? *Could be better*

PART THREE

COST/BENEFIT ANALYSIS

18. PAYOUT

"Most people have an aversion to risk, my college economics professor told me. Which means they have to be rewarded to take on that risk. The higher the risk, the higher the possible payout has to be for people to jump."

Michael Arrington

Once T returns to NYC we roll up our sleeves and get into it over Skype. The crux is, it's not working. What we now have is a radical reduction of what I want — or need. We have to end it. A lightness fills me as we come upon this resolution together.

We agree to keep talking, to process this together. Over the next few days, I lounge on the sofa as T and I negotiate our separation.

The conversation flows, kind and thoughtful, filled with apologies, sorrow, regret and tears followed by numbness, and punctuated with moments of litigious indignation from me, in which I hurl the book at him and itemise the arenas in which he has let me down:

"You have been ungenerous on occasions that matter to me — no flowers at opening, for example. You still haven't met my family. You never procured your UK passport and you have not acknowledged that you reneged on that promise. You never came to London for a month, and again, no acknowledgement that you said you would. You dropped therapy again and again. You haven't made a plan to see me on your upcoming trip to Europe. We had no plans for Christmas or New Year's Eve when I had all this time free. You have not made any effort to Skype with me.

And it breaks my heart that in all these years you have never seen one of my solo shows and you've not made it a priority."

He says, "I'm not with you because of your shows."

"My solo shows are a big part of my identity."

But as we unpack our relationship, T begins to question if separating is right after all. He says he flubbed it badly with Christmas and New Year's. He is coming to Europe for work in a few weeks and it makes sense to see each other. He says come to Budapest, please. At some point between conversations, he books a flat big enough for me to stay with him there. A tinge of the simpering puppy enters his voice when he tells me this.

A couple years ago, this gesture would have enchanted me, but now, I'm nearly unmoved. "You didn't check to see if those dates work for me," I say. But after all the circling, we find ourselves closer. Our candid conversations have dispelled tension and tightened our bond. I admit that I would like to see him, to say goodbye properly. We'll put the relationship to bed together in Budapest.

He also books a ticket to see *The Ex-Boyfriend Yard Sale* at the festival in Toronto in February, along with an airline ticket and an Airbnb. It'll be a bit strange having him there after we're broken up, but since we're committed to remaining friends — after all, that's what we actually are — this will be fine.

In Budapest, T and I pour all our affection and penitence into our best sex yet. It's clutching, gulping, desperate, let-me-have-you-while-I-still-can sex. Our flat is on the top floor of an art nouveau walk-up. At the head of the bed, a circular shaped window looks onto a clock-tower. Snow falls and I melt into colours, T's expert cunnilingus erasing my speech.

While he's out working on his story during the days, I chip away at the book proposal, covering the sloped attic walls with a rainbow of Post-its.

Bad moments are limited to T having a panic attack over dinner after I told him I was flat out of empathy for him. He'd started to get anxious about something and all I felt was my compassion being siphoned away.

"Your moods run this relationship," I tell him. "When you're in a bad mood nothing happens that you don't want to."

Eventually he says he has to get back to therapy. I make an "up to you" face and think, thank god he's out of my life soon.

The good moments are spent in bed and teetering through cobble stone roads, searching out the stuffed kohlrabi T is determined we try. In Budapest, with the pressure off, we break through to the other side of the pain that's plagued us with a force and clarity that renews my hope, and his commitment. And in the end, we can't end it. We are more attached and more connected after this trip. We rationalise it. As T's coming to Toronto next month for the show, we'll say goodbye then.

Back in London, the book proposal is meant to be my primary focus; however, Ísleif got pregnant over Christmas. Therefore an earlier moving date is thrust upon us both. Navid and I don't really say goodbye. We're ships in the night, each of us removing our personality from the flat. My plants go to Fi's garden. The theatre houses all the materials for the show. Devoid of our stuff, the flat is cooler and uncannily spacious.

I roam between Fi's future baby's room and Stan and Sue's in Tooting — the couple in their seventies who I lodged with before moving into Navid's — while I save money and search for a flat of my own. My propensity for writing from home drives this desire. I'm banking on an imminent book deal to make it feasible. Whatever money I "save" on rent is funnelled into restaurants and cafés. I don't track my finances because I know the numbers will distress me. The house hunt engenders anger at T. Why aren't we looking for *our* home?

Ollie says cohabitation is overrated. His flat in Singapore is serving as an excellent "revolving door" where no lover is permitted to spend the night.

At improv, my impulses bring forth violent scenes. I'm either playing fascist high school teachers, bloodsucking creatures or calcified middle-aged women. "Why do you like me?" I challenge my fellow player in an accusatory tone. My strident character had been harsh with him for the whole show, and he continually returned my snippy tone with adoration. My challenge gets a huge laugh and my scene partner and I start to corpse. "Give me a kiss," I order and he does. Our coach says it's the only kiss I earned all season.

Fi is in the audience alone this night, shrieking as she cackles. She's not pregnant anymore. She carried her last pregnancy for ten weeks before miscarrying. She and her husband have been fighting. He's in Majorca at a stag do this weekend. After the show she pulls the sweater I'm wearing off my torso, explaining in a delirious hush that she laughed so hard she peed her pants and needs to cover her wet bum.

T is in Toronto for two days. Knowing I'd be consumed with the show, he prepared himself to feel unsatisfied by our little time together. He sends a gift backstage before the show and rushes to my dressing room afterwards to kiss me. But as we trudge through the city's sidewalks of compacted snow after drinks with my friends, he admits that throughout the entire performance he wanted to scream, "You can't create an equation for the cost of love without the other person!"

I don't equivocate. (It's not an equation! It's a formula.) When we get inside the apartment, I just sob. The shower in the Airbnb is cold with low pressure. I climb into bed shivering and we don't have sex. I don't experience this as rejection. I don't want to be touched.

The next morning T admits that he didn't enjoy the role he

was relegated to after the show. He wanted to be his own person and not consigned to a beta.

I tell him I can see it was unfair that I interviewed many of my other exes and not him.

The following day he helps the team load out of the theatre, buys us expensive Thai food and gives me a soy-wax pine-scented candle for Valentine's Day.

How could this fly-by visit be our final goodbye? Things don't feel done. I want to see him in New York. Back in London, from my bedroom at Fi's, I book a flight — a renegade colluding with her boyfriend to disobey her big sister.

Fi has her fourth miscarriage in eleven months while I'm staying at her house. The mounting losses seem to belong between the two people involved in the endeavour, and yet I'm here, cast as a witness. And a buffer.

I yearn to make myself scarce. I tiptoe around, carefully eking on the shower tap, closing the cupboards gingerly. But Fi and Ru don't require or even seem to desire my efforts to disappear. They seem to crave a third party to focus their mutual attention on.

"I'm so ready to be a mother," says Fi. Hot water bottle on her abdomen.

I lie on her bed with her. Together we stare through the skylight. London's cloud-streaked sky, planes criss-crossing our view. I want to ask if they'd consider adopting, if it's really about being a parent and not about being pregnant. But this isn't the right time. It may never be. Besides, I know what it's like to have a vision for your life and a specific way you want to fulfil it.

When Ru gets home, I roll out of their bed, glad to have him replace me at his post.

I circle around the Hollow Ponds and wish I was walking with T. I miss Milo. I miss Ollie. I miss Toronto. I miss the possibilities of the many roads presented to me when I was twenty-one.

My money is dwindling. I'm in credit card debt again and only falling deeper in. I haven't had a voice job in almost six months and the book hasn't sold. I emailed my Joe-jobs to let them know I'm available, but my schedule's tricky to work around because I'm heading to NYC for a week and then I'm off to the Netherlands shortly after that.

Verity arranges meetings with more TV producers. I write pitches and do follow-up meetings on how we could transform the stage show into a fictionalised TV series, or a non-scripted one in which members of the public get to create a formula for their items for their exes, which I dub "The Broken Hearts Roadshow". I begin work on a podcast series, *The Cost of Love*, where I'll interview experts in tangentially related fields, from couples' counsellors, to divorce lawyers, economists and sex workers, about the intersection of love and money. I'm approached by several commercial theatre producers who want to capitalise on the stage show, scale it up and get it touring to regional houses for years. But I ask myself, how can I go on the road for that long? What if I get bored of the show? I'd have to trade my ownership of the show and my time. Plus how will I ever meet someone new if I never stop moving? So Verity and I pass on what once would have been a dream for me, without a morsel of regret. I take meetings with prominent presenting houses in London, including one from the West End. We talk dates for the transfer. And then they ghost us. All the theatres who'd been interested just stop replying. And the TV companies, though convincingly enthusiastic in our last correspondence, go silent too.

Since December, Thea's allowed me to defer therapy payments again. Now it's March and she says it's time to go on a payment plan. I steel myself as we hammer out a daunting schedule to ensure she's repaid over the next six months.

£ + ♥

After a tense half-day in NYC during which I confront T about his pursed-lipped breathing and anxiety about the blank page, we have our best visit yet. The day before I arrived I got my period — not that it's ever been an imposition, but I prefer not to deal with its custodial duties. Luckily, it only lasts three days. The East Village ensconces us as we ramble and swoon. But even despite this being the most relaxed we've ever been with the lowest quotient of strife, the underlying problems between T and me remain. We have no plan for a life together and T will not make any suggestions as to how we might make one.

Yet by the time I'm boarding the plane, we're so bonded that we would be bereft to cut ourselves off from each other. And in the weeks after my return to the UK, I can't end it. Neither can he. We're attached again. "Maybe we don't have to force it," we say. "We can let it dissipate on its own. It happens naturally anyway."

It takes longer than usual for our pattern to repeat.

The pattern repeats.

£ + ♥

On one of the first nights warm enough to sit out in the garden again, Fi asks how it's going with T.

"It's uh . . ." I decide not to lie, "bad."

"Well—" she's about to start in.

"See this—" I stop myself. "Actually, forget it."

"No, say it." She sweeps her stemless wine glass to the right, as if clearing the way for me.

"This is why I don't talk about it. I feel judged."

We're on the brink of an uncomfortable argument when John Lewis makes a strange howling noise and won't stop.

The next hour is a fever dream. Fi and I in an Uber, John Lewis convulsing, Fi yelling at the driver to go faster, Fi giving me her phone. Me explaining John Lewis's symptoms to the emergency vet, Fi coaxing him to breathe. Fluorescent lights of the waiting room. Fi pacing. John Lewis limp. Fi refusing to pay for a service that didn't save her dog. Me holding a garbage bag containing John Lewis's stiff body on my lap on the drive home.

"What's supposed to happen now is that our dog dies, but it's okay because I'm pregnant," Fi says when we get back in the house. "This is a mess. It's a fucking mess." While she cries and drinks red wine in the bath, I clear out the freezer and put the dog inside. Ru is in Romania on a work trip. I call and tell him John Lewis had a blood clot, which led to a stroke.

He says he'll try to get home as soon as possible but he might not be able to leave early. I bring a melting container of chocolate and banana ice cream to Fi in the tub.

She takes the next day off work and demands that I do the same. We dig a hole under the lemon tree in the back garden.

"I mean you know it's coming when you get a pet — you know they're going to die, but . . . You think it's going to be worth it. But I don't know why I would set myself up for this kind of . . . again." She folds into herself on the plush garden furniture and makes a sound I can only describe as keening — somewhere between a wail and a song. "When does it just stop being awful?"

"I don't know," is all I can manage to say. When I touch her back, she flinches.

We drink gin, expensive gin with fresh squeezed oranges, and when we run out of oranges Fi takes it on ice and gets mad when I switch to tea and tells me I need to eat more. Despite being insatiably hungry and eating constantly, my metabolism seems to be speeding up, and lately even a few sips of booze have been giving me serious headaches.

Later she wants me to tell her about T again, to be distracted.

I don't want to. "It's so trivial compared to what you're going through."

"It's all relative — suffering is suffering."

"Okay but I don't want a lecture."

"Yeah, maybe don't tell me then." She lies back on her sectional sofa and the tears flow. She releases a long, animalistic squall.

And I watch, embarrassed by the miniature nature of my woes.

£ + ♥

In the coming weeks two publishers, one in Canada and another in the UK, buy my book. I sorely misjudged the going rate for a book advance. It's markedly less than I'd promised myself in my mind. Nor did I realise the advance is paid in four instalments over three years, only two of which will I receive *in advance* of publication.

"What am I supposed to live off while I write it?" I ask my agent.

She's sympathetic. "Yes, that's the question for writers."

Luckily, as my brother says, I can sell my voice to the man. And that's what I will do. But the man doesn't want to buy me these days. The festival in the Netherlands is fun, but I come shy of breaking even. My credit card debt grows.

The flat hunt continues to appal me. Based on my most recent tax return, the estate agents say I can afford a place up to £1,053 per calendar month. If I want something more expensive than that, then I have to pay the shortfall upfront, along with a security deposit, which is six weeks' rent. I spiral: How am I going to get a place of my own if I can't get my shit together when I'm living for free? Is there any pattern I can break? What was the point of all those goddamn mantras and meditations about the goddess of money, if all that happens is me repeatedly lurching from feast to famine?

Fortuitously, in the span of a week, four disparate people ask me if I would ever teach a course on how to create a solo show. From my single bed at Stan and Sue's, a syllabus materialises. I type it up zealously, balancing the laptop on my stomach. With Thea's encouragement, I book a venue and advertise. The course

fills up so fast, I add another session. To celebrate, I unsub-
scribe from the catering company's emails.

With my newfound income stream, plus the book advance
and a one-episode TV gig that I landed a couple days after I
taught my first class, I scrape together the shortfall, security
deposit and first month's rent, and in May I sign a rental agreement for my own flat in south-east London.

The flat is in no man's land. The closest Tube stop is a ten-
minute walk *plus* a thirty-five-minute bus ride away. It's a
twenty-five-minute walk to the closest Overground and an
eighteen-minute walk to a Southern Railway train station. But
it is so bright and clean and warm and spacious that I am reticent to have people over, so ashamed of the riches the gods
have spoiled me with.

From a hotel room in Cardiff where I'm filming the TV show,
I try to explain to T the predicament I find myself in with him.
"There's this person I love and this kind of relationship that I
badly want, but I can't seem to bring them together. And it's
maddening."

T calls it our "cycle of pain". A pattern where the outcome is
always the same.

"It's the same because you don't change," I say flatly.

He says it's not that he doesn't think I'm terrific. He wants to
give me all the things I want, but he can't see the point of fighting for our relationship anymore.

No longer cool and detached, I ask why I'm not worth more.

"I hate when you phrase it that way, Haley. It's not a reflection of your value." He doesn't say it, but I can tell he wants to
tell me not to quote my own show.

£ + ♥

Ollie now swears he never wants more than casual intimacy.
He's recently started seeing someone new. This guy pales in

comparison to his ex but he's carrying on with him. I'm traipsing through the Victorian Market Building in Cardiff's city centre, admiring the fish and the flowers.

When I tell him that nobody is making him date this person, Ollie tells me the way we feel love when we're young is not replicable. "Once you're of a certain age, it's extinct for you. And everything available is a lesser version, a copy of a copy of a copy. Why try?"

"Ollieeee." I try to remind him of who he is by how I pronounce his name. "That's not true. It's not a mutated clone. It's a different thing."

"The 'different thing', then, is worse. Like muscles that atrophy. Skin sags, taste buds dull. The capacity for love withers."

"You don't know that."

"You're only saying that because you're an optimist."

"I'm not."

"Okay well, you're not a cynic." He drags on his vape pen. "For us cynics, what's the point in hoping if everything ends in either heartbreak or contempt?"

"As in familiarity breeds it?"

"Yeah."

He's got me. I'm walking through the market slowly. My knees have started to ache. Ageing is pain, I think. "Are you saying you really don't believe in any good, lasting love?"

"Who do you know who has it?"

I rack my brain for relationships I'd like to emulate. And it's true. There are very few. "I get it Ollie. When to quit or when to commit?"

"If every relationship encounters the same struggles does it really matter who we're with?"

"So, I should resign myself to a lifetime of struggle and woe with T — and enjoy the rare moments of bliss?"

"Just don't expect anything better with anyone else."

I sit on a bench and massage my throbbing kneecaps. "Sure,

no one's perfect but what about gradients of compatibility? And what about love?"

"What about love?" he says emptily.

£ + ♥

Back in London and in my new home, T and I agree to split again. We're not going to speak for a week, to ease ourselves out, informed by the failed cold turkeys of our past. When we hang up, I'm spooked by my heart racing. It's been doing that a lot lately. Your heart is breaking, I tell myself, no wonder it feels weird. Other things have been feeling weird too. The joints in my feet and hands ache in the mornings and I've had headaches that made me feel hungover without drinking at all. I've made an appointment to visit my doctor in a few weeks' time.

The next morning, I'm on track to be at my desk by nine and commence writing the book, but after making a coffee and walking to my desk, my heart is beating furiously. I lie on the hardwood floor in a cold sweat, shaking. I take my phone out of the pocket of my housecoat and measure my heart rate: 140 beats per minute.

At the hospital they keep asking if I've felt anxious or moody lately, to which I reply, "I've been anxious and moody my entire life." Ten hours and several blood tests later, I'm diagnosed with an autoimmune condition called Graves' disease. I have an overactive thyroid. I'd written off all my symptoms as insomnia, ageing and a fast metabolism.

From the hospital I call T. He's instantly researching thyroid conditions and joins a hyperthyroid chatroom as "haleyBF". At home, while I lie on the sofa, knocked out by beta blockers and a heavy dose of anti-thyroid drugs, he continually checks in from afar.

A fellow improviser, who is an osteopath by day, creates a dietary, sleep and meditation protocol for me that includes one phrase about overactive thyroid problems being triggered by stress, in particular, the threat of losing the person you rely on for emotional support. I don't relay this to T, but it comes to mind when he confides his fear that he's to blame for my medical issue. I assure him he's not. But I wonder what I'd done to bring it on myself.

I discuss with Thea what would be healing right now. Yet again, I screw my courage and in halting half-measures, I ask T to come and be with me for a few calm days together.

"I don't know if that's a good idea," he says in his social worker tone.

First, I castigate. "It's so fucked that you'll be back in Budapest in two weeks and you have made no plans to see me." Then, all my pride pushed to one side, I supplicate. "I don't have anyone else. I don't want to be alone."

He reminds me our relationship is painful. "And, Haley, we're breaking up."

"Then why do you keep calling me?"

He doesn't answer my question but says, "If you want me to come, I will give you that."

"I want you to want to see me."

I promise we'll sleep in separate beds.

I dutifully wash the sheets and towels for him and set up a mattress on the floor of my office where I'll sleep.

He asks if my therapist would be willing to help us break up. I love this idea. Thea considers and agrees to do it.

T arrives during a heatwave, but I now live too far from the Heath to go swimming. On the first day of his visit, he rubs my feet and buys me a fern in a terracotta pot. We're affectionate with each other but our lips don't touch. He offers to make tea but gets distracted with his phone. I dampen the urge to point this out and make it myself. He eats the grapefruit I bought in anticipation.

I shower in the evening. I have a full, luscious bush of pubic hair, unplucked nipples, fuzzy legs and armpits too. The beta blockers reduce me to three hours of energy each day; why would I have spent a portion of them on hair removal when we'd agreed not to sleep together?

As I tread from the bathroom to my office with a towel wrapped around my body, T intercepts me.

"I mean, I don't know Haley. I came here to be with you. We don't have to sleep in separate beds."

I hold the towel tight and look at the flecks of red nail polish that remain on my big toes. "No," I say, swaying slightly from one foot to the other, "I think it's good."

He looks pained.

"Kiss me and we'll try sleeping in separate beds tonight." We kiss soft and clean a few times, lingering, and then I tell him the keys are on the counter if he gets up first and wants to go out. "Don't wake me."

I sleep deep and long on the floor of my office. In the morning, I'm so glad to have slept alone so I could fart and take up space and not be impinged upon by worrying about annoying T.

He returns with more gifts: smoked fish, fresh eggs, a copy of *Monocle* and the *Observer*. He whips up a breakfast straight away, even though he's been caught in the flash thundershower.

We lie in each other's arms on the sofa. He strokes my hair and kisses my forehead. Outside the summer temperature rises again.

I get exasperated with a habit of his that I always forget about until we're reunited, where he asks me an open-ended question and as soon as I begin to answer, he walks out of the room, and I find myself shouting, panicked that I won't be heard. He apologises when I point it out but continues to do it. I decide to adjust and stop talking when he leaves the room.

That night we have sex. It's very good. When he asks if he should sleep in my bed with me, I say, "Nah." We both admit that we love sleeping in separate rooms.

The next morning an inordinate number of house flies have filled my flat. They spill out of a crack in the baseboard and smatter the walls. We lose hours smushing them with paper towels.

With great earnestness, T posits a biblical connection.

"Because we slept together?"

"Yeah," he says solemnly.

"No," I assure him. "That's ridiculous. It's the heatwave."

But later that day sitting in a beer garden, gobbling our Sunday lunch, house flies surround me. I survey the rest of the patio. No one else seems to be dealing with them.

With gravity, I ask T, "Is it *me*?"

He laughs. "No, babe."

We buy sticky fly traps and hang them from my light fixtures, but then spend a lot of time squishing the flies as their legs pedal the air, their delicate wings caught in thick glue.

Later T sobs and apologises for all the ways he has not followed through on his pledge. He sobs in an unhinged way. "There's something wrong with me," he says. He's sorry for all the ways he hurt me — that's what he was startled by in my show. "I'm so, so sorry. I'm just so sorry Haley. I really thought I could do it." The notion of hurting me causes him profound distress.

"It's okay it's okay it's okay," I try to soothe him as we lie face to face. I know he's not malicious. But with sudden plainness, I see how I've cast him in that part. Nobody made me stay here, with my hands on my hips, stomping my foot, asking him to change. And refusing to accept him for who he is. "It's okay," I repeat again.

His tears fall into my eyes and pool with mine. When they roll down to my mouth, I swear they taste different. I hold him for a long time, my palm pressed against the back of his neck.

I have accepted this relationship. More than that, I have co-created it. I have not held up my end of the bargain either, my end to not settle for less, to hold my ground.

Nobody made me stay, I think again, the concept taking hold. In fact, though the culture is all about securing a decent bloke in the nick of time, most of the people in my life counselled me to leave. And I, perhaps foolishly, thought — hoped — that our love would surpass all the impediments, not just the physical distance, but the inner barriers that have made it impossible for us to truly unite. I'm culpable.

It strikes me that a person's innate urges can't be manipulated. They can only evolve over time, at their own pace. T, behaving from a place of integrity, isn't able to give me what I've said I wanted. And only now has something shifted enough in me that I can no longer accept what he has on offer. And many people told me so, but I had to arrive at that conclusion on my own.

On T's final evening we sit on my sofa together and stare into my computer. From her office on the other side of the Atlantic, Thea offers to be our witness. T is initially resistant, but Thea wins his confidence quickly with her adept observations about our dysfunctional dynamic.

I start off by scoffing at my hard-nosed determination to stuff the connection T and I share into a relationship that doesn't fit.

"But Haley, look who is here beside you," Thea points out, "trying as well. You've never been alone in that effort."

"She's right."

The conversation rushes on and I grasp at phrases to store in my memory.

At one point, T says he knows I'm strong, but he feels like he's abandoning me and he's confused as to why. We talk about the polarised roles T and I have found ourselves in. By way of illuminating my attachment injuries, off the cuff, Thea says, "And of course, Haley, you have your thing of, 'Why will no one go to the wall for me?'"

At those words, my tears come on hard. A deluge from my solar plexus. Eventually I say, "I want to make my own family." I don't mean that I need to have a baby, but I want a partner that I create a family unit with, even if that's just the two of us.

"And what about you, T?" Thea asks. "Do you want to make your own family?"

He moves his jaw around but can't get words out. "I don't know. I don't know."

At this, she remarks that his perpetual ping-ponging around, his inability to make a commitment to a place, indicates a fear of commitment or intimacy, maybe a feeling of unworthiness of love. She and T agree that this is a neurosis that T needs to untangle on his own, because it's making a relationship impossible. T apologises for not doing therapy regularly, for dropping his end of the deal.

I forfeit the enlightened point of view I'd achieved a couple days ago and sling some mud. "I do blame you for us failing. And I don't understand how you could not have wanted to try harder?"

"Do you understand, it's not that he didn't want to, Haley, he couldn't?" asks Thea.

T corrects her, "Well, no. I didn't."

Gently, she pushes back. "Not that you didn't, T. You couldn't. It wasn't your authentic movement to do those things you promised, even if on a conscious level you wanted to."

"Right," T says.

And I know she's right too.

We seem to reach a point of mutual understanding but as we're winding down, I blurt out, "I know this is disruptive but I am really angry that T has never told me what he *wants*."

After some back and forth Thea says to T, "It sounds like, because Haley is able to tell you what she wants, there's been stuff you can do to help. But if she doesn't know what you want, then there's nothing she can do to meet you halfway. And I think, from what I'm hearing, that this has made her feel help-less in the relationship."

She floats that to break this cycle, we must do something drastic and brave. "How about no contact for a year with no obligation to meet on the other side?"

We're silenced by this but neither of us rejects it. We look at each other. It's a long time. But six months wasn't enough, historically.

"I'm scared of being tossed back out into the middle of the ocean."

T says he understands and he's there too. "I rely on you."

When we get off the call, T curls into himself and bawls. "No one's ever said I have a fear of intimacy or an unworthiness of being loved."

"Really?" This has been so obvious to me I never thought to raise it with him. I flick on the kettle, then head to the bath-room. I pee forcefully and pop an ingrown hair on my thigh, before washing my face.

When I return to the living room with two cups of tea, he's stretched out long, staring at the ceiling. I put the tea on the radiator, kill a few flies that have appeared on the window, and slither in alongside him. Breathe in his white T-shirt. We don't talk for a while. His hand rests lightly on my back. The sun sets over Lordship Lane. Purple and pink haze splashed with orange.

"I'm terrified."

"Me too."

Holding and kissing and clutching and cupping each other's faces and squeezing each other's arms and taking turns comfort-ing and rallying and "we tried", "we really did our best" and "when we're sixty we'll be friends and we'll laugh at how absurd it was that we tried to date". Finally, "I know I'm never going to find anyone better than you."

Then I cry. "I'm so, so sorry I wasn't more generous about your brother. I'm sorry I've been so angry and tight."

He says he understands and that I did nothing wrong.

In my bed we kiss with deliberate care and warmth and finality. He starts to go down on me and I remind him I haven't showered today.

He says, "I don't care. I love you, Haley." As if love usurps a gross-out factor, which, I guess for him, it does. And me too. This is the other side of the Ew Point, when someone at their dirtiest is still attractive to you. I zone out for a moment thinking, I must remember this peculiarity so I can write about it in the book. T is a chivalrous lover.

We sleep in separate rooms, even though he's leaving in the morning. When he wakes up he comes back to my mattress on the floor and we have sex again. Then we have breakfast.

Over scrambled eggs, we split the cost of the therapy session, but T misremembers the fee and transfers me ten dollars more than he needs to. When I try to give it back, he won't take it. "It was more than worth it."

T says that, as he suspected, coming together has made this decision to separate much harder. Especially now that we've figured out sleeping in separate rooms and couples' therapy are so useful. He's worried he's making the biggest mistake of his life.

"I'm not." It comes out before I even have time to brace myself or take a breath or think — it's out.

"You're sure?"

I nod. "We have to break up. There's no hope otherwise."

"We do." He almost laughs.

The only path to the love we want is by ending this. We discuss the terms of our non-talking for a year. We agree to trust the other is thinking of us.

He says it's okay if I find someone else. It's the risk he has to take.

I hope I do. I hope he doesn't. But I don't say that. I say, "If you do, just don't post about it on social media right away."

He promises he never would.

I say I won't either.

He says if I do, he can take it. And he wants me to be happy — he cares more about my happiness than his own. I believe him.

"And T," I say, "this is not your fault. And in my best self, I don't blame you."

He nods and leans back. Our plates empty now. Neither of us want to check the time.

"And just so you know," I say, "even if I don't put it in the dedication explicitly — the book is thanks to you."

He pinches the space between his eyes.

"So we're even. We're square."

He looks at me and puts a hand on my shoulder.

"I'll change details — I'll tell the truth but 'tell it slant'." I bend my fingers into air quotes, trying to lighten our last moments together.

"Or lie if it makes a better story," offers T. "It's not journalism."

I clasp my fingers around his wrist.

"Honestly though, Haley, you write what you need to."

We say our I love yous and thank yous. And we cry at the door. My tears wet on the chest of his white T-shirt. He swings his tatty duffle bag over his shoulder and inhales, stilling his lip. "Okay. Bye."

Cried dry, I take a shower. Then I rearrange the furniture in my bedroom, put fresh sheets on the bed and wait for grief to strike.

As I restore my office to order, my eyes land on my *The Ex-Boyfriend Yard Sale* notes, a pile of papers exploding from a binder — the mouth of an insatiable monster, food slopping down its front — a binder that barely contains all the hours of careful calculations and discussions and arguing about each data point and its ramifications.

I open it smack in the middle and read:

When I asked Riku about T, he said, "This person has already given you a lot."
And I thought, Fuck you Riku. He's given me nothing.

I thought — hoped — the payout would be a life together and a baby eventually.

I gleefully wrote another ending to the stage show where I said:

"I didn't want to write this ending. I didn't want to be a person who makes a show about break-ups only to fall in love. I didn't want to say, 'You guys, this T-shirt's not for sale anymore cause we're back together, he's moved to London, and this isn't a burrito . . .'" [pointing to my stomach]

I wrote that gleeful ending because when we had our fleeting honeymoon moment, swimming in the ponds, I was convinced that outcome was on the horizon. Right then, it looked like a real possibility that by the time I was performing the show I'd have to say:

"I'm sorry about the poetic timing but the truth is, the flowers rotting in the dressing room are from him and he's in the back row right now, hiding his grin. I don't have to go to market anymore!"

I'm embarrassed by how much joy it gave me to imagine that ending. I'm embarrassed by how quickly my disdain for the status quo melted away at the fantasy of living that ending.

The silver lining is that I have not fallen into that particular cliché. I have not managed to weather a difficult love to be rewarded with a big ol' sunset.

The payout is not a lifetime but release. I'm alone, but I'm not in a relationship that will quash me. I'm free.

THE LEDGER

Love	Finally broke up with T
	Single
Money	Was – £4,681.74 in debt
	Then got paid:
	+ £3,072 for teaching, round 1
	+ £2,477.45 for TV gig
	+ £5,733.28 for recent voiceover work
	+ £3,731 for teaching, round 2
	+ £4,735.27 for book deal
	Shelled out £6652.94 to secure my new flat in south-east London
	Now debt-free!
	I paid Thea £1,438.23 ($2,480, 31 sessions @ $80)
Career	*The Ex-Boyfriend Yard Sale* got a book deal & I'm writing a book
	Started teaching
	TV series gig
	Voice work is picking up
	No "right fit" for theatre transfers yet
Total	?

19. AFTERMATH

Aftermath, noun
1. *the consequences or after-effects of a significant unpleasant event.*
2. *Farming: new grass growing after mowing or harvest.*

> *"Classic economic theory, based as it is on an inadequate theory of human motivation, could be revolutionized by accepting the reality of higher human needs, including the impulse to self-actualization and the love for the highest values."*
> Abraham Maslow

When I get to the bank, I swing the door open with ease. Casilda is not here because I'm at a different bank in my new neighbourhood. I only decided to come to this bank after I called to make an appointment with Casilda and discovered she's on her second maternity leave.

At my new bank, I am assigned Carlos. I'm under instructions from my brother. Kian is back in his job in Vancouver. His year "doing good" gave him a new philosophy to live by: it doesn't matter *what* he's doing but *how* he's framing it in his mind. I admire his new approach, even if I'm not entirely persuaded. I suspect he'll always be wiser and more evolved than I am.

"I'm here to open a tax-free savings account." I beam.

"Sounds good," Carlos sings distractedly, spinning his chair to face the computer.

I tell him I've never had savings before.

"Oh savings," he says with longing. "Yeah. My wedding ruined me." He hums to himself as he clicks on his keyboard, then asks for my address.

I rattle it off and tell him I live there alone.

He says he'd be too lonely living solo. He's one of those people who hates being by himself.

"My friend Milo is like that," I say. I guess he's not my friend anymore, but he called a few days ago. He's in a new relationship with a dog trainer. It's splattered over all his social media. They appear to be in the eye of lust. And Julie has started a podcast about polyamory. Hearing his voice made me miss T.

T and I have committed wholeheartedly to our year of no contact. Other than intermittent spontaneous bouts of sorrow, I haven't been tortured by his absence. I feel more lucid than ever.

Fi said, "Thank Christ," and raised her hands to the heavens when I told her T and I had ended it, for real, with the help of a professional. She's been coming over a lot recently even though it's a ninety-minute journey for her. She and Ru have stopped trying to have a baby. "Too much heartbreak and we don't feel like having sex with each other anymore." It came out that he slept with someone else in Majorca. She's not going to leave him. When I suggested that she could, she told me not everyone is a break-up aficionado. She and her husband are now in what she calls "emergency couples therapy" instead. I'm humbled to learn people in committed long-term relationships can have their hearts broken too. No label or piece of paper or myriad of shared assets can protect us from it. And I'm aware there's enough good between them for her to stay.

Carlos talks me through the terms of the account I'm opening. It's a place where money goes in but can't come out for a fixed term. This is an act of faith, betting on myself to earn well regularly.

When I got paid up with Thea, she raised my fee again. Her stock is also rising. After some initial disgruntlement on my part, this too seemed like a token of faith in my evolution.

The day after T left, the voiceover work came back. A trickle at first and then in waves. I have kept selling my voice and when the payouts come, I squirrel them away, treating them as bonus money for this account. Without prompting, I tell Carlos I do voice acting.

"'She had a voice that sounded like money' — that's from *The Great Gatsby*," he informs me. "Love that book."

I tell him I'm writing a book. I tell him about the show and the formula and Gemma, who I'm meeting for dinner this evening.

Carlos says it sounds cool, but for him, once a relationship is done, he gets rid of all the stuff and cuts the person out completely. He says let's hope he never gets divorced, or he'll have to get rid of everything.

I say, "A lot of people do," recalling Milo's account of his trips to charity shops, his car stuffed with his exes' clothing and kitchen gadgets and novelty mugs. He moved out of Julie's eventually. I wonder if he did a purge then, or whether she did. Ollie, on the other hand, still has a small shrine of his ex's effects — two pocket squares, a razor and an expired credit card.

Carlos asks how much money I made from selling my items.

I explain that they're currently tied up in a larger investment. When he looks confused, I say, "I use them as props in the show."

He wants to know what my exes think about being in my book.

I smile. "I don't know."

I hope they feel valued. I want to do them justice, especially T. I want to honour the good stuff he brought me and that we cultivated. But it's hard to put it into words that don't come out saccharine or deluded or defensive. And my propensity for negativity has me typing epic accounts of the bad times — the petty grievances, circular disagreements, frustrations and agony. Perhaps it's easier to write the bad stuff because it reminds me why we're broken up.

I sign some papers and Carlos gives me a copy of the contract. The account is open and I'll soon be earning interest. He shakes my hand and wishes me good luck with the book and the show and all my "future endeavours".

When I emerge from the bank, I don't zip my coat. The crocuses have sprung through the soil. London is its subdued grey self. The pavement is damp. All I can smell is earth. I'm thirty-four.

There's an email from my editor with her notes on my most recent draft of the book. She said it came to an end too abruptly. She wants to know more about what I learned.

How can I extract individual lessons when the project and my life are intrinsically interdependent? I make a turn away from home and head to Dulwich Park to consider this in motion.

I recognise that I picked apart and evaluated component parts of my relationships for the sake of a price tag, but I don't know how to untangle the symbiotic elements at play for the sake of a tidy conclusion.

Thoughts comes quick then. I dodge two people roller skating and claim my spot on a bench. Pulling my notebook out of my purse, I write:

> I'll do my best to present my findings categorically but forgive
> me if they don't sit neatly on the ledger lines.

The dampness from the wooden bench seeps into my jeans, but I stay and begin to enumerate my gains, in love and money, as a by-product of creating the formula, performing the show and writing the book. I list the obvious things I learned:

- *How to give myself enough time and support to create and execute a project as I envision it*
- *Math is not objective — it's subject to manipulation*
- *Time is more valuable than money*
- *Positive and negative events that have a big impact are more valuable than meh experiences*
- *New info from an ex can augment how we view the past*
- *When it comes to projects, done is better than perfect – let go of control and share it with people*

A man pushes a stroller filled with two screeching babies as he talks into a wireless headset. I walk in the opposite direction towards the large sculptures.

The show itself has yet to pay off in a significant way. Beyond the unworkable offers from commercial theatre producers and being ghosted by the West End outfits and TV sharks, it looks like it'll return to Toronto for a run later this year, but the contract's not yet signed.

The book deal is a pay-off of sorts. It certainly has the potential to raise my profile and increase my cash flow. Fingers crossed the rest of the lawyer's prophecy comes to pass. And according to the astrologer, the stars say age thirty-five is when things will get really good for me. I hope she's right.

I now have £57,000 in the bank and I am debt-free. I wish I could say I arrived at this abundant bank account as a result of scrupulous money management and savvy entrepreneurial tactics, or at least a TV deal, but that would be a lie.

To give myself credit where due, I tracked my income and expenses for a year and got out of debt, then back in, and then out again. Throughout that time I learned about money, worked on my relationship with it — uncovering my limiting beliefs around "evil money" and "horrible rich people" with Thea, doing money meditations and reading self-help books — I stopped being afraid to look at my bills, started admitting I want to earn, and I figured out a way to make more and live within my means through teaching and acting work and the book deal.

The truth is, the bulk of the money came from my voiceover work, which, by some stroke, took off. I landed several advertising campaigns for different multinational companies in quick succession. Was it luck? Was it the power of manifestation? Being available during the weekdays? Was it that I'd improved my skills over four years? Or that I'd cultivated relationships and developed a positive reputation in the industry? Was it my meditations and my newfound relationship with money? Some indeterminable confluence? I don't know.

There were fallow periods; however, the voice work itself has come without struggle. I have a good voice, a strong ear, I take direction well and I'm reliable. But I'm not exceptionally gifted. I can't do a million accents. I just talk in my own voice. I didn't gun after it desperately or assiduously. I learned on the job. And enjoyed it. I wish I could apply this approach to my love life.

I'm no financial expert. I still have to learn about pensions, ETFs, mortgages and crypto-currency baskets. But I discovered the two-pronged approach, practical and mindset, weighted at 25 per cent practical and 75 per cent mindset, works for me. The fact that this combination worked in the money realm gives me hope that it'll work in the love realm too.

I haven't spoken to T in seven months. I have been lighter, moving faster and generally crying less since ending the relationship. Except for when writing the first draft of this book, especially recounting instances when T and I were kind to each other. Then I cried a lot.

I wasn't depressed to spend another Christmas alone. Bolstered by the thought that while I may not have been in the relationship I yearned for, I wasn't in a relationship I didn't want to stay in. I was in a neutral place. And that felt like progress.

Although when the new year rolled around, faced with the prospect of dating someone new, and in the throes of a full-on romantic ideation about one of my Inappropriately Attired team-mates, I found myself sobbing to a top forty pop song, levelled by the lyric, "If the world was ending, you'd come over, right?" It was easy to feel at peace with the split when I was entirely alone, but it seemed a betrayal of T to seriously consider someone new.

When I asked Thea if she thought my relationship with T was a sick compulsion or love, she asked me what kind of reality I wanted to choose to believe in. I guess I want it to be both. When I asked if the demise of the relationship could be boiled down to one core issue, she said it could. He fit perfectly into my "unavailable love object complex" and I fit perfectly into his "overcritical love object complex" — hand in glove and doomed. She said the only way out of a complex is to work through it. I want to know if I've done it. She said I wouldn't have been able to end it if I hadn't. She says I may always have a sense of sadness when I think of T, and that in the future unavailable men may be kryptonite to me, but I'll have the tools to spot it and move the other way. She called T my "noble friend". I like that.

I buy a peppermint tea from the kiosk in the middle of the park. I've been off caffeine since I was diagnosed with hyper-thyroidism last year, but I no longer have to take medication for it. Sitting at a picnic table, I make a list of the gains from my time with T:

- *How to advocate for myself, how to fight fair, how to lay down arms and admit another person is right*
- *The show, the book, half a decade of art*
- *That sensational sex isn't about acrobatics but connection*
- *To not take everything so damn personally*
- *What I want from a partner and what I won't accept*
- *The space and time to create The Ex-Boyfriend Yard Sale without the distraction/compromises/considerations of a partner in my daily life, without pressure to have a baby or take a holiday — the*

> *LDR protected me from falling into a co-dependent coma and*
> *fortified me against ever being in one*
> – *Just because all you have to show from a relationship is a*
>   *souvenir (not a family or a life together) doesn't mean the time*
>   *invested was a waste. You gain from love that "fails"*

The neutral place at Christmas was a pivotal moment; I had to choose to expand or contract. After asking out a guy I met at a party, getting rejected, hitting on my Inappropriately Attired teammate and getting rejected again, I put myself on the dating apps and corresponded with about forty-five men simultaneously for a couple weeks while I weeded my options. I went on dates, and once I proved to myself that I was capable of holding down a conversation with a stranger, it hit me that these fellas were pretty lucky to be out with me. My fears of not living up to my pictures were allayed when they looked older and less polished too. It amazed me that I wasn't hurt by their brush-offs, just like I wasn't flattened by the ghosting TV producers and theatre deals that weren't quite right.

I've spent the majority of my romantic life in a mode of "first I need a total buy-in from *you*, then I'll decide if I like you back". Now, men are on and off the table with incredible speed. After a rejection, my ego smarts for a couple hours but I'm coming out unscathed, and I'm glad I'm not lying or pretending or trying to convince them to like me.

Sunk Cost Bias is valuable too. Just because you've invested time and emotion and built something, doesn't mean you should stick it out and make it work when you find yourself faced with a decision to quit or commit.

I now believe the goal when we reach the quit or commit crossroads is to do the brave thing. The brave action is one that expands rather than diminishes you. And we know what it is. We know that we know, but we want to pretend we don't know, because it requires risk. In our risk/reward economy I am now an advocate of risking it — going for a good story with big impact over stagnation. The risk is saying what you actually want. And after that, if the other person can't meet you, or match you, then you walk away. And if they can, then you stay.

I started this project wanting to disprove my feelings of low self-worth by slapping a number on my failures. But as I discovered when we finished the formula, the price isn't really the answer. The result is that my value system has changed.

Your life isn't tragic, or a failure, if it doesn't *look* a certain way. Your life is tragic if you don't take action because you're afraid. Your life is richer every time you're brave.

It occurs to me that this is the difference between valuing integrity over dignity.

I think to be a person with integrity first requires the courage to examine what is actually going on inside, to identify what's out of alignment and to be honest with yourself about what you truly want. And then, it's about having the guts to share what you want with the people around you, relinquishing control of the outcome.

Living an integrated life means summoning the pluck, over and over, risking ridicule, embarrassment, vulnerability, rejection, alienation, dissent, disappointing others, being alone in the name of living a truer, richer life.

But of course, our inner truths shift, and therefore the outward expressions shift too. So to live with integrity is to continually make courageous acts, large and small, and to risk losing the things you have become attached to, in the name of being unified, honest and growing — to make meaning of your life by offering everyone you encounter your whole self.

From what I understand so far, the annoying thing is that you never achieve it; maintaining alignment is an ongoing pursuit. But you can start at any time. And when you falter, you can pick it up again. It's never too late to begin, or been too long a break to seek your own integrity.

Sometimes the people you risk losing will leave and some-times they'll stay. But their staying is not the prize. The prize, the gold, is the new paradigm in which you are never living a lie. You are true. And we know what the truth does. It sets you free.

I return my teacup to the counter and stroll out of the park's gates as the sky clouds over again.

I've been pontificating as if I'm an authority on integrity when I'm not. I'm a novice who's glimpsed it and wants more.

What do I know? I ask myself. I know getting back together with T was not a waste of time. It was a gift, because it proved that that relationship was never imaginary, but real.

And I know for sure that the formula for the cost of love, flawed as it is, spits out a number. And that is not nothing.

The wind picks up. My new flat is in sight.

It hits me. Working on the formula, making the show, writ-ing this book have taught me two big, irrefutable things that seem to be in contradiction, but both are of great value to me.

On one hand, relationships are uncertain, precarious, ever-changing and completely out of our control. And this is something we know and forget, and we know and forget, and we know, and we know that we know. And we forget that time will keep moving and your life will keep unfolding and how you assess your previous experiences will keep changing. The assessment — the number — the value — is always temporary, never fixed.

And, on the other hand, when you forget, and you pause to take stock — when the ledger of your life feels like a big fat zero — I have crunched the numbers. I have proof. The ledger is never zero. It's not.

THE FORMULA FOR
THE COST OF LOVE

To enjoy the formula in all its glory, cut along the dashed lines and assemble with tape as the letters indicate.

I've also included a few notes and a legend so you can squeeze the most out of it.

Notes

There is a certain amount of "behind the scenes" math at play in this rendering of the formula. For the purposes of style, legibility and elegance we decided to omit some of those nuts and bolts, but wanted to mention a few that might be of interest, especially if you happen to be a more mathematically-minded person than I am.

Many of the symbols you'll see on the formula represent several pieces of math. For example, the *quality of sex* variable, which you'll find in the Relationship Index, is determined by measuring the quality of sex (1–10, no 7) at the beginning *and* at the end of the relationship and taking an average.

Lots of variables have been "scaled", meaning taken up or down in size, depending on their emotional impact in relation to other variables, or level of importance within my personal value system. For instance, if something was rated a 2, we could include it as 0.2, 1.2 or 2. Since Wild Cards are taxes (or multipliers) that already scale the entire price, we scale them down by adding the number one at the beginning of the phrase and then multiplying the phrase by $(1 \div 100)$.

If these notes feel too esoteric for you, please enjoy the formula as is and trust that it really works.

LEGEND

Market Value (MV)

This phrase is all about the hard, financial costs associated with the item for sale

CMV	Current market value
GT	Median of Gumtree offers
aw/o	Audience bids without context
aw	Audience bids with context
EM	Cost of repairing any damages
D	Value of any embellishments or improvements made to the object
Purh £	Purchase price*
Mth £	Your estimation of the ex's monthly income*
[gift icon]	Level of gift
[thought icon]	Level of thought put into the gift

Together these two make up relative generosity

Narrative Impact (NI)

Narrative Impact captures the value of a particular relationship in retrospect

H	Quality of the healing
W	Magnitude of the wounding
LL	Value of the big life lesson the relationship provided
[baggage icon]	How much baggage you left with
age	Your age at the time of the break-up

$\sqrt[N]{\begin{smallmatrix} S \\ K \\ I \\ L \\ L \\ S \end{smallmatrix}}$	The Nth root of the value of the practical skills and knowledge acquired in the relationship where N equals your age at the time of the break-up
ROP	The significance of the rites of passage experienced in the relationship
$\underline{gS}$	How many good stories the relationship contributed to your life story
# Rel	The total number of significant relationships you've had in your life
↑ ☮	Level of friends you are with that ex now

Dollar Today (DT)

This phrase represents how the live show impacted the value of each object

$\frac{?}{£}$	My perception of the ratio of who paid for more things in the relationship
⌂#	How many people are in the house (audience) that evening
(☹)	The emotional toll of working with the object
$\log(\square)$	Logarithm of the ticket sales to date
$\log(p.£)$	Logarithm of my potential earnings
$\log(★)$	Logarithm of my celebrity status
$\log(t+hc)$	Logarithm of the costs of creating the show in time and money
$\log(avg. £ in rel)$	Logarithm of my average earnings in the relationship
RANK 1 - 8	Where the item ranked (1-8) based on the audience's initial bids without context
% AIR TIME	The percentage of airtime the object receives in the show

Time Invested (t)

This is about the amount and quality of the time spent in a specific relationship

TSR	Total time spent in the relationship
%.life	Percentage of my life the relationship occupied at the time of our break-up
%.⊖	Percentage of the relationship spent in transit to see the ex
%.⑤	Percentage of relationship spent on relationship admin (especially time with their friends and family out of obligation)
STAKES	How high the stakes were when you got together*
↑ approp.	How appropriate it was to date that person at that time in your life*

Together those two variables capture the timing of a relationship

Relationship Index (RI)

The Relationship Index reflects the quality of a particular relationship while you were inside it – it's the brass tacks stuff you can measure for just about any relationship

K↑	Key highs
K↓	Key lows
☺	Fun
☹	Misery
LoL	Laughter
⟨POW⟩	Fighting
♥	The quality of the biggest romantic gesture they ever performed for you
rely	How reliable they were on a day-to-day basis
↑♀	How much you liked their people
y♀	How much your people liked them
↑SEX	The quality of the sex

⏰	The regularity of the sex
XXX	The amount of new sexual territory they introduced you to
use	How useful that new sexual territory was in the future
by	How well and often they took care of you
bt	How well and often you took care of them
? ❤	Who broke up with who?
WANT 2	Did you want to break up?
❤	The power of whether or not you were in love

Rose Tint Corrector (RTC)

The Rose Tint Corrector was implemented by Gemma to counteract how my nostalgia was affecting my assessments of my exes, especially after I interviewed them

INT → 🗓	Amount of time between interviewing the ex, if applicable, & filling in the spreadsheet
❤ → 🗓	Amount of time between break-up & filling in the spreadsheet

Wild Cards

Wild Cards are like taxes or credits and are only applied or deducted if any of the following were present in a specific relationship. These are even more particular to my experiences:

'Collateral Damage'

This applies to other physical items that were damaged as a result of a particular relationship

C repair	Cost of repairing or replacing the item in question
M £d	My monthly earnings at the time of the relationship

Crying Tax

0.95	Less 5 per cent for any object given to me before 2012, to compensate for all the garbage I dumped into those relationships that actually belonged in therapy

The Martha Card

Inspired by the Tom Waits song, this represents the rare, lasting effect a precious few may have on us, which is that no matter the outcome with them, they occupy a space in us that no one else can touch.

1.1	Plus 10 per cent if applicable and more than 10 years have passed since break-up

'Bad Shit Happened to Me'

☺	How much fun I was having while he was enacting his pattern with me
↑CR	How creative the elements of the pattern were
PAIN	The amount of pain I feel now about being put through the pattern
THEN	The level of pain I experienced upon discovering his betrayal
↑res	How well he's taken responsibility for his actions since
⌐	How much I ignored red flags
$\sum_{i=1}^{x} \frac{1}{2^{i-1}}$	Law of diminishing bad shit, where x equals the number of times they did the bad shit
⚑/.	Percentage of the relationship he was pursuing & wooing other women

'I Did Bad Shit'

☺	How much fun I had while I was doing the bad shit
↑got away	How well I got away with it
↑apol.	How well I apologised
⌐	The red flags my ex ignored

$\sum_{i=1}^{x} \frac{1}{2^{i-1}}$	The law of diminishing bad shit, where x equals the number of times I did the bad shit
$\overset{\cdot\cdot}{\frown}$ /.	Percentage of the relationship I was engaging in the shitty behaviour
GuILT	The guilt I felt then
Now	The guilt I still feel now

'Bodily Harm'

LT ☹	The long term (LT) emotional impact of a singular event's ramifications
☹	The emotional impact of the original (og) event
LT 🧠	The amount of headspace the ramifications have occupied in the intervening years
%. og 🧠	The amount of headspace the original event has occupied
t	The long term impact on me physically and on my relationship with my body
LT :👤:	The original event's impact on my body
T $	The total financial costs of the event and subsequent ramifications for me
◎	The size of the inciting incident, in number of words spoken

Unspeakable Bliss

If the relationship in question contained a moment of unspeakable bliss, the buyer must include a non-monetary payment, in the form of a story from their own life of equal emotional weight, in addition to the cash price.

¥	This is the symbol that represents Unspeakable Bliss. It's inspired by the Japanese symbol for 'cloud nine'

$$\left(\frac{CMV + G + awlo + aw}{4} + EM - D \right) \times \left[\frac{Push\ \pounds}{Mth\ \pounds} + \left(\boxplus \times \bigcirc \right) \right] \times$$

MARKET VALUE

NARRATIVE IMPACT

$$\left(\left(\frac{1 + (H+W)}{age} + \frac{LL + \square}{\frac{SCC - RS}{N}}\right) \times \left(ROP + \frac{SS}{\#Rel}\right) \times \bigcirc\right) + $$

$n = \frac{age}{e}$

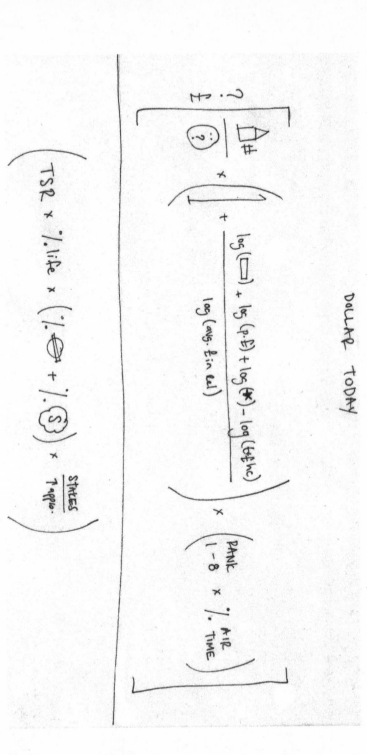

TIME INVESTED

$$\left(\text{TSR} \times \% \text{ Life} \times \left(\% \text{⊘} + \% \text{\$} \right) \times \frac{\text{STAKES}}{\text{Topic.}} \right)$$

X

RELATIONSHIP INDEX

$$\frac{\left(\dfrac{KT}{KI} + \dfrac{☺}{☹} + \dfrac{LoL}{fml} + (📺 \times 🍔) + (🍷 \times 🍴) + \dfrac{SEX}{🕐} + (xxx \times 💋) + (😊 \times 👕) + \dfrac{?}{WANT} \right)}{1,000}$$

X

INT →

X

PURE TINT CORRECTOR

X

WILD CARDS

$\times \left(1 + \dfrac{C_{repair}}{M \pm \Delta}\right)$ COLLATERAL DAMAGE

$\times (0.95)$ CRYING TAX

$\times (1.1)$ MARTHA CARD

$\times \left[\left(\text{😊} \times TCE\right) \times \left(\dfrac{PAIN}{THEN}\right) + \left(\uparrow res - 1\right) \right] \times \left(\sum_{i=1}^{x} \dfrac{1}{2^{i-1}} \times \text{🐛\%} \right)$ 'BAD SHIT HAPPENED TO ME'

$\times \left[\left(\text{😊} \times \uparrow_{today}^{guilt}\right) + \left(\uparrow apol. - 1\right) \right] \times \left(\sum_{i=1}^{x} \dfrac{1}{2^{i-1}} \times \text{🐛\%} \right) \times \dfrac{guilt}{NOW}$ 'I DID BAD SHIT'

UNSPEAKABLE BLISS

$+ \left[\left(\text{😊}_{LT} - \text{😊} \right)^2 + \left(\text{🥔}_{LT} - (\text{🥔} \times t) \right)^2 + \left(\text{😶}_{LT} - \text{😶} \right)^2 + \left(T\# - \text{🎯} \right)^2 \right] \div 100$ BODILY HARM

TIPS FOR BREAKING UP

- Do it as close to the Ew Point as possible
- Don't dovetail one relationship into the next
- Remember there's value in being "cruel to be kind" – when you tell the truth you set yourself *and the other person* free
- You can't control another person's reaction and they're entitled to their reaction
- But you don't have to stick around if you don't like their reaction
- Everything you want lies on the other side of an uncomfortable fifteen-minute conversation
- Don't attack, blame or list faults
- It's about your feelings. You're not feeling or seeing a future together. It's an instinct you have to listen to – no one can argue with your feelings
- Thank them for the good stuff they gave you
- Agree to a period of no contact and keep your word
- Don't shit-talk them, especially not to mutual friends
- Unfollow and don't stalk on social media
- Make a list of reasons why you split and look at it to remind yourself when you feel lonely
- Cool your jets and don't jump into something new ASAP – feel what it is to be single
- Consider what the relationship taught you, about yourself and what you want and how you were complicit in creating something that wasn't satisfying – think about how you can integrate that learning moving forward

ACKNOWLEDGEMENTS

Writing this book has been the realisation of a dream I didn't let myself dream. There are so many people I want to thank for believing in this idea and supporting me while I toiled away.

Thank you to –

My editors Hannah Black, Lily Cooper and Natalie Young. I'm so fortunate to have been guided through this process by a team of whip-smart women who know what's up and to have had your deft hands helping me separate the wheat from the chaff.

The marvellous team at Coronet and Hodder, especially Erika Koljonen, marketer Helen Flood and PR Rebecca Mundy, for their attention to detail, patience and sensitivity. To Claudette Morris and Rachel Southey in production.

My agent, Kirsty McLachlan, for finding me, championing this story and fielding my panicked calls with grace and kindness.

The whole team who got the live show off the ground. To Brian Logan and the staff at Camden People's Theatre, my long-time collaborator, director Mitchell Cushman, my creative team: Zoe Robinson, Rose Hockaday, Anna Reid, Kieran Lucas and Lucy Adams and my most wonderful assistant and friend, Eliza Cass. To my outside eyes: Deborah Pearson, Phillip McKee, Holly Beasley-Garrigan and Richard Corgan. To experts Lee Smolin and Robert Elliot Smith. To all the theatre companies and organisations who supported the show's development and brought it to audiences and every audience member. Without you this book would not exist.

Melanie Frances, my math whiz. Thank you for diving in and showing me all that numbers could do. You are remarkable. Brains, care, creativity, humour. How'd I'd get so lucky?

My most faithful friends, who've borne witness to all the crushes, flirtations, flights of passion, boredom, heartbreak and despondency of my romantic life: Teddy, Milena, Daniel, Taylor, Talia, Carlyn, Marla, Shannon, Brittney and Jared. Thank you for your ears, advice, comradery, joy and depth.

My London contingent: Mike, Liz, Rebecca, Dave, Paula, Robert, Jonathan, Debbie, Morgan, Alan, Rajiv, Matthew, Simon, Marta, everyone I improvise with at the Free Association, all my students, my agents at Yakety Yak and Geoff at SDA. You've helped make this new place home.

The extraordinary women who taught me math in high school: Mrs. Packull-McCormick and Mrs. Biffis.

Jennifer Adams, my high school drama teacher, who called me an actor, and Sheldon Rosen who taught me writing at theatre school and called me a writer. Thank you for seeing me.

Mary Ellen. Your brilliance, insight and generosity have shepherded me into the life I've always wanted. I'm so glad I found you.

Robert, who couldn't have come at a better time.

My family for their steadfast support, encouragement and boundless love; my parents for showing me how to work hard, raising me to have the confidence to go my own way and for never telling me the arts weren't a viable career choice (sorry about the double negative Dad!), my aunt Lynda whose sense of humour and creativity have shaped how I see the world; my brother Rory for his wisdom, friendship and truth-telling.

My exes, for all the riches you've bestowed on me. Thank you for teaching me about love.

And finally, thank you to you, dear reader, consider this sentence my ponytail sweeping the stage floor in a humble bow. Your reading this has made it all worth it.

AUTHOR BIOGRAPHY

Haley McGee was born and raised in Kitchener-Waterloo, Canada. At 17 she moved to Toronto, where she received a BFA in Acting from Ryerson University and subsequently worked as an actor and playwright until she relocated to the UK in 2016.

Heralded as "the formidable Haley McGee" (*Globe* and *Mail*), her award-winning, critically acclaimed solo shows have played in thirty-six venues in eleven countries and been translated into four languages.

Haley lives in south-east London, where she thrives on variety—she writes, acts, performs improv, does voiceovers, teaches artists in a variety of online courses and hosts *The Cost of Love* podcast.

She loves pancakes, being outdoors and reading. This is her first book.

www.haleymcgee.ca

FORMULA

Written by Haley McGee and Melanie Frances
And all copyright shall be reserved and retained by the Owner:
© Haley McGee